# THE
# CONSULTING
# TRAP

# THE
# CONSULTING
# TRAP

### How Professional Service Firms
### Hook Governments & Undermine Democracy

## CHRIS HURL &
## LEAH B. WERNER

Fernwood Publishing
Halifax & Winnipeg

Development editor: Fiona Jeffries
Copyeditor: Amber Riaz
Text design: Brenda Conroy
Cover design: Evan Marnoch
Printed and bound in Canada

Published by Fernwood Publishing
Halifax and Winnipeg
2970 Oxford Street, Halifax, Nova Scotia, B3L 2W4
www.fernwoodpublishing.ca

This book has been published with the help of a grant from the Federation
for the Humanities and Social Sciences, through the Awards to Scholarly
Publications Program, using funds provided by the Social Sciences and
Humanities Research Council of Canada.

Fernwood Publishing Company Limited gratefully acknowledges the
financial support of the Government of Canada through the Canada Book
Fund and the Canada Council for the Arts. We acknowledge the Province
of Manitoba for support through the Manitoba Publishers Marketing
Assistance Program and the Book Publishing Tax Credit. We acknowledge
the Nova Scotia Department of Communities, Culture and Heritage for
support through the Publishers Assistance Fund.

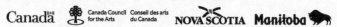

Library and Archives Canada Cataloguing in Publication
Title: The consulting trap: how professional service firms hook governments
& undermine democracy
/ Chris Hurl & Leah B. Werner.
Names: Hurl, Chris, 1978- author. | Werner, Leah B., author.
Description: Includes bibliographical references and index.
Identifiers: Canadiana (print) 20240288076 | Canadiana (ebook)
20240288130 | ISBN 9781773636672 (softcover)
| ISBN 9781773636825 (PDF) | ISBN 9781773636832 (EPUB)
Subjects: LCSH: Political planning—Case studies. | LCSH: Consulting firms—
Case studies. | LCSH: Privatization—Case studies. | LCGFT: Case studies.
Classification: LCC JF1525.P6 H87 2024 | DDC 320.6—dc23

# Contents

# Acknowledgements

To critically investigate the consulting industry is to acknowledge the profoundly social character of knowledge — to recognize where it comes from, the conditions under which it produced, and who stands to gain from it. Indeed, the central criticism in this book is that consulting firms tend to disavow the social conditions under which their knowledge has been produced. Adopting a transactional approach, these firms have aimed to foster a scarcity of knowledge in order to defend their privileged position and continue selling their products. Confronting a variety of gatekeeping mechanisms, critical researchers and investigative journalists face a daunting task when attempting to access and make sense of their formulae and methods.

Through the course of our research, we have set out to challenge this transactional approach by working with others to cultivate a surplus of knowledge about these firms and their operations. We could not have done this alone. The work has demanded building social relationships and speaking with public officials, critical researchers, and community groups that have encountered and generated knowledge about these firms.

We are grateful to activists in Toronto, Barnet, and Cape Town who took the time to speak with us.

We have benefited from the contributions of Anne Vogelpohl, Larissa Hallis, Alia Nurmohamed, and Valerie L'Heureux, who worked on the wider research project.

We would like to thank Michelle Girash, Michael Howard, Nick Hildyard, Tom Baker, Jamie Brownlee, and the anonymous reviewers for their comments on the manuscript.

And we are grateful to Andrew Sturdy, Denis Saint Martin, Matthias Kipping, Howie West, Jordan McAuley, Paul Finch, Kevin Walby, and Munira Lokhandwala for their input and insights through the course of the project.

Thanks to Fiona Jeffries and the Fernwood team for all their support in publishing the book.

Finally, we are grateful to our loved ones for their encouragement and support through the course of the project and for their tolerance in hearing us babble on about municipal service delivery reviews.

# Preface

# Never Let a Good Crisis
# Go to Waste

In late September 2020, as the United Kingdom was struggling to keep up with a deadly second wave of COVID-19 infections, the transnational professional service firm Deloitte invited a group of local health officials to a demonstration of their new test and trace system. Developed in partnership with the software company Salesforce, the firm promised that this "totally paperless," quick to deploy "local contact-tracing solution" would help alleviate the pressure of recent outbreaks on local health teams.[1] Deloitte's initiative was, however, swiftly and roundly condemned — not surprisingly, given the firm's already poor track record in rolling out a test and trace system at the national level. How was it possible, a Director of Public Health wondered, that "the ongoing failure of NHS [National Health Service] test and trace is being turned into an opportunity for one of the companies engaged in it to profit"?[2] And how was it acceptable that the national system's "apparently inept leadership either isn't aware of this or actually allows one of its delivery companies to blatantly sell 'solutions' to councils?"[3] Deloitte was accused of coming "round the back door to profit" from a worsening health crisis to which they themselves had contributed. The Shadow Health Secretary at the time, Jonathan Ashworth, noted that local councils, as members of the NHS, "should be getting this [system] anyway."[4]

At that point, Deloitte had already raked in millions to manage and coordinate the NHS test and trace program, which Prime Minister Boris Johnson claimed would both be "world-beating" and form the backbone of the United Kingdom's pandemic response.[5] The firm's work included managing test centres, appointment bookings and laboratories, collecting statistics and hosting and maintaining the NHS test tracking digital platform that "holds data captured by the registration system and makes it available to the NHS."[6] Deloitte was not the only professional service firm involved in assisting the UK government's test and trace program. The outsourcing giant Serco was heavily involved in the work of tracing.

1

And McKinsey & Company was hired to define the "vision, purpose and narrative" of the program — a program that was, incidentally, led by McKinsey alum Dido Harding, who had been appointed by the UK government to be the interim executive chair for the newly established National Institute for Health Protection.[7]

By the time Deloitte pitched their offer to local councils in September 2020, a slew of problems had been plaguing the national program. For example, in April 2020, some local hospitals had requested to take control of the Deloitte test centres because "test results of NHS staff [were] being lost or sent to the wrong person."[8] By May, local authorities and general practitioners had complained that Deloitte was not sharing testing data with them, which left them with little knowledge of where local disease clusters were located. Deloitte's testing system also failed to collect key data — such as people's ethnicity or whether they worked in health or social care — making it impossible to gather information on those most vulnerable to the disease.[9] The British Medical Association reported that "outsourcing the coordination of testing" was likely "resulting in adverse effects"; NHS staff were, for instance, waiting seven days to receive their COVID-19 test results from Deloitte test centres, while local NHS labs could have completed the process in just six hours.[10] And when Serco began recruiting contact tracers, the firm "accidentally shared 296 contact tracers' email addresses," and it was later reported that the firm was failing regularly to trace up to 30 percent of contacts.[11]

Yet, despite this growing list of complaints, the firms continued getting lucrative contracts — often without competitive tendering processes.[12] By October 2020, the number of consultants from Deloitte working on test and trace was equivalent to a small government department.[13] With a total of 1,230 consultants working on the program — the majority from Deloitte — the ratio of consultants to civil servants working for test and trace was, at its height, one-to-one. Despite the government's commitments to reduce the number of consultants working on the program amid growing criticism, a House of Commons report found that the number had only risen from December 2020 to April 2021.[14]

And these consultants were being paid hefty daily fees. In the summer of 2021, it was revealed that the average rate for a test and trace consultant was £1,100 per day, with some senior advisors billing for over £6,000 daily.[15] This meant that the government was shelling out over £1 million per day to Deloitte.[16] And all this was for work on a scheme that, by the fall of 2021, was deemed to have failed in its objectives to "help break chains of COVID-19 transmission and enable people to return towards a more normal way of life."[17]

By this time, it was becoming increasingly evident that the over-reliance on consultants for the program was achieving poor results, and that consultants were far more costly than civil servants or temporary staff from other public services.[18] But the Department of Health defended its use of consultants, arguing that it had been necessary "given the emergency nature of the initial response and the need to scale up operations at speed" because "many of the skills required were not available from the civil service within the timeframe"; therefore, "it had to use the private sector to respond quickly under power of the emergency regulation."[19]

Deloitte, for its part, appeared unfazed by the criticism and maintained, against all evidence, that it was "proud of its work" on test and trace in the United Kingdom.[20] Perhaps Deloitte could afford to remain confident, as, despite the documented failures of the program, it continued getting contracts for test and trace systems in other jurisdictions around the world. For example, across the Atlantic, in the Canadian province of Alberta, Deloitte was hired in April 2020 to build and launch COVID-19 contact-tracing app ABTraceTogether. The Albertan government — at that point the first province to introduce a COVID-19 tracing app — paid nearly CAD 1 million to Deloitte to build the app with IBM providing the infrastructure; the app itself, however, was based on open-source software code that had initially been developed and freely shared by another software developer based in Singapore.[21] Although the app developed by Deloitte required some customization to implement in Alberta, many wondered why the firm had been hired and paid such a steep price to adapt it from free source code, especially when, as some pointed out, the work could have been done through the local tech community in Alberta for little to no cost.[22]

Not surprisingly, the app faced a myriad of problems in Alberta, problems that had already been documented in Singapore. It couldn't run in the background on iPhone operating systems; it was failing to record cases; and, as opposed to the federal app that would send out notifications of positive diagnoses automatically, it relied on manual entries of notifications by provincial contact tracers, which could take several days to process. There were also concerns around data privacy, with one privacy expert arguing that the app was "so flawed it shouldn't have been introduced."[23] By the summer of 2020 — only a few months after its launch — the province decided to switch to the federal tracing app, ditching ABTraceTogether for which they had already paid Deloitte CAD 1 million.[24]

Despite these failures, however, Deloitte was hired by the Canadian federal government in January 2021 to create and implement a digital COVID-19 vaccination tracking system — earning an initial $16 million for its efforts. The decision was met with some skepticism since, as had been the case with the Alberta app, Deloitte was largely importing a system from the United States, which, critics noted, had been plagued with problems since its inception.

Indeed, a few months earlier, in September 2020, the US government awarded a sole-sourced contract to Deloitte to build a vaccine administration management system (VAMS) — a new vaccine tracking system using software from Salesforce. Initially, some health officials and observers wondered why a new system was necessary in the first place as an existing vaccination program had already been in use for many years by state governments and the Centers for Disease Control and Prevention (CDC) without any problems.[25] The government insisted that a new digital infrastructure was needed given the scale of the emergency, and some critics conceded that there was room for improvements to the existing system. Improvements were, however, far from what people got. The system was supposed to provide a free "one-stop shop where employers, state officials, clinics, and individuals could manage scheduling, inventory, and reporting for COVID shots" with ease, but it was riddled with bugs.[26] Among other problems, people were unable to sign in or connect to the system, it was confusing patients with health care providers, and it only worked on one internet browser. Elderly people — those most in need of vaccines — were facing difficulties booking appointments. People reported showing up at their appointments to get vaccinated but being turned away because the system had not registered their meeting or had wrongly registered them as already vaccinated.[27] In response to the problems with VAMS, Deloitte maintained, as they had in the UK, that the firm was proud to support the vaccine campaign and "help with ending the COVID-19 pandemic so that our families and communities can recover and thrive."[28]

In total, Deloitte was paid $44 million to build VAMS, which, due to concerns over usability, only nine states chose to employ — and several of those eventually abandoned it.[29] As in Alberta, many questioned the government's decision to hire Deloitte at such a steep price for this work. And in February 2021, allegations surfaced that Deloitte had stolen the idea for the system, though the firm dismissed those claims.[30] In April 2020, Tiffany Tate, executive director of the nonprofit organization Maryland Partnership for Prevention presented her platform, PrepMod — based on a flu vaccine registration program already in operation — to officials from CDC and the American Immunization Registry Association. In these meetings, consultants from Deloitte had been present. Despite expressing interest in buying PrepMod, the CDC instead hired Deloitte in May 2020 to implement VAMS, which, according to the allegations, "'mirror' the system Ms. Tate created — including a 'new feature' that 'eventually found its way into VAMS.'"[31] In fact, Tate claims that Deloitte even offered to hire her to roll out the system that she had devised, after the firm had won the contract on a bid that was $600,000 higher than her own.[32]

Such cases raise important questions that we investigate in this book: How did an accounting firm like Deloitte become a central broker of knowledge about public health? Why, amid serious problems and ballooning costs, did Deloitte keep getting contracts? Why wasn't the firm held accountable for their work when it was negatively impacting millions of people? And to what extent has the pandemic enabled these firms to expand their foothold in government, growing their range of services and extending their influence around the world?

As we show, the COVID-19 pandemic was no anomaly. While it was an exceptional moment — an opportunity for firms like Deloitte to expand their operations — the role of these firms during the pandemic calls attention to more longstanding and deep-seated trends in government outsourcing. It underscores the tremendous scale of transnational professional service firms and their capacity to mobilize personnel, policy programs, and infrastructures around the world. It speaks to the tremendous scope of these firms, as they have come to provide a myriad of services to governments. Not just consultants anymore, the pandemic highlights the transition of these firms from advising governments on an ad hoc basis to providing entire governance platforms and administrative infrastructures, developing more extensive and continuous ties with governments. Moreover, it speaks to the changing orientation of these firms as they have attempted to rebrand themselves as information technology (IT) firms, investing in cloud computing, artificial intelligence (AI), and extensive data infrastructures. Finally, taking advantage of their scope and scale, it also calls attention to the methods through which these firms have been able to influence governments.

In this book, we show how transnational professional service firms have been able to entrench themselves in the infrastructures of government, fostering dependencies — which we refer to as a "consulting trap" — from which it can be difficult for governments to extricate themselves. Through their command of such infrastructures, they are able to extract exorbitant rents while at the same time avoiding public scrutiny under the auspices of commercial sensitivity and cabinet confidence.

The book explores how these firms have been able to generate such influence and how this influence has impacted government. As we will show, the problems with Deloitte's work in the UK, the US, and Canada during the COVID-19 pandemic are just a drop in the bucket when it comes to consulting scandals around the world. Like Deloitte, transnational professional service firms (TPSFs) such as Boston Consulting Group, EY, IBM, KPMG, McKinsey, PwC, and Serco have rapidly expanded their operations over the past two decades despite mounting controversies. These firms have profited greatly from a growing volume of lucrative government contracts, often leaving in their wake a trail of problems, and are rarely held accountable for the outcomes of their work — work that directly impacts people's everyday lives and costs the public sector colossal amounts of money.

This guidebook shows where these firms come from, the programs they provide, the strategies through which they generate influence, and the ways they have been resisted. We hope that it will supply people with a resource that can be used to help challenge the power of these firms, overcoming government dependency on consultants and fostering more democratic pathways for policymaking and public administration.

# Chapter 1

# What Is the Consulting Trap?

The growing reliance of governments on transnational professional service firms (TPSFs) has recently ignited fiery debates and stirred up controversy. Across the political spectrum, critics have called attention to the outsized influence of firms like Boston Consulting Group, Deloitte, EY, KPMG, McKinsey, PwC, and other larger firms in shaping public policies from behind the scenes.[1] Critics have challenged the opacity of their work and the difficulty of holding these firms to account. They have exposed the role of these firms as "shock doctors" taking advantage of crises to implement unpopular policies.[2] They have condemned the exorbitant price of their services, which could be undertaken by public-sector employees for a fraction of the cost.[3] And they have warned of their role in "hollowing out the state"[4] and "infantilizing government," cultivating long-term dependencies that ultimately incapacitate the civil service.[5]

Indeed, a brief look at some of the recent scandals demonstrates the degree of public distrust for these organizations.

In France, the clout of TPSFs became an election issue that threatened to topple President Emmanuel Macron's government after opposition lawmakers found that contracts worth 2.4 billion euros had gone to private consulting firms between 2018 and 2022.[6] This figure had more than doubled over the course of two years, and critics raised concerns that this trend could lead to a "relationship of dependence" on these firms. At the same time, it was revealed that McKinsey — which had benefited greatly from all these billions — had not paid corporate taxes to the French state for at least 10 years. This scandal was dubbed "McKinseyGate," as critics noted the extensive ties between McKinsey and Macron's La République En Marche party, igniting further controversy and prompting many to wonder how much influence the firm had on the government.

In South Africa, several firms — including Bain, KPMG, and McKinsey — were embroiled in the largest corruption scandal in the country's history since the apartheid era, as it was revealed in 2016 that they facilitated the looting of public contracts over the course of three years under the presidency of Jacob Zuma. The scandal was so egregious that it was investigated by public officials as a problem of "state capture" — a process by which private individuals and companies "take over state agencies to redirect public resources into their own hands, while weakening the institutions for ferreting out that corruption."[7] As the auditors responsible for keeping tabs on public agencies, KPMG played a central role in rubberstamping financial arrangements enabling the corruption. As for the role played by McKinsey, the National Prosecuting Authority reported in 2016 that the firm had been instrumental "in creating a veil of legitimacy to what was otherwise a nonexistent unlawful arrangement."[8] Bain's work restructuring the South African Revenue Service to minimize its oversight and regulatory capacity was seen as such a grave offence that the firm was, in 2022, temporarily barred from tendering for public contracts in South Africa and the United Kingdom — a rare instance of these firms being held accountable for their actions.[9]

Meanwhile, in the United States, McKinsey was under fire for its role in fuelling the country's deadly opioid crisis. At a time when the dangers of opioid use were apparent, the firm advised the drug company Purdue on how to — in McKinsey's words — "turbocharge" opioid sales while they were simultaneously guiding the Food and Drug Administration (FDA) on restructuring the Center for Drug Evaluation and Research — the public agency responsible for approving the use of opioids.[10] Public officials called out the firm for the potential conflicts of interest that this clearly raised. A government investigation ensued, and in its wake, McKinsey agreed to pay more than $600 million in penalties to the government, though the firm denied any wrongdoing in the matter.

In Canada, as KPMG was advising municipal governments across the country on how to slash public spending and cut services in the aftermath of the 2008 economic crisis, the firm was quietly devising offshore tax haven schemes enabling wealthy Canadians to avoid paying taxes. Described by public officials as "a sham ... intended to deceive" federal authorities, these schemes allowed wealthy families to set up shell companies in the Isle of Man from which they could receive tax-free "gifts" in return.[11] And while the scheme was a costly affair for the Canadian state, KPMG faced no consequences.

And in the United Kingdom, outsourcing firms Serco and G4S have repeatedly been caught defrauding the government in their public service contracts. This has included understating profits and overstating delivery. For instance, in their work in the health sector, Serco admitted to giving false data to the National Health Service (NHS) over 250 times on the performance of its out-of-hours GP service. And in their electronic monitoring contracts they were caught charging for "tagging people who were either dead, in jail, or had left the country." The director of the Serious Fraud Office (SFO) undertaking the investigation concluded that the firm had "engaged in a concerted effort to lie to the Ministry of Justice in order to profit unlawfully at the expense of UK taxpayers."[12]

Yet, despite these ongoing scandals, the power and influence of TPSFs have only grown. Government spending on consultants has increased dramatically over the past decade. While the bulk of consulting revenue continues to come from the private sector, a growing share comes from government (11.8 percent) and government-adjacent services, such as energy and utilities (9.3 percent) and health services (11.3 percent) amounting to more than USD 261.5 billion in global annual revenue as of 2023.[13] In the UK, government spending on consultants jumped from £0.7 billion in 2016 to £2.5 billion in 2021. In Australia, spending on the "Big Seven" consultancies increased from under AUD 400 million in 2013 to over AUD 1.2 billion in 2020. In Canada, government spending on "professional and special services" — which includes consulting as well as other services — increased from CAD 10.4 billion per year in 2016 to CAD 17.7 billion by 2021.

And the spending has continued to grow as governments around the world turned to these firms as first responders in confronting the complex public health, social, and economic problems that emerged in the wake of the COVID-19 pandemic. Never letting a good crisis go to waste, these firms managed to even expand their roles during the pandemic as they moved from advising on government policies to rolling out entire pandemic response infrastructures. As we saw with the example of Deloitte recounted in the preface, TPSFs offered a wide range of services to governments during the pandemic — at no modest price. These services included everything, from building COVID-19 tracking and tracing apps[14] and coordinating vaccination campaigns to designing and administering governance response structures,[15] and advising on post-pandemic recovery[16] — all with limited public oversight or attention.

Indeed, the rapidly expanding scope and scale of TPSF procurements by governments is striking, raising the question: how did these firms come to occupy such a prominent role in public administration?

In this book, we aim to shed some light on their path to power — a path that continues to widen as these firms act not only as advisors to governments but also increasingly take on the role of public service providers. We explore how TPSFs have become entrenched in public administration over the past three decades, investigating how they have combined consulting services, accounting frameworks, and information technology (IT) infrastructures to develop more continuous and multifaceted relationships with governments. In the process, we explore the growing dependencies that have emerged as different levels of government have come to rely on these firms for policy advice, public administration, and service delivery. This reliance has, over time, given rise to what we describe as *the consulting trap* wherein these firms organize and value public services — services that they themselves are hired to advise on and deliver — in ways that benefit them and that deepen their influence. By fostering a style of governance by contract — advising government to deepen their outsourcing arrangements while in turn standing in to assess these same arrangements, and directly administering services under these arrangements — the power of these firms can be self-perpetuating, constituting a vicious cycle that erodes democratic decision-making and accountability over time.

Such structural transformations are often overlooked as critical researchers and investigative journalists tend to focus on the personalities involved — the Ivy League connections, campaign donations, and cocktail parties. From this perspective, the critical literature tends to frame the government as a tool or instrument that has been colonized by consultants who mobilize it for their own selfish purposes. This can foster narratives — at times, verging on conspiracy theories — that focus more on the interests of these firms than on their practices. Who is really running the show? What is their hidden agenda?

Although exposing the allegiances of consultants is informative (as we discuss in Chapter 4), focusing only on the "who" rather than the "how" can, at times, reinforce a sense of powerlessness, counterposing the lonely muckraking journalist to the shadow state. It can also exaggerate the purity of the state — as if a once pure public interest has been corrupted through the incursion of outside interests. In contesting the power of these firms in governance, we contend that it is not enough to simply name names. Rather than treating consultants as "outsiders" seeking to take control of the state as a tool or instrument to pursue their own interests, we are interested in how professional service firms have contributed to reconfiguring the state through cultivating new ways of seeing and governing, and — through these novel vantage points — developing different relationships between public officials, private actors, and the communities they govern. From this perspective, our focus is not as much on who is pulling the strings as it is on investigating the "ties that bind."[17]

Over the past fifty years, TPSFs have popularized a particular set of ideas, a particular way of seeing the world, and a particular set of norms through which to appraise the quality of governments. They have assembled communities and instituted relationships around these ideas. They have codified and commodified products that make these ideas modular, capable of being packaged and sold across different contexts. They have built up sociotechnical infrastructures that enable the entrenchment of these ideas, allowing them to operate silently through everyday institutional routines and procedures.

The ideas promoted by these firms are often connected with neoliberalism, an ideology that is associated with less government, less regulations, lower taxes, and fewer gatekeepers. Rather than "rowing" — directly providing services themselves — proponents of neoliberalism argue that governments should be "steering," delegating services to those actors best able to provide them, who are invariably located in the private sector. By making public services more "market-like," it is argued, those delivering services will be incentivized to optimize their work, providing lower cost and better-quality services. Behind these ideas are social arrangements that have given a central role to TPSFs. Over the past fifty years, these firms have positioned themselves as the central intermediaries and arbiters of governance, rolling out arm's length, privatized, and financialized forms of governance while at the same time claiming to be the best able to assess their value. Through their capacity to stand across domains or jurisdictions, they have come to serve as powerful intermediaries brokering access to ideas, personnel, and infrastructures. And, in a context of economic globalization where enterprises and governments must increasingly operate across a fractured and complex regulatory landscape, they have played a key role as wayfinders, helping public and private officials navigate uncertain worlds and wicked problems.

Although they promise to empower governments through such methods, the result is often the opposite. Their business model — which is driven by the commodification of policy ideas and administrative infrastructures — has been premised on deepening dependencies. TPSFs set out to maintain and extend power asymmetries by creating the impression that they have access to ideas, services, and technologies that their clients cannot get elsewhere. Economists Mariana Mazzucato and Rosie Collington liken it to "a psychotherapist having no interest in her clients becoming independent with strong mental health, but rather using that ill health to create a dependency and an ever greater flow of fees."[18] Thus, these firms withhold access to their formulae and models, datasets and infrastructures, and client lists. Moreover, to maximize business opportunities, TPSFs have expanded the range of products they sell. This has set the trajectory of many large firms, as they have grown from providing ad hoc advice to governments to offering administrative infrastructures and governance platforms. Through maximizing the contact points with governments, these firms have consequently been able to establish multifaceted and ongoing relationships with their clients, establishing what Antonio E. Weiss describes as "hybrid" governance arrangements[19] and refashioning themselves as partners in governance.[20]

Through the course of this book, we provide a road map of how these firms have risen to such power and prominence. Our format is simple. First, we examine the makeup of TPSFs, discussing their history, structure, and operations. Second, we survey the services that they provide for governments and explain how they have contributed to consolidating a neoliberal regime of governance premised on austerity, financialization, and privatization. Third, we explore the strategies that these firms deploy to generate influence and entrench themselves in government. Finally, we discuss how the power of these firms can be confronted, exploring strategies that have been taken up in challenging the influence of TPSFs in government.

## What Are Transnational
## Professional Service Firms?

So, what are TPSFs? How are they established? And how do they operate? Despite all the scandals, there is not much research on the structure or history of these firms. The studies that have been done tend to focus on their role as consultants to governments and corporations.[21] However, as we show in this book, TPSFs often play a much larger role. Governments now depend on these firms to deliver a range of services that go beyond simply advising policymakers.[22] Many self-branded professional service firms offer a multitude of services to governments, including legal, actuarial, financial, and accounting services. They provide IT infrastructures, such as cloud computing, management information systems, and administrative platforms; they also offer advice on everything from lean production and labour market restructuring to digital governance, snow clearing, waste collection, prison reform, building smart cities, and public health issues — the list is endless. Considering how all-encompassing they have become, how can we go about locating their expertise?

They are also slippery organizations. They brand themselves as "professional," but one does not actually need to be accredited as a professional to serve as a partner in many TPSFs, unlike more specialized professional enterprises like law firms or medical practices. No special degree is required, even though these firms present themselves as experts in a variety of areas.[23] In fact, EY and PwC removed university degrees from their requirements for entry-level positions altogether in 2016, stating that there is "no evidence" that success at university correlates with achievement in their firms.[24] So, in the absence of a licence or degree, what makes these firms "professional"?

As we show in the second chapter, the ability of TPSFs to brand themselves as jacks-of-all-trades is the outcome of a distinctive historical trajectory based on the subsumption of different professional identities under a distinctive organizational form. We begin by historically locating TPSFs at the nexus between the fields of management consulting, cost accounting, and IT services. Drawing from the work of business historians, such as Antonio Weiss,[25] Matthias Kipping, and Ian Kirkpatrick,[26] we identify four waves of advisory services to governments that have shaped the trajectory of modern TPSFs over time:

1. Scientific management and cost accounting — which focuses on optimizing processes within organizations (1900s onward);
2. Strategy and organization — making sense of the relative position of organizations in a larger environment, field, or market (1950s onward);
3. IT services — providing administrative infrastructures to organizations (1970s onward);
4. Outsourcing — directly delivering public services for governments (1990s onward).

This corresponds to four types of TPSFs (see Figure 1.1) that we explore as prominent actors in the privatization of public administration: auditing firms (the so-called Big Four firms — Deloitte, PwC, EY, and KPMG), strategy firms (the so-called Elite Three firms — McKinsey, Boston Consulting Group, Bain), information technology firms (IBM, Accenture, CGI, Microsoft), and outsourcing firms (Capita, Serco, G4S, Atos).

**Figure 1.1 Transnational Professional Service Firms by Field**

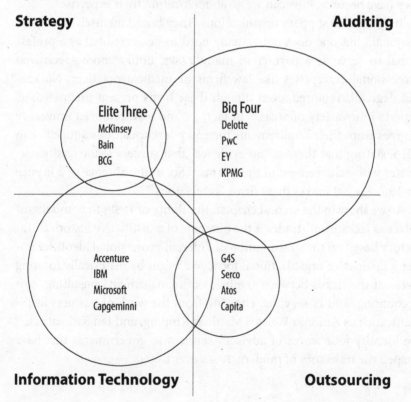

**Strategy**

**Auditing**

Elite Three
McKinsey
Bain
BCG

Big Four
Delotte
PwC
EY
KPMG

Accenture
IBM
Microsoft
Capgeminni

G4S
Serco
Atos
Capita

**Information Technology**

**Outsourcing**

Although these four waves of advisory services have contributed to the emergence of TPSFs, it is only since the 1980s that firms have branded themselves as "professional service firms," beginning with Price Waterhouse (before it became PwC) in 1986. Since then, many other organizations have followed suit, starting with accounting firms like Deloitte, KPMG, and EY, and expanding to include a range of other organizations. The organizational shift to professional service firms, we argue, reflects a convergence between consulting, auditing, and IT services. As we show, the nature of consulting has changed with the development of expansive IT infrastructures. Alongside offering bespoke expertise, these firms now serve as data brokers enlisted by governments for their capacity to collect, collate, and analyze information. This, in turn, has transformed the nature of audits. As firms have developed the ability to gather more information about institutions and their operations, there has been a shift from using data to verify accounts to speculative and strategically oriented forms of assessment that are more akin to consulting.[27] It has also opened the doors for these firms to directly administer services, as they move from consulting to selling whole management information systems and IT infrastructures to governments. Along these lines, we argue that auditing firms like KPMG, strategy firms like McKinsey, and IT firms like IBM are converging their business models, which is reflected in the growing overlaps in the services that these firms provide.

As such, their scope of operations has widened from simply providing ad hoc advice to governments to providing more thorough data and IT infrastructures, and, ultimately, services to the public. This has led to more continuous and multifaceted relationships between TPSFs and governments. It has also granted these firms enlarged influence over a broader area of public policy, enabling them to infuse their ideas and values into government. Indeed, during the pandemic, we saw how TPSFs were invited by public officials to take charge of core aspects of governance, including developing the strategies and implementing the structures and processes through which the pandemic response was coordinated. As we recounted in the preface, Deloitte was hired in the United Kingdom to set up a network of drive-through rapid testing centres designed to be central to the government's plan to control the spread of COVID-19, and EY was put in charge of managing publicity around a program to track people infected with COVID-19 and to improve the purchase of personal protective equipment. In Canada, in addition to managing the federal vaccine rollout, Deloitte also played a major role in setting up Québec's COVID-19 screening system and developing the vaccination campaign in Ontario. As industry magazine *The Canadian Accountant* noted during the pandemic, these kinds of contracts show how these firms "are no longer strictly auditors but technology companies as well."[28]

Moreover, the turn to professional service firms reflects the changing scale of professional enterprises. These firms have experienced meteoric growth over the past three decades. In a context of economic globalization, financial deregulation, corporate mergers and acquisitions, privatization, and debt restructuring, these firms have rapidly grown, both in

**Table 1.1 Transnational Professional Service Firms by Employees and Revenue, 2022**

| Firm | Employees (number) | Revenue (USD, billions) |
|---|---|---|
| **Accounting Firms** **The Big Four** | | |
| Deloitte | 411,951 | 59.3 |
| PwC | 328,000 | 50.3 |
| EY | 365,399 | 45.4 |
| KPMG | 236,000 | 32.1 |
| **Strategy Consulting** **The Elite Three** | | |
| McKinsey | 38,000 | 10.6 |
| Boston Consulting Group | 30,000 | 12 |
| Bain and Company | 15,000 | 6 |
| **IT Firms** | | |
| Accenture | 721,000 | 61.59 |
| Capgemini | 358,400 | 22 |
| IBM Consulting | 160,000 | 19.1 |
| **Outsourcing Firms** | | |
| G4S | 533,000[a] | 8.94[b] |
| Atos | 112,000 | 11 |
| Capita | 61,000 | 3.6 |
| Serco | 50,000 | 5.6 |

Note: a. Data is from 2021; b. Data is from 2020.

employees and revenue (see Table 1.1). For instance, McKinsey's work-force nearly doubled over the course of thirteen years, growing from 17,000 employees in 2009 to 30,000 in 2022. Over the past sixteen years, Deloitte has tripled in size, growing from 135,000 employees in 2006 to 411,951 employees in 2022. And Accenture has grown from 177,000 employees in 2009 to 721,000 employees in 2022. TPSFs are also extend-ing their reach to more places, with the largest firms — such as PwC, McKinsey, and Accenture — operating in over 100 countries around the world as of 2022.

Their formidable institutional footprint gives them access to substan-tial resources, personnel, and infrastructures, enabling them to com-pete with governments in their command over data. As we show in this book, this has led to practices of epistemic arbitrage, as these firms are able to "exploit differences in professional knowledge pools for strate-gic advantage."[29] Indeed, many governments now rely on these firms for their capacity to mobilize data and policy ideas that they would be oth-erwise unable to access. Through their capacity to span jurisdictions, these firms can expropriate data and policy ideas for cheap from other jurisdictions, acting as curators of policy ideas and technologies, which they then selectively sell back to governments at exorbitant prices. And TPSFs have been able to leverage such dependencies in order to further entrench their power. As they have successfully installed themselves as brokers of administrative infrastructures, we argue — drawing from sociologists Marion Fourcade and Jeffrey Gordon — that governments have increasingly ceded to these firms certain "forms of social regulation and economic control historically reserved for the sovereign."[30]

## Where Are Transnational Professional Service Firms Located?

For our research, we have taken Canada as our starting point. Canada is in the Anglo-American heartland of the consulting industry. As nu-merous scholars have noted, professional service firms have had a long-standing presence in the Anglo-American world, particularly in the United States, Canada, and the United Kingdom, where these firms played a central role in stitching together the North Atlantic economic order.[31] As of 2019, the United States and the United Kingdom remain the top two markets for consulting services (at USD 71.2 and 10.88 billion respectively), followed by Germany (USD 10.4 billion), Australia (USD 6.08 billion), France (USD 5.6 billion), China (USD 5.44 billion) and Canada (USD 4.32 billion).[32] Regionally, North America and Europe account for over 77 percent of the market, while the rest of the world accounts for just 23 percent.[33]

These firms have been especially influential in liberal market economies, where direct government intervention in the economy has been treated with suspicion. As we discuss in Chapter 2, the big accounting firms all got a substantial boost during the Great Depression, when governments mandated that companies hire an outside auditing company that could attest to their books.[34] In the absence of strong regulatory oversight, these firms have played a central role in facilitating the coordination of economic activities at arm's length from the state, providing a means by which private companies could communicate their activities to their shareholders and the wider market. Likewise, after the adoption of anti-trust legislation in the early twentieth century prohibiting companies from communicating directly with one another, strategy consultants like McKinsey played a central role in facilitating the communication of management information between the largest corporations.

Drawing from longstanding ideologies that government should be run like a business, and close connections between government and private enterprise, such firms were early movers in advancing managerial reforms in the Anglo-American heartland. Even before the onset of neoliberalism, they advised governments in Canada, the United Kingdom, and the United States on how to make their services more business-like, as we will see in Chapter 2. For instance, in the early twentieth century, municipal governments employed efficiency engineers in implementing scientific management and cost accounting programs, and strategy consultants were taken up in applying multidivisional corporate structures to an increasingly complex welfare state during the 1960s. Saint Martin notes that these legacies paved the way for the state restructuring of the 1980s and 1990s, as consulting firms leveraged their strong links with governments in Canada, the United Kingdom, and the United States to advance a program of New Public Management based on deregulation, privatization, and contracting out.[35]

Starting from the Anglo-American heartland, we explore how these firms have enabled the spread of accounting standards, managerial best practices, and financialized forms of control to other places, playing a key role in coordinating economic relations across empires.[36] As we will see in Chapter 2, TPSFs like McKinsey played a central role in helping American corporations set up shop in Europe after the adoption of the Marshall Plan and an infusion of American capital into Europe during the 1950s and 1960s, paving the way for their sizable presence in Germany and France today as the world's third and fifth largest markets for consultants respectively. And in the wake of the global economic crisis in the 1970s, professional service firms expanded their operations to other parts of the world. Through their work with transnational institutions and regulatory bodies, such as the International Monetary Fund (IMF) and the World Bank, these firms got their foot in the door in the Global South advising on government restructuring in the wake of sovereign debt crises.[37] As a condition of receiving funding from the World Bank, governments around the world have often been required to enlist consultants to advise on structural adjustment programs involving deregulation, cutbacks, and the privatization of state-owned enterprises. Likewise, with the fall of the Iron Curtain in 1989, consulting firms expanded to the postsocialist countries to advise on rolling out market economies and privatizing state-owned enterprises.

In a context of economic globalization, these firms have come to position themselves as transnational intermediaries brokering the circulation of ideas, personnel, and infrastructures to governments across the globe. Although their influence remains uneven, their global footprint gives them considerable leverage in translating policy programs across jurisdictions, assisting public officials with making sense of an increasingly complex regulatory landscape, and quickly mobilizing resources in response to crises. In this context, they have been able to dis-embed their knowledge from its specific professional, institutional, and geographical location and present it as universal "best practice."[38] However, as we demonstrate in Chapter 3, this has entailed a very specific program for government.

## What Services Do Transnational Professional Service Firms Provide to Governments?

TPSFs like to portray themselves as impartial actors, but neither the advice nor the services they offer are "neutral." Their programs and technologies have made certain kinds of problems "legible" and "actionable" while occluding alternative lines of understanding and decision-making. As we show in Chapter 2, by providing the government with "operating systems" that entrench public-sector austerity while facilitating tax avoidance for the wealthy, TPSFs have contributed to the hardwiring of neoliberal policy priorities into the public sector.

On the one hand, firms have taken advantage of their comprehensive knowledge of government standards and regulations to orchestrate tax avoidance for economic elites and transnational corporations, enabling the wealthy to pick and choose which tax regulations they will abide by. Drawing from Katharina Pistor, we consider them to be "masters of code," seeking to "exploit gaps and ambiguities in the law for structuring new financial assets or intermediaries that are formally compliant with the law while escaping the costs associated with it."[39] As of 2021, it is estimated that nearly $500 billion per year is lost globally due to the tax avoidance industry. As documented by investigative journalists, whistleblowers, government commissions, and the academic literature,[40] the Big Four firms have been the key architects in enabling tax avoidance, taking advantage of their global reach in rolling out programs that starve the state of revenue.

On the other hand, these firms have leveraged their position as standard-setters in rolling out programs that enable governments to impose austerity, entrenching normative aspirations to minimize public spending through their command over benchmarks and best practices. As we demonstrate, TPSFs have played a key role in expanding the scope of public-sector audits. While audits were previously taken up to assess the fiscal state of organizations, they are now frequently used to evaluate the performance of governments and their services. As the architects of such assessment regimes, TPSFs have come to exercise a substantial degree of power in gauging the performance of governments, with the aim of doing more with less. In this way, we argue that they have contributed to the entrenchment of a "lean" state in service delivery.

Moreover, in a context of austerity, they have played a central role in the marketization of public services, creating lucrative opportunities for institutional investors to extract rents from public infrastructures and social services through transforming them into objects of financial speculation. Drawing from case studies of Public–Private Partnerships (PPPs) and Social Impact Bonds (SIBs), we explore how these firms have designed vehicles for public service delivery that are premised on hybrid public-private governance arrangements, while at the same time positioning themselves as neutral third parties in assessing their value. In the process, TPSFs have popularized dubious financial models and metrics that legitimize the high costs of privately financed infrastructures, while marginalizing "traditional" forms of public procurement. Drawing from such models, we explore how TPSFs have been able to entrench themselves as key intermediaries in the assessment and administration of public infrastructures.

Finally, we look at how TPSFs have spearheaded the outright privatization of public service delivery. In addition to advising governments, these firms have been enlisted to directly deliver a growing range of services. We saw this during the pandemic when TPSFs were contracted to provide COVID-19 tracking and tracing apps. But this was also happening well before the pandemic. Since the 1970s, firms such as IBM and Arthur Andersen have been enlisted by governments to roll out IT infrastructures in public agencies, often with unsuccessful outcomes. Despite their epic failures, TPSFs have been able to extend their reach. We discuss how firms like G4S, Capita, and Serco leverage their extensive data infrastructures in order to coordinate operations in a wide array of areas, including everything from prisons and immigration detention centres to social assistance, health services, and urban planning, replacing front-end service delivery with a "call centre" model. We explore how this has played out in the United Kingdom, which has been an epicentre for these kinds of firms, with approximately 30 percent of *all* public spending (or approximately £250 billion) going to contracted-out professional service firms.[41]

Through programs such as these, we argue that TPSFs have played a central role in reformatting the state. They have established a machine that opens loopholes for the rich and powerful while tightening the screws for everyone else. And they have done this with very little public oversight or scrutiny. In effect, these firms often play a central role in drafting the rules that govern their own conduct and the conduct of their clients; and, perhaps not surprisingly, this is often to the benefit of themselves and their clients and at the expense of the public sector.

## How Have Transnational Professional Service Firms Been Able to Influence Governments?

So, why have governments turned to TPSFs for these services? Why not turn to public officials, think tanks, community organizations, or universities? In Chapter 4, we look at the specific practices through which TPSFs achieve power in the public sector. By leveraging strategies of networking, institutionalizing, commodifying, and brokering, we argue that these firms have been able to influence core principles and values that shape public policy outcomes while extending their range of authority in policymaking. In the process, local knowledge is sidestepped, government decision-making is removed from public scrutiny, and a public-private interface is entrenched in the design and delivery of public services.

Very often, investigative journalists have focused on the social networks linking together consultants and public officials, as we see with the McKinseygate example in France. Potential conflicts of interest abound as private sector consultants actively colonize the public sector, replacing public servants as decision makers in areas that often benefit their clients. Moreover, they establish "revolving doors" that entrench these relationships over time, as public officials go on to serve these firms after completing their terms. Critical researchers often frame this as a problem of "consultocracy," in which "long-term civil servant work" is replaced by "short-term outsourced expert knowledge production."[42] Certainly, there is some truth to these claims. Drawing from a case study of elite networks in infrastructure procurement, we demonstrate how TPSFs entrench their influence in public agencies via the movement of personnel.

However, it is also important to look at how these firms generate leverage from other sources of power, alongside social networks. As TPSFs become progressively more embedded in public policymaking, we explore how they exercise what political scientists Marius Busemeyer and Kathleen Thelen describe as "institutional business power."[43] This form of corporate power flows from the growing dependency of governments on these firms for the delivery of public goods and services. As public agencies come to rely on these firms for their infrastructures and institutional memory, it can become increasingly difficult for them to disentangle themselves from these relationships over time.

Moreover, we discuss how TPSFs have been able to install themselves as key intermediaries in the policy process through actively appropriating and commodifying policy knowledge. TPSFs rely on the enforced scarcity of policy knowledge to generate profits. Along these lines, TPSFs carefully guard access to their formulae and methods. We discuss the intellectual property regime constituted by these firms and how it contributes to augmenting the position of these firms as knowledge brokers to the public sector, while removing core aspects of policymaking from public scrutiny under the auspices of "commercial sensitivity."

Finally, we consider how these firms generate power through their capacity to collect, process, and circulate data. TPSFs have invested heavily in data infrastructures, cloud computing, and machine learning in ways that now rival the state's command over data. Through the scale of their operations, these firms can broker access to data, acting as intermediaries that governments depend on to learn about policy ideas and services in other parts of the world. Moreover, through these networks, they can also contribute to accelerating the policymaking process, quickly packaging programs and circulating them in response to social, political, and economic crises. Drawing on the pandemic as a case study, we show how they have been able to leverage their scale and scope in rapidly mobilizing "fast policies" across jurisdictions and regions.

Through such processes, we argue that TPSFs have become thoroughly entrenched in public service delivery giving rise to what social scientist Ivan Horrocks describes as "power loops"[44] between these firms and governments. The more these firms become entrenched, the more governments come to depend on them to perform tasks and deliver services formerly done in-house, which, in turn, only reinforces their influence and power. This can create a vicious spiral in which the power and influence of these firms in government become self-reinforcing, raising the question: How can they be challenged?

## How Can the Power of Transnational Professional Service Firms be Challenged?

While TPSFs can quickly package and circulate ideas across the globe, the struggles against them have often been restricted to local and temporary campaigns. Thus, public officials, community activists, and critical researchers are often re-inventing the wheel when consultants come to town. In this context, it is vital to circulate our own stories, sharing lessons from our struggles, to foster collective capacities to challenge this regime of knowledge production. In Chapter 5, we consider how the authority of TPSFs can be contested, and discuss some of the strategies that have been deployed in confronting the incursion of these firms into public policymaking and service delivery.

Here, we provide examples of local coalitions that have countered the thin, commodified, and opaque policy ideas and infrastructures produced by these firms with community-based knowledge of public services that are situated in the experiences of public service providers and users. Beginning with a case study of the 2011 struggle against the KPMG Municipal Service Delivery Review in Toronto, we explore how community groups have been able to effectively challenge the claims of TPSFs through intervening both in and outside the consultation process, ultimately discrediting their reports and preventing their recommendations from being implemented. In exploring these struggles, we identify four different strategies for resistance.

First, we explore how activists have engaged in People's Audits, actively gathering and analyzing legal contracts and financial records in interrogating the relationship between governments and TPSFs. This has been a popular strategy in the United Kingdom, where activists have used People's Audits as a means of getting access to contracts and financial records. As we show, this has enabled them to identify and confront institutional blind spots in the procurement process, demonstrating the state's incapacity to provide oversight for such arrangements and documenting all the fine print and extra costs appended to contracts through forensic accounting.

Second, we explore how activists and critical researchers track the movement of personnel between TPSFs and public agencies. This involves turning from finances and contracts to focus on people. Engaging with the work of William Carroll, Tom Juravich, and Jane McAlevey, we explore strategies for gathering data on the circulation of personnel that can be deployed in social struggles.[45] Through methods such as social network analysis, critical researchers can investigate the ways in which connections are forged. This can involve focusing on interlocking directorates, exploring how public and private officials come together on the boards of advocacy organizations and regulatory bodies. It can also include investigating the biographies of personnel, exploring the "revolving doors" that are generated as personnel pass from TPSFs to public agencies and vice versa. Through such investigations, critical researchers can identify the allegiances of these firms and their personnel as well as potential conflicts of interest that may arise.

Third, we explore how activists have used access to information requests to gain access to materials on TPSFs and their relationship to government. This includes a discussion of the "access regime" through which information is brokered and the strategies deployed by activists, researchers, and journalists in getting access. As we show, the process of undertaking access to information requests provides an important strategy for not just getting access to files but also confronting the privatization of policymaking under the auspices of "cabinet confidence" and "commercial sensitivity." Through skillfully engaging with the access regime, we show how critical researchers can identify and confront the thresholds where policy knowledge is transformed into private property.

Fourth, we explore how community groups can gather alternative sources of knowledge, drawing directly from the experiences of public services providers and users. Through building grassroots networks, we argue that community groups can challenge the thin knowledge generated by these firms, calling into question the way comparisons are made and commensurability is established. Moreover, they can help foster more enduring and democratic spaces for gathering knowledge and making sense of policies.

## Why Does This Matter?

In investigating the influence of TPSFs on government, we have framed this book as a sort of citizen's guide. Our hope is that it will give the reader a good sense of what TPSFs are and how they impact the public sector. We also hope it will provide insights into what their growing authority and influence means for the public, for democracy, and for the state.

As we show, the growing reliance of governments on TPSFs is cause for concern. By investigating the role and influence of these firms in government, we demonstrate the negative implications of outsourcing professional services to private corporations. As TPSFs increasingly entrench themselves in government, they threaten to remove whole areas of public administration from democratic oversight. Operating at arm's length, they often bear little accountability for the advice that they provide or the services that they deliver. With a focus on cost-cutting, reducing service levels to their bare bones, and outsourcing "non-core" services to the private sector, they have adversely impacted the quality of public services. In facilitating these austerity measures for the public, they have created opportunities for private sector actors (including themselves) to profit immensely.

Such arrangements have transformed the relationship between governments and firms. While governments have outsourced professional services to outside actors for decades, we argue that what makes TPSFs distinctive is the extent to which they have become interlinked with governments on an ongoing basis. We argue that this gives them the capacity to exercise institutional business power, taking advantage of the governments' dependencies to further extend their reach while extracting exorbitant rents from the public.

Along these lines, our book contributes to a growing literature highlighting the damage that these firms have done to democratic policymaking. In much of the literature, the picture that is painted is one of political disempowerment, in which an outside consultocracy actively colonizes the public sector. And while we contribute in part to this picture, we also believe that the story should not end there. By foregrounding the enclosure and commodification of public administration as a process, we want to call attention to the ways in which it can be contested. Indeed, as we show, the commodification of public administration is not a foregone conclusion. There are ways we can actively resist these firms' influence in policymaking. The struggles against these firms can set in motion other ways of knowing, arranging, and valuing public services. This can include efforts to challenge the monopoly power of these firms through disaggregating their services — as we have seen recently in the United Kingdom[46] — and establishing in-house public sector consulting agencies — as we have seen in Australia and Germany. It can also contribute to efforts to establish grassroots community networks for knowing public services differently as we have seen in Toronto, London, or Cape Town.

Beyond challenging the privatization of public administration, then, we hope that this book will also be useful for people seeking to develop more democratic pathways for public service delivery and policymaking.

# Chapter 2

# Actors:
# The Rise of Transnational
# Professional Service Firms

## What Are Transnational Professional Service Firms?

In 1986, Price Waterhouse rebranded itself as a "full-service business advisory firm."[1] Other firms — such as Deloitte, EY, and KPMG — quickly followed suit. As purveyors of a wide range of services — including management consulting, tax advice, auditing, legal services, and management information systems — these companies came to frame themselves as jacks-of-all-trades: "professional service firms." However, while transnational professional service firms (TPSFs) have become preeminent organizations in many professional fields over the past four decades, their shape and structure has often been taken for granted. What exactly were the conditions of possibility for the emergence of these kinds of firms? And how have they become so entrenched in the operations of governments around the world?

While TPSFs like to present themselves as neutral third-party service providers to governments and corporations, this chapter traces their roots in distinctive ways of knowing and administering public and private enterprises. We locate TPSFs, as we know them today, at the nexus between the fields of management consulting, accounting, and information technology (IT) services. Drawing on the work of business historians,[2] we identify four waves of consulting to governments that have paved the way for modern TPSFs. Beginning in the late nineteenth century, we note the ascendancy of "efficiency engineers" selling scientific management and cost accounting as the first modern consulting products with a focus on optimizing processes within organizations. By the 1950s, the focus was extended to strategy and organization — looking at the relative position of organizations in a wider environment, field, or

market. Then, in the 1970s, firms also began providing management information systems and administrative infrastructures to organizations.
Finally, building on these administrative infrastructures, firms have
gone on to directly deliver many public services, leading to the rise of
outsourcing firms in the 1990s. This, in turn, corresponds to four types
of TPSFs that we explore as prominent actors in public policymaking and
service delivery today: auditing firms (the so-called Big Four firms —
Deloitte, EY, KPMG, and PwC), strategy firms (the so-called Elite Three
firms — Bain, Boston Consulting Group, and McKinsey), technology
firms (Accenture, IBM, CGI, and Microsoft), and outsourcing firms (Atos,
Capita, G4S, and Serco).

By historically contextualizing these firms and their work with governments, we show that they have been involved in public-sector reform
for a long time. Well before the advent of neoliberalism, governments
relied on earlier incarnations of these firms to introduce new forms of administration and accounting to public agencies.[3] However, under neoliberalism, there has been a historical convergence between these four kinds
of services. This is reflected in the blurring of the line between auditing
and advising, as the orientation of audits has shifted from seeking to cer-
tify the finances of organizations to more speculative and strategically
oriented forms of performance assessment and risk management.[4] It is
also reflected in the role of new information technologies in reconfiguring accounting and management consulting practices through intensive-
ly mining and processing data. The growing integration of accounting
and consulting with new management information systems, we argue,
has contributed to the converging business models of auditing firms like
KPMG, strategy firms like McKinsey, and IT firms like IBM, which is reflected in the growing overlap in the services that these firms provide.

After demonstrating how these firms' services are converging, we then
discuss the role they play in state restructuring. Through the integration
of consulting, accounting, and IT infrastructures, TPSFs have been able
to expand their roles in both policymaking and the provision of public
services. The role of these firms in providing management information
systems to governments, we argue, has contributed to the hardwiring of
neoliberalism in a new kind of hybrid public-private state.[5] It has also
enabled the development of more continuous relations between governments and these firms, fostering long-term dependencies that have
given TPSFs greater leverage in the governance process.

**Table 2.1 TPSFs in Context, Four Waves of Development**

| Wave | Origins | Principal Service Offering | Leading Firms |
|---|---|---|---|
| Efficiency engineers and cost accounting | 1900s–1930s Taylorism and scientific management | Maximizing productivity through scientific management techniques and accounting practices | AIC; PA Management; P-E Consulting; Urwick, Orr |
| Organization and strategy | 1950s–1960s Popularization of systems theory and strategy in analyzing the organization's position in a wider field | High-level management issues such as organizational structure and corporate planning | Arthur D. Little; Boston Consulting Group; Booz Allen Hamilton; McKinsey |
| Accounting and IT infrastructures | 1970s–1980s Development of large-scale management information systems and IT infrastructures | Technology focused work; information system design and installation | Arthur Andersen; Capgemini; Coopers & Lybrand; IBM; Marwick, Mitchell; Peat, Touche Ross |
| Outsourcing | 1990s–2000s Move toward greater competition in public service delivery and an opening up to non-state providers | Running backup support functions with some advisory work | Capita; EDS; Serco |

Source: Adapted from Antonio Weiss, *Management Consulting and the British State* (London: Palgrave Macmillan, 2019), p. 27.

# First Wave: Scientific Management and Cost Accounting

When we think about the work of TPSFs in government today, what often comes to mind are the buzzwords of "efficiency," "optimization," "stream-lining," and "value for money." Indeed, many TPSFs frame themselves as "efficiency engineers" that can provide tools and methods by which governments can "do more with less." For instance, McKinsey offers to "streamline" government services through an analysis of their "end-to-end processes."[6] Deloitte offers to "deconstruct (then reconstruct) work" in order to "capture efficiency gains through human-machine collaboration."[7] And, in confronting the "need to achieve maximum results from increasingly scarce financial resources," KPMG provides public-sector agencies with "methodologies for achieving continuous improvement in internal processes, as well as outcome- and performance-based models of engagement."[8]

Such programs for reengineering public services build on these firms' roots in cost accounting and scientific management. For more than a century, consulting firms have been commissioned by governments to advise on the efficiency of their services. Beginning in the late nineteenth century, the first wave of management consultants focused on dissecting the labour process within large industrial enterprises, aiming for "systematic observation, optimum organization and stimulation of individual activities."[9] This involved breaking down services into their component parts, analyzing how these parts all fit together, and then reassembling them with the aim of optimizing service delivery.

The starting point was Frederick W. Taylor and his theory of 'scientific management' — often described as the world's first modern consulting fad.[10] Taylor's background and approach are emblematic of a particular kind of management consulting that rose to predominance during this period. An American mechanical engineer, Taylor started his career in the US steel industry in the 1870s and 1880s. Building his reputation on years of experience within the industry, he sold his services as a "Consulting Engineer" specializing in "systematizing shop management and manufacturing costs," as his business card proclaimed at the time.

The language of science suggests that Taylor applied an objective approach to the problems of management in the workplace. And, indeed, he claimed that his approach was "objective," believing that there was "one best way" to do things, and that management consultants could discover it, implementing changes that were beneficial for both employers and workers. However, as Harry Braverman presciently observed in his comprehensive study of scientific management, the approach advanced by Taylor did not begin from the standpoint of workers or set out to understand their view of their own work.[11] Rather, it began from a standpoint of suspicion, which aimed to divest workers of their knowledge and capacity to make decisions about how they did their work. The central problem for Taylor was control: How could management minimize the discretion of workers in their jobs and maximize its capacity to control the labour process in the interests of increasing productivity? In this sense, Braverman argues, scientific management entered the workplace "not as the representative of science, but as the representative of management masquerading in the trappings of science."[12] It was not a "science of work," but "a science of management of others' work under capitalist conditions."[13]

Through his time in the steel industry, Taylor became obsessed with the problem of "soldiering," in which, he argued, workers deliberately slowed the pace of their labour to make their jobs easier for themselves. Taylor was convinced that most industrial workers operated with "the deliberate object of keeping their employers ignorant of how fast work can be done."[14] For Taylor, this meant that workers had an intolerable degree of control over the labour process.

In shifting the locus of control from labour to management, he advocated for the systematic observation of the labour process through programs such as time-motion studies, in which efficiency engineers meticulously documented and measured the worker's every movement. Once this data had been collected, the work could then be reconceptualized by management consultants, who broke down the labour process into its component parts with the aim of deskilling and simplifying the work, ensuring that workers used their time in the most productive way possible.

Such ideas gained ground in restructuring government work in Canada and the United States during the early twentieth century. In fact, through this time, the historian Magali Larson notes that Taylor's ideas were more attuned to the work of governments than the private sector, where business executives often did not want to share control with outsiders.[15] Central to the civic reform movements of the period was the belief that governments should be run like businesses, based on the principals of efficiency, bureaucracy, and centralization. This included a commitment to the optimal use of administrative resources based on "gathering and interpreting 'facts' about how a department or office functioned as opposed to what its officer stated."[16]

While Taylor himself did not advise governments, his disciples, such as Morris Cooke, were quite influential in introducing scientific management techniques to local governments. In restructuring Philadelphia's public works in 1911, Cooke advocated "conducting municipal experiments on the most productive way to accomplish relatively routine tasks such as removing snow or paving streets."[17] As part of this work, he procured two hundred "expert" engineers to supervise highway workers, which he claimed saved the city five million dollars. In the early twentieth century, consulting engineers circulated such ideas through associations across Canada and the United States, such as the National Civil Service Reform Association, the League of American Municipalities, and the National Assembly of Civil Service Commissions. Through these networks, consultants travelled between cities advising on how to maximize productivity in easily quantifiable services, such as waste collection and street cleaning, using time and motion studies. They also undertook comprehensive surveys of municipal services, with the aim of fully documenting and comparing costs between cities.[18]

Building from such reform movements at the municipal level, consultants were then able to scale up their advice to civil service reforms at the state/provincial and federal levels. The role of consultants in designing federal civil service reforms are notable here. For instance, after advising on restructuring the City of Chicago, Arthur Young and Co (which later became one half of the firm Ernst and Young or EY) played a central role in civil service reforms for the Canadian federal government, giving the Civil Service Commission the power to conduct investigations into the efficiency with which government business was being conducted. Drawing from Taylor's work, there was an emphasis on scientific observation, gathering systematic data about the civil service, which could then be applied by efficiency experts in breaking the organization down into its component parts. This culminated in the publication of a *Book of Classification* in 1919, which classified the federal civil service according to 1,729 different kinds of work. For each position, an "efficiency rating" was provided, which set out to quantify the evaluation of public services. According to the *Book of Classifications*:

> The rating of an individual must as far as possible eliminate personal prejudice, or what might be called the variation of the human equation, which occurs when even the most conscientious of men is asked to give his written opinion and recommendation concerning a number of persons with whom he has had more or less personal relations. This is the object of the 'numerical' or 'percentage' system, whereby the efficiency of an applicant can be expressed in arithmetical terms capable of mathematical weights and comparison.[19]

The intent of scientific management was to eliminate patronage from the civil service and enable the objective assessment of civil servants based on their merit. However, as Roberts (1996) documents in his history of the reforms, it culminated in the formation of a hopelessly complex and unaccountable system, often out of touch with the realities of public administration on the ground. As one critic noted at the time:

> Instead of visiting the departments and offices and, as far as possible, acquiring a first hand knowledge of affairs, [consultants] took their information from a card index. Instead of calling all deputy ministers and heads of branches and consulting with them, and thus getting a fully orbed view of Civil Service operations, they called only a few, or depended on volunteer information.... It is easy to see that by this method they would get a distorted view ... of the importance of some individuals and branches.[20]

Under scientific management, the separation of conception and execution in the delivery of public services has often led to the production of knowledge that is out of touch with the day-to-day realities of public service delivery.[21] Through monopolizing knowledge at the top, based on the premise that there is "one best way" to do things under the purview of scientific experts operating at arm's length from those delivering or receiving public services, the voices of those on the frontlines, actively engaged with the delivery of public services are often discounted. This can contribute to the depoliticization of public services, constituting what Wendy Brown calls an "anti-political" regime. Under such a regime, she notes, "public life is reduced to problem solving and program implementation, a casting that brackets or eliminates politics, conflict, and deliberation about common values or ends."[22] Moreover, expropriating all the brain work involved in the delivery of public services has often contributed to the deskilling and intensification of the labour process for public-sector workers, creating a public service that is profoundly alienating for both workers and service users. As we see in the next chapter, this legacy continues to inform the programs of TPSFs today, as they set out to offer technical solutions to political problems.

Three principles emerged from the scientific management movement that set the stage for TPSFs. First, the popularization of mechanical metaphors elevated the principle of efficiency as a normative ideal in the operation of organizations. As Henry Schacter notes, "productivity, discussed under the rubric of efficiency or optimizing output/input, emerged as an important criterion in assessing public and private organizations."[23] Second, efficiency engineers like Taylor popularized the idea of management as a generic science that could be uniformly applied across different industries. If the organization was imagined as a machine, then it was not necessary to understand the distinctive cultural milieux in which people worked, with their own rules of operation or knowledges. The same methods could be applied to governments as to private enterprise, without regard for their distinctive missions, values, or methods of working. Third, scientific management was premised on the asymmetrical control of information. Workplace knowledge was expropriated from workers, and codified and transformed into the property of a distinctive managerial class. By denying workers access to such data, efficiency engineers could then use their "monopoly over knowledge to control each step of the labor process and its mode of execution."[24]

## Second Wave: Organization and Strategy

In the late 1950s, the first wave of consulting engineers gave way to a new generation of consultants focusing on issues of corporate organization and strategy. Going beyond the minutiae of operations on the shop floor, attention turned — with the growth of international trade and corporate expansion — to assessing how operations compared across a wider organizational field.[25] In his history of strategy consulting, Walter Kiechel describes this movement as "Greater Taylorism," insofar as it extended "the corporation's application of sharp-penciled analytics this time not to the performance of an individual worker — how fast a person could load bars of pig iron or reset a machine — but more widely to the totality of its functions and processes."[26] This involved two components: First, consulting firms developed more macro-level organizational analyses, interrogating the overarching structure of public and private enterprises. Second, they developed methods for gauging the strategic positioning of these enterprises in a wider "market." Through such methods, consulting firms contributed to reorienting political decision-making toward accounting logics, establishing complex metrological regimes through which to "manage by objectives," and positioning consulting firms as central intermediaries in brokering access to a picture of the wider "field."

### Organization

During the 1950s and 1960s, the focus of consultants shifted from investigating the minutiae of the labour process on the shop floor to assessing the broader structures of public and private enterprises. Responding to the growing scale and complexity of operations during this time, consulting firms such as McKinsey, Price Waterhouse, and Boston Consulting Group helped burgeoning multinational corporations to establish more decentralized organizational frameworks, adopting relatively independent divisions coordinated by a corporate head office (described at the time as the "multidivisional form" or "M-form").[27] For many consultants, this organizational form promised greater flexibility, giving corporate divisions the freedom to adapt to their distinctive milieu while facilitating the development of overarching strategies from the head office above.

The model was in demand from multinational corporations seeking to better coordinate their work in a context of rapid expansion following the Second World War. As American corporations set up shop in the United Kingdom, France, and Germany with the influx of American capital after the adoption of the Marshall Plan, they faced challenges in coordinating their operations across the Atlantic. During the 1960s, strategy consultants, particularly McKinsey, played a key role in helping them adapt, using the M-form to decentralize their organizations. In the process, Matthias Kipping notes, "multinationals based in America performed an important bridging function" in popularizing American consultancies and their associated management ideas in Europe.[28] In seeking to tap into this new business, strategy consultants established offices in Europe through the 1960s and 1970s, beginning with McKinsey in 1959, contributing to the formation of a transatlantic consultancy complex.

Consultants applied similar organizational frameworks to state restructuring, as they were commissioned to advise on the coordination of expansive and dispersed services across a burgeoning warfare and welfare state in the wake of the Second World War.[29] Confronting challenges associated with the rapid expansion of social security and the nationalization of industries, alongside the growth of a military industrial complex enlisting a multitude of public agencies and defence contractors in the procurement of weapons and equipment, consulting firms reimagined government as a multidivisional enterprise and set out to enable more flexible and decentralized administration while facilitating the implementation of overarching strategies by the executive.

A common consulting program at the time involved undertaking comprehensive surveys of government operations. For instance, in 1962, Price Waterhouse provided the Ontario government with a "Survey of

Organization and Operations" for hospitals, which had been recently brought under the administration of the Hospital Services Commission with the adoption of public health insurance. The survey focused on "appraising [the commission's] organization, staffing, methods, procedures and discharge of responsibilities under provincial legislation, and ... suggest[ing] such changes and improvements as would lead to greater efficiency and economy in operation."[30] This included advising on the appropriate relationship between the commission and the hospitals, as well as establishing a uniform system of employment classifications and salary administration. They also recommended creating a Hospital Operating Standards Department, which would operate like a "reputable management consulting firm," acting as advisers to hospitals, "encouraging them and, if necessary, requiring them to install modern, efficient systems, procedures and methods in all areas of hospital administration and operation."[31]

Consultants during this time often made inroads into public administration via government commissions advising on public-sector reforms, such as the Hoover Commission on the Organization of the Executive Branch of Government in the United States (1947), the Fulton Committee on the Civil Service in the United Kingdom (1966), and the Glassco Commission on Government Organization in Canada (1960). Setting out "to inquire into and report upon the organization and methods of operation" of government to "best promote efficiency, economy and improved service in the dispatch of public business," the Glassco Commission recommended that the government "let the managers manage," free from executive control and with the capacity to devise methods to suit their own needs.[32] The Hoover, Fulton, and Glassco Commissions were largely staffed by management consultants, as governments set out to integrate private sector management techniques into the public sector. According to political scientist Denis Saint Martin, at least six of Glassco's project teams were under the direction of senior partners in Canada's largest and most important accounting and management consulting firms and half of the 170 specialists were associated with accounting and management consulting firms.[33]

Rather than relying on political control over government departments from above, consultants promoted new forms of arm's length fiscal control via performance-based budgeting. In the United States, Canada, and the United Kingdom, consultants played a central role in designing and rolling out the Planning, Programming and Budgeting System (PPBS), which set out to "unify the planning, programming and budgeting functions" of public agencies via new forms of analysis and assessment.[34] Building from scientific management principles, these reforms were fuelled by the motivation to account for performance outcomes in public-sector budgets, enabling greater capacity for budgetary control from administrative centres. "Instead of fiscal appropriations being handed down from Congress to meet operational needs," historian S.M. Amadae notes, "defense planners would articulate their needs using presumptively objective and thus incontrovertible cost-effectiveness studies."[35]

While some public officials valourized such methods for their objectivity, others warned of the implications for democracy. As political scientist Frederick C. Mosher warned at the time:

> At no point does one gain the impression that the budget process is a "due process" of administration wherein the facts, the analyses, the interests, the politics and the prejudices of people enter. Much of the literature of PPBS resembles that of the technocrats of the thirties; its aim seems to be to eliminate *politics* from decisionmaking.[36]

In her history of PPBS, Amadae documents how such methods contributed to a reconstitution of political power in the United States, effectively empowering new technocratic elites recruited from consulting firms to gauge the success of public policies via new accounting technologies.[37] "The new decision techniques," she notes, "replaced the traditional approach in which persons of equal status reached decisions in open discussion with the idea that trained analysts should provide leaders with studies of how efficacious various policy proposals would be in meeting 'objective' national goals."[38]

Spearheaded by the RAND Corporation, PPBS was introduced to the US Department of Defense by Robert McNamara in 1960 and became adopted as standard operating procedure for US federal agencies by 1965.[39] It was rolled out by the Canadian federal government in 1969 and further consolidated by consultants in orchestrating the expansion of the Office of the Auditor General in 1970 which was "given important new powers in the area of 'value for money' management and subsequently became one of the main access points through which consultants diffused managerialist ideas in the Canadian federal state."[40] This was reflected, for instance, in the 1974 Financial Management and Control Study, which incorporated a substantial number of personnel from the largest accounting and management consulting firms.[41] Under the leadership of Auditor General James Macdonell — previously head of Price Waterhouse's management consulting division and cofounder of Canadian Association of Management Consultants — the audit's mandate was extended to include performance management. The Auditor General was empowered to call attention to cases where "money has been expended without due regard to economy or efficiency; or satisfactory procedures have not been established to measure and report the effectiveness of programs, where such procedures could appropriately and reasonably be implemented."[42]

With their focus on fiscal discipline through new forms of audits, Saint Martin notes, such programs paved the way for neoliberal programs of governments and the rise of New Public Management ideologies in the 1980s and 1990s, laying the groundwork for new forms of performance-based audits.[43] Moreover, they gave consultants a foot in the door through which they expanded their influence through the 1980s and 1990s. Implementing new performance-based accounting systems created a demand for data, leading to investments in management information systems and opening the door for the computerization programs of the 1970s and 1980s.

## Strategy

During the 1950s and 1960s, consultants also popularized the notion of "strategy" in public policymaking. Prior to the Second World War, Kiechel notes, the notion of "strategy" was not widely taken up in gauging the position of public or private agencies; the term was largely confined to military planning.[44] Through the 1950s and 1960s, however, a whole new generation of consultants came to the forefront who extended the notion of strategy to questions of business administration. McKinsey led the way, as it shifted focus in the late-1930s, under the direction of Marvin Bower, from cost accounting to business administration. Boston Consulting Group (BCG), established in 1963, followed suit, and then Bain, which was made up of former BCG consultants. While the first wave of efficiency engineers appealed to their industry experience for credibility, the second wave relied on their pedigree. Rather than recruiting engineers or accountants, they hired MBAs, as business schools became increasingly professionalized through the 1950s and 1960s, with firms competing to recruit top ranked candidates from Ivy League schools, fostering what anthropologist Karen Ho describes as "elite kinship" networks[45] (see Chapter 4). Under the leadership of Bower, McKinsey provided the template, as it was reorganized to resemble a high-end law firm, adopting a professional partnership model and "up-or-out" promotion policies.[46]

In framing strategy as an everyday practice for both governments and corporations, consultants extended their focus from investigating questions of process to questions of positioning. Along these lines, the central question in the private sector was how a firm compared with rivals in its market. The notion that this required fact-gathering was a novel insight as companies previously did not have much information on how their products compared with their competitors. In an era of anti-trust, when companies could not directly communicate in setting prices, consultants played a vital role in showing firms how they measured up through market analysis, giving companies access to "unprecedented amounts of data on costs, markets, and competitors."[47] From there, they could identify strategic advantages that could be leveraged via price-setting, vertical integration, and economies of scale in establishing market dominance.

Beginning in the late 1970s, such methods were also applied by consultants to the public sector, showing public officials how they measured up against other governments. In response to growing national rivalries in the midst of economic stagflation, consultants introduced the notion of "competitiveness" to the political vocabulary, with the key question being how states could foster "competitive" economies. Strategy consultants played a central role in introducing this language beginning with the *Global Competitiveness Report*, which was first published by the World Economic Forum in 1979 under the guidance of Swiss management scholar Klaus Schwab and strategy guru Michael Porter (whose consulting firm The Monitor Group was later acquired by Deloitte in 2013). Ranking governments by their degree of "competitiveness," the report enabled public officials to see, for the first time, how they measured up against their "rivals," fostering a sense that they were all part of the same field with the same ultimate goal — that of becoming more "competitive." Sociologist William Davies argues that the significance of the report lay in its "self-conscious construction of a common global language through which business and political leaders could discuss how public policy influenced corporate and entrepreneurial performance."[48] In adopting the language of competitiveness, public officials were invited to see themselves as akin to corporate CEOs, making decisions with the aim of minimizing costs and maximizing productivity. In the process, a new vision of political authority was fabricated: one that treated governments as comparable to corporations.[49]

Consultants played a key role as intermediaries in translating this framework for public officials. As Davies notes, it was their function to "constantly alternate between representations of equivalence and differentiation, on the one hand representing the shared global reality that all decision makers need to recognize, and on the other representing the qualitative and quantitative differences which define rival national communities in the global 'race.'"[50] In appraising the relative competitiveness of a country, consultants rolled out new kinds of metrics that promised to inform governments on where they stood in relation to their competitors. During this time, "benchmarking" — a technique first developed in Japanese manufacturing in the 1950s and exported by management consultants to American corporations in the 1960s — was extended to the assessment of governments.[51] The term had initially been taken up by private corporations to itemize their industrial processes and gauge their competitiveness at each level of their organization. However, by the 1980s, consultants extended such metrics to governments. This involved developing methods through which different aspects of public policymaking could be translated into figures, rendering disparate qualities equivalent through new forms of quantification, all of which built on scientific management principles. New calculative methods enabled governments to be sorted and ranked in an apparently objective manner, with the consulting firms presenting themselves as mere witnesses, simply reporting the results rather than offering any substantive political advice.

Such a regime contributed to developing popular metrics through which governments around the world could be ranked; everything from education and health standards to smartness, openness, and quality of life came to be benchmarked and compared. TPSFs have positioned themselves as key intermediaries in brokering access to these rankings in a wide array of areas. For instance, McKinsey has rolled out a "Public Sector Journey" Benchmark, to assess "customer experience satisfaction" in accessing public services.[52] EY has developed an international benchmark survey on COVID-19 crisis management. Deloitte's Centre for Higher Education Excellence now offers an interactive "student success" benchmarking tool, which enables institutions to see how they compare with their peers "across a wide range of student success and equity measures."[53] The IBM Global Institute for Business Value offers to benchmark cities by their level of 'smartness.'[54] And, as we will see in Chapter 3, KPMG has set out to establish a global benchmark by which to gauge the efficiency of city services.[55]

By making public services commensurable in this way, TPSFs have contributed to reconstituting the terrain of governance, establishing a regime that pits governments against one another in competition for rankings. In the context of urban governance, management scholars Martin Kornberger and Chris Carter argue that such practices have "usher[ed] into existence a new form of competition that transforms the relationship between cities fundamentally: rankings create hierarchical relationships; they are not about singular relations between cities but generalizable characteristics that establish a homogeneous ordering framework."[56] TPSFs have been able to exercise considerable influence as the architects of such benchmarks, exercising soft power over governments by defining the norms and standards to which public officials should aspire. Moreover, as brokers of "best practices," they wield significant influence in operationalizing the practices of "optimally" performing governments that they then package as commodities to be sold to governments around the world, while simultaneously singling out those that deviate from the norm.

The regime of benchmarking and best practices has given TPSFs a tremendous amount of power in defining the very terrain through which governments understand themselves. As public policy scholar Peter Triantafillou notes, such practices have produced "a form of knowledge that strongly urges if not forces those organizations that fall below the normal to launch procedural or organizational changes."[57] As their league tables are taken up by a growing number of governments to understand their performance, these firms become deeply entrenched in defining the political landscape, establishing the standards to which governments should aspire, and disciplining wayward governments who deviate from them. This, in turn, generates a market for their services, as anxious public officials seek outside assistance to improve their rankings. As

André Broome has demonstrated in his research on benchmarking, "a reliance upon global benchmarks for diagnostic, design and evaluation purposes in reform programs ... increases demand for consultancy services by maintaining regulatory reform as a problem requiring ongoing external expertise and strategic advice."[58] Indeed, a central aim of these firms has been to both define the rules of the game — establishing norms, standards, and guidelines that apply to everyone — while simultaneously providing those who are willing and able to pay with the ability to game those same rules. This constitutes a source of their power.[59]

## Third Wave: Management Information Systems and Data Infrastructures

The first two waves paved the way for TPSFs, but these enterprises had not yet branded themselves as "professional service firms." They were framed more as consultants that were commissioned through ad hoc procurement arrangements to provide advice to public and private sector clients. It is only over the past forty years — since the 1980s — that these firms have expanded their mandate to include a range of other professional services and develop more continuous and multifaceted relationships with governments.

The "Professional Service Firm" label became widely popularized in the 1980s with a third wave of professional outsourcing that involved IT procurement and the implementation of management information systems in government. As consulting guru Tom Peters observed in 1988: "professional service firms are not just advisors. They are full-scale partners in information-collection and manipulation networks."[60] Through this time, firms pursued lucrative contracts to roll out IT infrastructures, enabling public agencies to gather and analyze data in areas such as service delivery, payroll, procurement, demographics, decision-making, and citizen engagement. This transformed the relationship between private consultants and public agencies, as TPSFs shifted from providing ad hoc advice to becoming entrenched in the machinery of public service delivery on an ongoing basis. Indeed, as we see in Chapter 4, it has also fostered a growing dependency by governments on these services, which has made them prone to institutional capture.[61]

Although consultants had provided such administrative infrastructures to public agencies since the beginning of the twentieth century, their procurement by governments accelerated from the 1970s onward in response to technological innovations and broader political and economic changes. Kipping notes that, in a context of stagflation and growing economic competition, "global financial markets pressured companies to concentrate on core competencies and adopt leaner management structures. Coordination of activities both within companies and with suppliers and customers became a crucial competitive advantage."[62] The demand for new management information systems was driven, in part, by the changing shape of the firm, which moved from bulky multidivisional structures to complex, just-in-time outsourcing arrangements contracting "noncore" work to low-cost suppliers often based in the Global South. This led managers to focus less on corporate organization and strategy and more on management of the value chain. Along these lines, the development of IT infrastructures was deemed essential to "obtain necessary data to maintain control over such a networked organization."[63, 64]

Such coordination problems became more pronounced in a context of deregulation and economic liberalization through the 1980s and 1990s. Once it became easier to move capital and assets around the world, multinational corporations turned to professional service firms for advice on entering new markets, allocating capital, and negotiating a complex array of jurisdictions in minimizing their costs and maximizing their returns.[65] In the process, these firms began framing themselves as "transnational" intermediaries. As a study from 1998 demonstrates, these firms came to "present themselves increasingly as supranational agents of capitalism that transcended the 'imagined communities' [...] of nations, national economies and nationalism."[66] Promising to make sense of fractious global financial networks and supply chains for government and corporate clients, these firms contributed to constructing the global architecture of neoliberalism through spreading corporate best practices, setting global accounting standards, and offering specialized services to corporations to help them run geographically dispersed operations. It was at this time that they expanded their institutional footprint — helping companies set up shop in the Global South while advising governments facing fiscal discipline from the International Monetary Fund (IMF) on how to successfully "integrate" into the global economy.

In this context, both accounting firms and IT firms have been able to leverage immense organizational footprints in their respective fields as a means of expanding their operations, shifting from providing ad hoc advisory services to providing more enduring administrative infrastructures. Through incorporating consulting, accounting frameworks, and management information systems in novel packages, they have been able to take advantage of their control over existing infrastructures to sell value-added services to their clients, paving the way for more continuous and multifaceted relationships between governments and TPSFs today.

## The Rise of the Accountants

Accounting today is dominated by the Big Four professional services firms (Deloitte, EY, KPMG, and PwC). Together, they audit more than 97 percent of publicly traded companies in the United States, all the United Kingdom's top 100 corporations, and 80 percent of Japanese listed companies.[67] As of 2022, they employed more than 1,464,000 people in 150 countries,[68] more personnel than the six most valuable companies in the world combined.[69]

Established during the Second Industrial Revolution at the end of the nineteenth century in a context of growing disconnection between managers and owners, these firms made their business attesting to the credibility of accounts of joint stock companies. As stockholders became increasingly distant from their assets, they were trusted as neutral third parties to provide an impartial account of the enterprise.[70] The Big Four professional service firms today each trace their roots back to this period (EY's ancestors date back to 1849; Deloitte's and PwC's to 1858; and KPMG's to 1818).

These firms further solidified their position in the wake of the Great Depression as governments adopted legislation requiring publicly traded companies to enlist an outside accounting firm to report their earnings, effectively creating a state-guaranteed market for auditors.[71] In many countries, especially in the liberal market economies of Canada, the United Kingdom, and the United States, government oversight of the profession was limited, and accountants were granted substantial power in governing their profession through self-regulating associations dominated by the largest firms. As management scholars note, this was a part of a "regulative bargain" by which "the state grant[ed] professions autonomy and a monopoly over a defined jurisdiction in return for self-regulation and reciprocal assistance in maintaining state authority."[72] As we see in Chapter 4, this has given these firms substantial power in shaping reporting standards and regulating personnel, which they have often designed to protect their own interests and the interests of their clients.[73]

Being mandated by governments to audit the books of publicly traded companies gave auditing firms a stable source of business, as well as a foot in the door in selling a range of other value-added services. Through the twentieth century, the big accounting firms also offered consultancy services — which they classified as "special work" — for companies looking to implement new accounting systems, restructure their operations, or adjust to new government regulations.[74] However, while they maintained a presence in the consulting field during the first two waves, their principal business came from auditing and accounting. As the auditing market became increasingly saturated through the second half of the twentieth century, with little room for further growth, these firms expanded their operations to other fields, establishing separate management consulting arms of their operations by the late 1960s.[75]

Building on their work advising governments in cost accounting and organizational restructuring, accounting firms extended their expertise to rolling out new management information systems by the 1970s. As Thomas Armbrüster notes, these firms were well-equipped to make the transition from accounting to IT infrastructures as they had been early movers in adopting IT infrastructures themselves to assist with the work of auditing.[76] With the rise of new information technologies, a central part of their business became computerization work, as they received "lucrative fees for work concerned with management information systems and computer technologies."[77] Through this time, governments employed these firms to computerize public administration services in lucrative multi-year contracts. For instance, in his history of consulting in the UK, historian Antonio Weiss recounts how, over the course of 14 years, from 1977 to 1991, the accounting firm Arthur Andersen played a central role in rolling out the UK government's Operational Strategy, which set out to computerize the administration of benefits and social security across the country with at least £315 million spent on consultancy fees.[78]

This not only involved rolling out software, but also triggered a range of other advisory services in preparing organizations for the implementation of these systems. "As part of their work on the installation of [Enterprise Resource Planning] systems," Armbrüster notes, "management consultancies quite naturally came to deal with organizational issues."[79] There was a blurry line between IT advice and organizational restructuring, which created opportunities for firms to roll out a range of different services at the intersection of the technological and the political realms. As one consultant at Andersen noted:

> Andersen Consulting was dominated by IT implementation work. But what we started to realize was that, although we could win specific battles, we could not win the war: in order to be able to deliver results to clients we needed to be able to put other processes around IT — change management, business strategy, analysis of core competencies, and so on.[80]

In the process of organizational restructuring, opportunities for cross-selling services emerged that incentivized these firms to expand their operations.

As their focus shifted to consulting and IT procurement, accounting firms began to rebrand themselves, adopting the moniker of "professional service firms" by the 1980s, starting with Price Waterhouse in 1986 and the other Big Eight firms[81] following suit.[82] Beginning in the 1980s, management consulting overshadowed auditing in these firms, with fees earned from consulting growing from 9 percent to make up almost half of their revenues.[83] Fees earned from auditing and related assurance activities now only make of 39 percent of their income worldwide. From the late 1970s onward, large accountancy firms eclipsed both the efficiency engineers and strategy firms as the dominant players in the consulting field, effectively subsuming consulting as one branch of their operations. While efficiency engineers experienced a substantial downturn in business during the economic crisis of the 1970s, the accounting firms had competitive advantages in entering the field through their economies of scale and substantial investments in IT infrastructures. Moreover, their position as auditors helped them get a foot in the door as consultants to existing clients. As Weiss notes,

> The increasing use of accountants for state work had a substantial knock-on effect on the ease in which they could offer their expanding consultancy services. Not only had relationships already been developed through the audit work of accountants, clients could save on the inevitable transaction costs associated with hiring new professional service providers.[84]

Through economies of scale, the Big Four firms were able to secure lucrative contracts with governments, building on their reputation as auditors to do work in new areas. The intertwining of auditing and consulting forged connections that linked bookkeeping with speculative and strategic logics, opening the doors to new forms of performance-based audits and management information systems, as we explore in Chapter 3.

As they expanded in scale (operating across the globe) and scope (providing a growing range of services), these firms came to command a substantial degree of autonomy in defining the nature of their work. As Suddaby, Cooper, and Royston note, they had effectively "outgrown" regulation by the state, becoming "less the subject and more the site of professional regulation."[85] This raised questions of ethics and accountability as firms came to identify more with the commercial interests of their clients than the publics that they ostensibly served. As early as 1976, a US Congressional report *The Accounting Establishment* noted: "It appears that the Big Eight firms are more concerned with serving the interests of corporate managements who select them and authorize their fees than with protecting the interests of the public, for whose benefit Congress established the position of independent auditor."[86]

As they used auditing to get the opportunity to sell more lucrative consulting services, public officials raised concerns that the interest of professional service firms in getting further contracts could undermine their neutrality, providing incentives to skew audits in the interests of their clients.[87] This became a major issue in the wake of the Enron scandal in 2001 — the largest audit failure in US history at the time — as Arthur Andersen was caught aiding the energy company in inflating its profits and hiding its debts. According to a *New York Times* article, Arthur Andersen had

> so thoroughly blended its corporate DNA with its client's that a steady stream of Andersen employees came to work for Enron at the trading company's futuristic downtown tower.... One Enron vice president, who was laid off in December, said Andersen often had as many as 250 employees working inside Enron's 50-story skyscraper. "They were involved in about everything there," the vice president said.... This physical proximity was accentuated by the fact that so many Enron employees had once

worked at Andersen;... the company's chief accounting officer, Richard A. Causey, had started at Andersen.... "I remember them saying that once you got to a certain level at Andersen, they would suggest you tried to get hired by a lot of clients like Enron," the former Enron vice president said. "This would provide them with access to more accounting jobs."[88]

In the wake of Enron's collapse, governments around the world attempted to address this problem by prohibiting firms from advising clients they were also auditing. For a short time, in the early 2000s, this led the Big Four firms to divest their consulting arms, selling them off to the big IT consultancies, as we see in the next section. However, they bounced back as they rebuilt their consultancy wings in the mid-2000s, which very quickly returned to being principal sources of revenue, rekindling debates on the proper relationship between auditing and consulting that remain ongoing.[89]

## The Rise of Information Technology Consultancies

As the Big Four accounting firms moved into IT infrastructures in the 1970s and 1980s, IT companies like Capgemini, EDM, and IBM moved in the opposite direction — shifting from IT acquisitions to consulting. As with the Big Four accounting firms, many of these companies have a long history of designing and implementing IT infrastructures for governments. For instance, IBM got its start producing machines for the tabulation of census data in the late nineteenth century, providing logistical support during the two world wars, and information processing capacities to rapidly expanding welfare and warfare states through the 1950s and 1960s. In the United States, these firms became central to a growing contractor state that emerged in the wake of the Second World War, particularly in the areas of defence and aerospace contracting, which was coordinated through a complex web of outsourcing arrangements. In this context, as McKenna notes, "technocratic consulting contracts replaced organizational studies as the primary source of consulting assignments within the federal government."[90]

However, while the contractor state had already been well-established in the United States by the 1960s, government outsourcing to IT firms really got going in the 1970s for both political and technological reasons. The development of the first microprocessors in 1971 opened a whole new market for management information systems in government. Facing a growing fiscal crisis, neoliberal reformers in many countries attacked the capacity of civil servants to deliver such systems, framing the private sector IT firms as more innovative and efficient. "Encouraged to follow private-sector fashion," Agar notes, "government departments chose to concentrate on 'core competencies,' which did not include computing."[91] In this context, governments turned to private companies for the development and maintenance of management information systems. Over four decades, these firms integrated IT infrastructures with consulting in rolling out new management information systems to governments. This served as a very lucrative market for consultants, with outsourced IT services forming a market of $12.7 billion in the United States by 1994 and growing markedly through the 1990s and early 2000s.[92]

Although IT firms initially focused on providing the hardware for governments, by the 1990s, the market for IT infrastructure had become saturated and many IT companies turned their attention from hardware design and production to software development and consultancy. Along these lines, Microsoft established the Microsoft Consulting Services Group in 1990 with the aim of helping large clients "better use Microsoft products to build complex information systems."[93] IBM established a consulting wing in 1992, recruiting heavily from the Big Four accounting firms and the Elite Three strategy consultancies with the aim of extending its operations into traditional management consulting, including strategy consulting and process reengineering.[94] The firm expanded even further with its purchase of PwC consulting in 2002, bringing another 30,000 consultants into its operations. From there, it sold its PC division to Lenovo in 2004 in order to "move up the value chain" into "more lucrative fields."[95] Likewise, the French IT company Capgemini acquired the consulting arm of Ernst & Young for $11 billion in 2000, and Atos Information Technology acquired KPMG consulting in 2000 for EUR 657 million.

Through this time, new kinds of partnership arrangements emerged, fostering more continuous relationships between governments and TPS-Fs. This included everything from "ad hoc consultancy, through project tendering or facilities management, to systems integration projects or even 'strategic alliances' and 'partnership agreements.'"[96] Very often, IT companies deliberately bid very low for contracts "in the expectation that, once dependence had built up, costs could be recouped at a later date." For instance, Ross Perot's company, EDS, got its foot in the door by offering system development at no cost to the contractor in return for a share of the business gains. Agar characterizes the dynamic as a self-perpetuating spiral: "As outsourcing companies pick up more business, their expertise grows."[97] Correspondingly, as government expertise falls, government bodies become ever more dependent on companies to which business has been outsourced. In this way, TPSFs moved to hardwire neoliberal operating systems into the state, as advice was no longer provided intermittently on an ad hoc basis but became entrenched in real-time management information systems. This transformed both consulting work and IT infrastructures, opening the doors to the direct delivery of public services, as we see in the next section.

## Fourth Wave: Outsourcing Firms

Following the computerization campaigns of the 1980s and 1990s, we can add a fourth wave of consultants who have actively taken on the delivery of public services alongside the provision of data infrastructures. From the 1990s onwards, firms like G4S, Capita, Serco and Atos Origin expanded their mandate from consulting to acquire contracts in "back-office" services that were deemed to be outside of the 'core competencies' of governments. According to historian Antonio Weiss, this shift from advisory work to direct service delivery has marked "a significant discontinuity from historical precedent," which speaks to the changing relationship between the public and private sector going into the twenty-first century.[98]

With the rise of Compulsory Competitive Tendering under Thatcher — which required that public agencies open in-house services to private competition — the United Kingdom provided a beachhead for such operations. The story of Capita is notable here: Established in 1984 as part of the Chartered Institute for Public Finance and Accounting, a national membership-based association that provided IT systems and training to staff in local governments, the organization was acquired by investors in 1987 and transformed into a private consultancy. While initially advising local governments in the United Kingdom on how to implement and adapt to central government legislation, the firm moved to directly delivering computer services for local governments by the late 1980s. By taking these services under their wing, the firm enabled governments to make cutbacks without fear of public reprisal. In a context of austerity, Weiss notes, "Capita would take on responsibility for the employment of staff in outsourced services and therefore take the public blame for compulsory redundancies."[99]

Building on these roots in local government outsourcing, Capita grew rapidly through the 1990s and early 2000s, and, as of 2020, serves more than 20,000 clients, including regional, local, and central governments, providing services in everything from health and education to transportation, insurance, and pensions. As journalist Joel Benjamin notes, "Capita became the Vampire Squid of business process outsourcing, its money grabbing tentacles extending through every layer of Government."[100] In some areas, Capita had even assumed control over a majority of services for local governments. For instance, the London borough of Barnet adopted what it called an "easyCouncil" model (inspired by the no-frills airline "easyJet"), in which the firm took charge of over 70 percent of the services in two decade-long, multi-million-pound contracts, including care for people with disabilities, legal services, cemeteries and crematoriums, IT, finance, human resources, planning and regeneration, trading standards and licensing, council housing, environmental health, procurement, parking, and highways (see Chapter 5).[101] Building on its base in local government, Capita has also scaled up its operations to central government, collecting the BBC licence fee, operating the Criminal Records Bureau and managing electronic tagging of offenders, and taking charge of food inspection services.

Through the 2000s, outsourcing firms quickly extended their operations to other countries. As of 2022, Capita has offices in over 450 locations, including Ireland, India, China, the United Kingdom, the United States, South Africa, the United Arab Emirates, Germany, Austria, Switzerland, and Poland. G4S operates in over ninety countries around the world, including Canada, where the firm holds the contract for passenger and baggage screening at airports. Serco operates in thirty-five countries, including managing electronic monitoring systems for parolees in four Canadian provinces. It has also assumed responsibility for providing Driver Examination Services, life insurance agent certification, and security guard/private investigator accreditation services in Ontario. And it has facility maintenance contracts at two key Canadian military bases.[102]

Such firms have substantially reshaped the relationship between the public and private sector. In the early years of the twentieth century, these firms largely operated as consultants, providing ad hoc advice to governments, but these days they are directly providing many day-to-day public services. Weiss notes that "this public-private relationship helped to cement the new mixed economy of public and private sector bodies working in partnership."[103] As we see in the next two chapters, this has fostered dependency relationships. As Weiss concludes, it has "changed the nature of what the state does (at least temporarily) and because it proved difficult to take such functions back into the public sector once they had been outsourced, thereby compromising the future effectiveness of any state model which did not look to the private sector for support."[104]

## Putting It All Together

Tracing the history of these four waves helps us understand the role of TPSFs in governance today. In each case, we can see the ascendancy of certain management ideas, professional identities, organizational frameworks, and sociotechnical infrastructures in providing services to governments. While smaller firms made up of experienced engineering consultants were ascendant in the early twentieth century, and strategy consultants with MBAs became prominent in the 1950s and 1960s, these days we see the ascendancy of large multidivisional professional service firms equipped with armies of IT consultants and back-office workers. While earlier incarnations of consultants were much more reliant on human capital as they drew on experience and reputation to deliver their services, these days TPSFs have come to draw much more on extensive data infrastructures to circulate information across jurisdictions.

Of course, we should be careful not to draw too clean a line; it would be easy to frame each successive generation as a changing-of-the-guard. But each wave did not simply replace the previous one; rather, each wave has incorporated earlier models into its repertoire.[105] As Armbrüster notes, "different kinds of services often overlap within a single consulting project, and the separation and distinction of these services is often artificial."[106] Hence, we can see many TPSFs continuing to provide services such as efficiency engineering alongside cost accounting, service benchmarking, IT apps, and cloud computing. Moreover, these programs are often blended, with TPSFs offering data infrastructures to assess, process, and benchmark services in real time. For instance, IBM's Smart Cities campaign — promoted as a way of modernizing urban governance — contains all four elements. Launched in 2008, it involves scientific management through its focus on accumulating data on city services, which can be broken down into their component parts and restructured to optimize efficiencies. It also pursues benchmarking, providing cities with tools through which they can gauge their degree of "smartness." And, of course, it also offers IT infrastructures and management information systems, including the platforms through which cities can deliver and assess services in real time.[107]

By blending cost accounting, benchmarking, IT infrastructures, and service delivery, TPSFs have been able to rapidly expand, achieving market dominance by taking advantage of network effects and cross-selling to entrench themselves in governance. This has enabled the concentration of power within the field of professional services themselves. Firms that command more expansive data infrastructures can generate economies of scale, making it cheaper and easier to gather and process data.[108] It has also enabled the establishment of economies of scope, though which firms can gain competitive advantages by extending their infrastructures to offer a range of services.

Still, we should be careful not to conflate these different firms; each firm bears its stamp. For instance, the Big Four firms have leveraged their oligopoly in auditing to gain a foothold in management consulting. However, they are not as prominent in the field of IT infrastructure, which continues to be dominated by IT firms like IBM, Microsoft, and Capgemini. McKinsey continues to be heavily oriented toward high-level strategy consulting, remaining more invested in human capital, and does not provide adjacent services like accounting or, until recently, IT infrastructures. In fact, as Armbrüster points out, it is precisely because they do not dabble in such "lower fee" services that they have been able to preserve their reputation as an "elite" service provider.[109]

The continued differentiation of the field is also reflected in government procurement, with many governments spending substantially more on IT consulting. For instance, an appraisal of Canadian federal spending on "professional and special services" between 2011 and 2022 shows that over 66 percent of spending went to IT consultants, with large contracts going to IT companies like IBM and Accenture and only 30 percent of spending going to management consultants, which were more the domain of the Big Four firms and McKinsey (Professional Institute of the Public Service of Canada [PIPSC]; see Figure 2.1). The top professional service providers for the Canadian federal government are overwhelmingly IT firms, with IBM and Microsoft bringing in over $15 billion and $10 billion respectively between 2010 and 2020, while PwC and Deloitte brought in $800 million and $580 million over the same period. Clearly, the market continues to be segmented.

Nevertheless, there are indications of convergence. The Big Four firms have recently made heavy investments in IT services, as they have prioritized acquisitions of smaller IT companies specializing in artificial intelligence (AI), blockchain, and other technologies. They rely on tech start-ups to innovate, and then scoop up the companies that have been successful. A Deloitte Canada representative recently noted that "the [IT] market is like an incubator for smaller players, and then they are acquired."[110] Such trends accelerated during the COVID-19 pandemic, as professional service firms competed to extend the range of services that they offered to testing and tracing apps, vaccine trackers, and other platform-based forms of service delivery. This explains the increase in government spending on the Big Four firms during the pandemic, as they received more contracts to provide IT infrastructures.

As we will see in the following chapters, the convergence of accounting, consulting, IT infrastructures, and service delivery raises troubling questions regarding the relationship between TPSFs and governments.

**Figure 2.1 Federal Spending on Personnel Outsourcing, 2011–22**

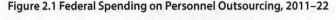
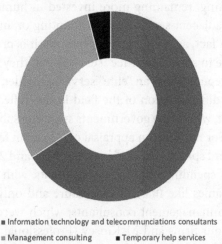

- Information technology and telecommunciations consultants
- Management consulting   - Temporary help services

Source: Reprinted with permission from the Professional Institute of the Public Service of Canada (PIPSC); based on data collected from the proactive disclosure of contracts.

As these firms have moved from being ad hoc consultants to providing ongoing services to governments, there is a problem of dependency. As public agencies lose their capacity to deliver services themselves and become reliant on privately owned infrastructures, it can be very difficult for them to exit these relationships.[111] This can give TPSFs leverage in extracting exorbitant rents from the public sector. ·

Moreover, while these firms have assumed control over the core hardware of governance, they are not often accountable for the services they provide. Public officials are directly responsible for the delivery of public services, but these firms operate at one step removed. Their performance is mediated by contracts whose contents and deliverables are often not disclosed for reasons of cabinet confidence and commercial sensitivity, which makes it almost impossible for the public to hold them accountable for what they deliver. Additionally, with the loss of public personnel capable of assessing contracts or services, it can be difficult for governments to provide oversight of their operations. In fact, it is often TPSFs themselves that are commissioned to assess the delivery of outsourced services. This raises questions of allegiance, as often these firms are simultaneously advising private companies and individuals on how to navigate the very same regulations that the government has enlisted them to design and deliver. For instance, McKinsey notoriously advised Purdue on how to keep opioids legal while they served as advisors to the US Food and Drug Administration where they helped restructure the agency responsible for regulating opioids.[112] And in many countries, representatives from the Big Four firms serve on accounting standards boards, responsible for drafting new tax regulations, while at the same time advising their wealthy clients on how to take advantage of loopholes in those same regulations, as we saw in 2023 with the PwC tax scandal in Australia.[113] In both cases, the advice that these firms provide to the public is compromised by their allegiances to their private sector clients.

As we see in the next chapter, such conflicts become apparent in the programs these firms deliver, which have enabled corporate elites to evade oversight or regulation, while, at the same time, subjecting public programs to cutbacks and privatization.

# Chapter 3

# Programs:
# Evading, Auditing,
# Financializing, Privatizing

As discussed in the previous chapter, management consultants, accountants, efficiency engineers, and strategy gurus were involved in public-sector reform in the Anglo-American heartland well before the neoliberal era. However, it is only since the 1980s — in a context of economic globalization, financial deregulation, corporate mergers and acquisitions, privatization, and debt restructuring — that these enterprises have been able to expand the scope and scale of their operations to become transnational professional service firms (TPSFs). And, as they have transformed their identities, they have transformed their relationships with governments, shifting from ad hoc advisory services to providing some of the basic infrastructures of service delivery. In this chapter, we look at how TPSFs have contributed to the hardwiring of neoliberal operating systems into the state.

Neoliberalism is a political project that sets out to make markets the principal framework for ordering society. It is premised on a normative vision that sees markets as the most efficient, ethical, and transparent means of organizing social life.[1] As the neoliberal economist Friedrich Hayek (1945) famously argued, state planners can never match the capacities of markets to circulate and process information.[2] By refraining from exercising control from above and letting information circulate freely via price signals, neoliberals argue that society can most efficiently respond to challenges and optimally allocate outputs. This vision is premised on the twin pillars of market naturalism and market justice.[3] On the one hand, the market is viewed as a "biological-like organism" tending toward "law-like equilibrium and prosperity as long as it is free of government coercion and moral interference." On the other hand, it is argued that "distributional outcomes produced by legally voluntary market transactions operating in a neutral price system" are morally just.[4]

In the wake of the economic crisis of the 1970s, governments around the world have been guided by neoliberal policies that set out to cut taxes, deregulate markets, slash government spending, and privatize public services under the auspices of "choice" and "competition." Along these lines, neoliberalism has been associated with two interrelated sets of strategies: starving the state of revenue and doing more with less.

Responding to the economic stagflation of the 1970s, neoliberal politicians spearheaded taxpayers' revolts taking aim at "reckless" government spending, targeting public-sector workers and "special interest groups," who, it was argued, were taking advantage of their position to extract exorbitant rents from the public.[5] Neoliberals have positioned themselves as acting in the interests of the taxpayer and have prioritized low taxes as a means of eliminating waste and fostering economic growth. Moreover, they have pursued policies of financial deregulation enabling the free movement of capital across borders. Along these lines, neoliberal policies have taken aim at bureaucratic red tape that was deemed to hinder financial innovation.

They have also set out to make governments more market-like in their operations. This has involved taking up the principles of New Public Management (NPM), aiming "to make government more efficient and responsive by employing private sector techniques and creating market conditions for the delivery of public services."[6] Rather than *rowing* — directly delivering services themselves — strategy consultants David Osborne and Ted Gaebler popularized the idea that governments should focus on *steering*, delegating services to those who are best able to deliver them.[7] Under these policies, political and economic elites have pursued the privatization and outsourcing of public services. On the basis that market competition is more efficient than state planning, they have adopted policies that give private sector actors a greater role in financing and operating public infrastructures and social services, and where they cannot outright privatize services, consultants and policymakers have set out to transform the public sector into a market-like arena in which public agencies are incentivized to compete against one another for scarce funding.

As we demonstrate in this chapter, this utopian vision of market libertarianism is far from the reality. While, in principle, neoliberalism promises transparency and accountability, in practice it has fostered fragmentation and opacity. Rather than enabling the free circulation of information, processes of marketization under neoliberalism have contributed to the enclosure and monopolization of data, which is hidden away in enclaves and carefully guarded by private gatekeepers under nondisclosure agreements and confidentiality clauses. To gauge the profits and losses of large corporations, for instance, one must navigate a tangled web of shell corporations and Special Purpose Vehicles dispersed across diverse jurisdictions and subject to different regulatory standards and reporting requirements. Power, in this context, is generated through the capacity to leverage information asymmetries.[8] Through accumulating information across different markets and regulatory regimes, actors are then able to engage in *arbitrage*, taking advantage of price differences across markets to generate profits.[9]

The capacity of private firms to leverage information asymmetries in establishing monopolies has been perhaps the most alarming in the area of information technology (IT).[10] As digital economies specialist Nick Srnicek notes, the digital platform has become a model "to monopolize, extract, analyze and use increasingly large amounts of data being recorded."[11] Many books and articles have illuminated how Big Tech — including firms such as Amazon, Google, and Facebook (now Meta) — take advantage of information asymmetries, filtering data up the system while restricting users' access to information to generate profits.[12] "In their position as an intermediary," Srnicek argues, "platforms gain not only access to more data but also control and governance over the rules of the game."[13]

However, alongside Big Tech, TPSFs are also positioned to thrive. While serving as so-called thought leaders responsible for promulgating the fantasies of libertarian market utopia, TPSFs have made it their business to collect, codify, and assess business practices, government standards, and regulatory practices across domains and regions. As Julie Eckl and Tine Hanrieder show, the power of these firms derives from their capacity to stand as *curators* of information: "Serv[ing] as a nodal point towards which knowledge flows," these firms "can determine which knowledge is shared with others."[14] From this perspective, their power is double-sided. On the one hand, power is generated through the capacity to acquire information across domains and regions. Those firms that are able to achieve economies of scale and scope are consequently better positioned as information brokers.[15] On the other hand, by selectively allocating information to clients, these firms exercise power through cherry-picking ideas, benchmarks, and best practices that serve their purposes. The whole thing only works to the extent that their clients do not have access to the entire archive or the formulae themselves. Hence, while these firms promise to give their clients more information, their business model is premised on practices of strategically withholding information, which, in turn, generates ongoing demand for their services. In this sense, the entire business model of TPSFs is premised on opacity and dependency.

This is reflected in the services offered by TPSFs. In tax consulting, auditing, financializing, and privatizing, the power of these firms is premised on their role as intermediaries upon which clients must rely to be able to understand and negotiate the wider field. In these areas, TPSFs have positioned themselves as both the standard-setters, responsible for establishing the norms governing the allocation of capital, and the *arbitrageurs*, granting those who are willing and able to pay the capacity to game these same standards.

In the first section, we discuss their role as architects of tax avoidance. Here, the Big Four firms have been able to take advantage of their economies of scale in auditing as a means of selling instruments of regulatory arbitrage to the wealthy and to large corporations. Through their comprehensive knowledge of different tax regimes around the world, they can act as masters of code, "navigating the complex interdependencies of multiple legal systems from which they pick and choose the rules."[16] As we show, this has contributed to a substantial drain on public resources, fundamentally restricting the mandate of governments to deliver services and infrastructures.

While their command of the archives enables TPSFs to sell instruments of regulatory arbitrage to the wealthy and to multinational corporations, these instruments can also be put to work by TPSFs to enforce discipline and restraint for the public sector. In the second section, we explore the work of these firms in rolling out new forms of audit to the public sector. By merging bookkeeping with strategic planning, we explore how firms take advantage of their private archive as a means of setting benchmarks and best practices for public agencies. Through the advancement of benchmarks, as sociologists Wendy Espeland and Mitchell Stevens note, there is a slippage between the normal in the statistical sense and the normal in the moral sense, as "the 'outliers,' 'under-achievers,' and 'under-performers' produced by performance measures become targets of manipulation, disapproval and anxious self-scrutiny."[17]

Moreover, their command of the archives has also enabled these firms to make the public sector more market-like. In the third section, we explore how these firms have set out to transform public services into objects of financial speculation. Here, firms have taken the programs through which investors ring-fence liabilities and obfuscate account-ability in the private sector and applied them to the public sector, ena-bling governments to invest in infrastructure in a context of austerity through complex vehicles for private sector financing, often at an ex-orbitant cost. As we show, TPSFs now serve as powerful gatekeepers in creating and popularizing the techniques through which the value of public infrastructure projects is assessed. Again, while their methods set out to demonstrate that such arrangements are more transparent and cost effective, public access to the formulae and calculations through which decisions are reached is denied, making it impossible to gauge their veracity.

Finally, TPSFs have been key actors in advancing the outright privati-zation of public services. In the last section, we explore how the process of archiving and processing information is automated and transformed into an infrastructure to which governments can subscribe for a fee. Here, firms are often able to generate leverage through their ownership of the sociotechnical infrastructures and expertise necessary to admin-ister management information systems, fostering dependency relation-ships over time and making it difficult for public officials to extricate themselves from such arrangements.

We show that the net effect of such practices has been to amplify social inequalities, contributing to a vicious cycle in which declining tax revenues, brought about in part by the tax avoidance industry, pro-voke periodic fiscal crises. And, in the context of these crises, TPSFs are then taken up as consultants who provide advice and technologies that facilitate greater austerity and privatization, shrinking the state further while creating new markets for outsourced services. As we will see in the next chapter, this process has fostered path dependencies between the state and TPSFs, enabling the increasing entrenchment of these firms in public policymaking while, in turn, expanding these firms' business opportunities.

## Tax Avoidance: The Pin-Stripe Mafia

On a global scale, the amount of revenue lost due to corporate tax avoidance is enormous. As of 2021, the Tax Justice Network estimated that governments around the world were losing a total of $483 billion a year due to tax avoidance (not including illegal tax evasion).[18] In Canada, studies have found that, on average, $22 billion per year has been lost to tax avoidance from 2014 onward, with the figure increasing each year.[19] This money could be used to improve public services, providing accessible and affordable childcare (estimated at $10 billion), free tuition for postsecondary students ($10 billion), or a national pharmacare program ($15 billion). Instead, these practices often lead to the opposite — public service cuts and austerity measures.

Sitting on government commissions, accounting standards boards and self-appointed regulatory bodies, TPSFs — and in particular the Big Four firms (KPMG, PwC, Deloitte, and EY) — have played a central role in establishing the regulatory frameworks, benchmarks and best practices through which global financial flows are managed.[20] Governments have relied on these firms as the keepers of accounts for their comprehensive knowledge of tax policy and on-the-ground experience with their clients. At the same time, it is precisely because of their comprehensive knowledge and institutional reach that these firms have been able to game the system, establishing a global tax avoidance regime that starves the state of revenue, restricting the democratic mandates of governments by undermining their fiscal capacities. In a recent study of the "Wealth Defence Industry," Lena Ajdacic, Eelke M. Heemskerk, and Javier Garcia-Bernardo note how these firms leverage access to information and loose reporting requirements to exercise power:

> As auditors, accountancy firms accumulate a high level of knowledge about their clients. When checking financial statements, they have direct access to a broad range of information concerning organizational, financial and operating activities of the corporation under audit. Due to the high complexity of information in the development of wealth defence strategies and the limited reach of regulatory actors, there is room for "creative accounting" and legal innovation.[21]

Indeed, the International Consortium of Investigative Journalism have described the Big Four firms as "central architects of the offshore system — and key players in an array of cross-border transactions that raise legal and ethical questions."[22] For this reason, British accounting professor Prem Sikka calls them the "Pin-Stripe Mafia."[23]

While the practice of tax avoidance is not new, these firms have played a pivotal role in transforming what Brooks describes as a "relatively amateurish minority sport" into a worldwide industry.[24] As early as 2005, the US Senate Permanent Subcommittee on Investigations noted that

> the tax shelter industry had moved from providing one-on-one tax advice in response to tax inquiries to also initiating, designing, and mass marketing tax shelter products ... dubious tax shelter sales were no longer the province of shady, fly-by-night companies with limited resources. They had become big business, assigned to talented professionals at the top of their fields and able to draw upon the vast resources and reputations of the country's largest accounting firms.[25]

Yet, while red flags have been raised for many years, the tax avoidance services pioneered by the Big Four firms continue to proliferate. Tax consulting services make up much of the Big Four firms' business, which, in 2022 alone, generated over USD 40 billion in global revenues.[26] While "some tax advice results in transactions or restructuring that are undertaken for commercial reasons and are neutral," a UK House of Commons (2013) report notes, "much of the advice is aimed at minimising the tax that wealthy individuals or corporations pay."[27] The Big Four firms have played a leading role here. UK government figures reported that "three quarters of tax avoidance schemes were 'purchased from the big accountants.'"[28] These firms have invested substantial resources — including money, personnel, and technologies — into packaging and promoting these schemes. For instance, in the United States, KPMG established a "Tax Innovation Center" and "Tax Services Idea Bank" with the aim of developing tax avoidance schemes that would increase the firm's revenue. Personnel then received training at a "Sales Opportunity Center," which included telemarketing staff who would make cold calls to find wealthy buyers.[29]

In Canada, KPMG's role in tax avoidance became a scandal in 2015, when news broke that a wealthy family — the Coopers — had paid virtually no taxes for eight years.[30] This, of course, raised a myriad of questions around how the family had managed to do this while simultaneously slipping under the radar of the tax authorities. The family claimed that they did not know that the scheme they had been using to avoid paying the state taxes was illegal. They had, as they said, simply arrived in Canada as newcomers and, not knowing much about Canadian tax laws, had approached what they considered to be one of the country's most respected accounting firms to manage their wealth.

KPMG had designed the scheme that allowed the family to dodge taxes for years. It worked by way of hiding money in offshore accounts on the Isle of Man, where investment and other income would be reported as being given as gifts to offshore companies and therefore be nontaxable. KPMG also sold this scheme to twenty-one other wealthy individuals in Canada, many of whom remained anonymous in their statements against the firm fearing the consequences of doing otherwise. While clients alleged that they thought they had complete control over their money, KPMG claimed that clients were explicitly told that they were giving up control of their assets — a claim made despite the firm's own documents disputing these very facts.[31] As one observer noted, "nobody gives 20 million dollars away to an Isle of Man company with no strings attached, not for a 100-grand cheque you just wrote to KPMG."[32]

The origins of the scheme can be traced back to 1999, when KPMG sent out a "product alert" to their personnel, instructing them to target wealthy Canadians worth at least $10 million by offering them the ability to receive "free of tax" money. KPMG asked for a 15 percent cut of the taxes dodged so it was a lucrative arrangement for the firm. From the Coopers, KPMG collected CAD 300,000 between 2002 and 2008, and the family themselves had $26 million hidden in offshore accounts.

Drawing from their global footprint and extensive knowledge of tax laws, the Big Four firms have orchestrated similar schemes in countless countries around the world.[33] In 2012, the Tax Justice Network estimated that 21 to 32 trillion USD, a "significant fraction of global private financial wealth ... has been invested virtually tax free through the world's still expanding black hole of more than 80 offshore secrecy jurisdictions."[34] More recently, a 2021 report from the National Bureau of Economic Research in the United States estimated that by using "sophisticated accounting techniques that are difficult to trace, such as offshore tax shelters, pass-through businesses and complex conservation easements," the wealthiest Americans "hide more than 20 percent of their wealth," with "the top 1 percent of earners accounting for more than a third of all unpaid federal taxes."[35]

While assisting the wealthiest members of society avoid their taxes, the Big Four firms have also enabled tax avoidance for corporations. As early as 2001, Deloitte reported that, in the United Kingdom, 52 percent of multinationals used "novel tax planning ideas which they would expect the Revenue to challenge and/or test in the courts."[36] And, as a 2021 study on tax haven networks demonstrates, there is a clear connection between the size of a multinational enterprise's tax haven network and their use of a Big Four firm for auditing purposes.[37] Indeed, the study presents evidence that suggests a causal relationship between the two on a global scale: multinational enterprises that "take on a Big 4 accountancy firm subsequently increase the size of their tax haven networks, relative to those firms which do not take on a Big 4 accountancy firm."[38] Likewise, Ajdacic, Heemskerk, and Garcia-Bernardo have documented that clients of the Big Four have a higher number of subsidiaries placed in jurisdictions that provide secrecy and low corporate taxes.[39]

Some well-known examples of corporate tax avoidance schemes include EY's "tax-efficient off-market swap" arrangement and PwC's "Double Irish Dutch Sandwich," which took advantage of "complex corporate structures to exploit tax treaties and tax rate differentials and arbitrage global tax systems."[40] PwC was also at the heart of the LuxLeaks scandal which broke in 2014 when the International Consortium of Investigative Journalists revealed the firm's collusion with Luxembourg to manufacture tax avoidance schemes on a massive scale for some of the world's biggest corporations, including Amazon, Koch Industries, Disney, Pepsi, Ikea, Accenture, and more.[41]

Such scandals have fuelled widespread distrust of the Big Four firms. A recent Organisation for Economic Co-operation and Development (OECD) study surveying 1,200 tax officials from 138 countries found that most of these tax officials believe that "the Big Four accounting firms try to exploit loopholes in laws to help clients at least some of the time."[42] Only a quarter believe that the Big Four "consistently follow the spirit of the law," while 30 percent said the firms "never did so or did so in only a few cases."[43] Yet, these firms' monopoly within the industry often makes it difficult for authorities to take substantive legal action. In his book, *Bean Counters,* Richard Brooks recounts an ex-KPMG lawyer telling US senators: "There was a 'too few to fail' attitude, that all of the firms, the Big Four and Big Five accounting firms, are doing this and they cannot shut down all of us."[44]

Consequently, their practices are often exonerated by public agencies. In the Canadian KPMG case, for instance, while investigations were ongoing, the Canada Revenue Agency (CRA) offered amnesty to all 21 KPMG clients under the sole condition that they pay back the taxes owed to the Canadian state. Then, CRA dropped any plans to further investigate KPMG as well. Even in situations where firms have been fined by governments, they often face no other legal consequences and continue to be treated as neutral (and beneficial) actors and partners by governments, as we show in the next sections.

Moreover, the firms often take advantage of the limited capacities of tax authorities to investigate these types of schemes. The risk of getting caught is factored into their analysis in deciding on whether to go ahead with their schemes. For instance, in a hearing by the UK House of Commons Committee of Public Accountants in 2013, a senior PwC employee provided evidence that the firm "had a policy that stated that they sell tax avoidance schemes that have a 25 percent chance of withstanding a legal challenge."[45] In other words, they sell schemes to clients that have a 75 percent chance of being deemed illegal.[46] Others "admitted that they sell schemes that they consider to have a '50 percent chance of being upheld in court.'"[47] And if these schemes should be subject to an investigation and end up in court, the firms often conclude that the risk of getting fined does not outweigh the profits made through crafting and selling these schemes. Penalties are written off as just another cost of doing business.[48]

Through such practices, the Big Four firms have substantially limited the capacities of governments around the world. Through their role in depleting the public purse, preventing governments from fulfilling the "social investment" mandated through the ballot-box," critical accounting scholars argue that they "exercise the ultimate veto on democratic choices."[49] Nevertheless, as we see in the following sections, this has not stopped governments from giving these firms substantial influence over public policymaking. Indeed, public officials often turn to these same firms in the context of fiscal crises to balance the books.

## Austerity: Wolves in Sheep's Clothing

As discussed in the previous section, the Big Four firms play a significant role in starving the state of revenue. Through devising and selling tax avoidance schemes, they have taken advantage of regulatory loopholes that have enabled billions of dollars to be squirrelled away in low tax jurisdictions each year. In this context, the tax revenues of many countries have either stagnated or declined over the past forty years. Facing declining revenues, governments have experienced periodic fiscal crises from the 1970s onwards. And, in a context of fiscal crises, these same firms have stepped in again to advise governments on cutting costs and privatizing services.

Indeed, TPSFs have played a crucial role in popularizing the narrative that austerity is necessary — that there is no alternative but to cut costs. This was a central line pushed by these firms in the wake of the 2008 economic crisis, just after governments around the world spent billions bailing out the banks. Here, we find KPMG at the centre again. In 2009, KPMG commissioned a study interviewing 124 senior state officials from six countries to understand the impact of the global economic crisis on the public sector. Entitled *The Wolf Is at the Door*, the findings of the study were stark: "Governments around the world will urgently need to save money. This time it's for real and not a false alarm."[50] To cope with the state's ballooning fiscal deficit and the growing demands for services from an aging population, they argued that "radical" changes to public services were urgently required. In effect, "the whole business or service delivery model of the public sector must change … the wolf really is at the door"[51] And KPMG would provide the tools necessary to deal with it.

Building on their background in scientific management and cost accounting, TPSFs — especially the Big Four accounting firms and the Elite Three strategy firms (McKinsey, Bain, and Boston Consulting Group) — have played a central role in providing governments with programs and technologies to find cost savings. Special auditing methods and tools make up a key product line of these firms that are then marketed to governments as a means of achieving austerity. Indeed, the centrality of audits as policymaking instruments, and the role of TPSFs in delivering them, has been a distinctive feature of the neoliberal era. As accounting professor Michael Power notes, prior to the 1970s, auditing only played a relatively minor role in policy discourses and was assigned relatively "low epistemic and symbolic status."[52] However, over the past four decades, there has been a veritable audit explosion, as a growing number of policy areas have become framed as "auditable."[53] This reflects the expanding mandate of the accounting sciences, which has come to be used not simply as a means of financial reporting, but also in overseeing new performance-related mandates in government.[54]

In an era of neoliberal restructuring that sets out to achieve "value for money" for the taxpayer, governments have turned to TPSFs to undertake this kind of work. This has been most readily apparent in the United Kingdom, where TPSFs played a central role in expanding the mandate of auditing with the aim of creating an *enterprise culture* in government. This led to the establishment of the Audit Commission under Thatcher in 1984, which became a powerful gateway for the entry of TPSF personnel into government and policymaking. In recounting the rise of "audit culture," Cris Shore describes its founding as

> the key moment in British history when the discourse and practices of financial accountancy shifted and expanded to include the "monitoring and performance" and identification of "best practice." Audit no longer meant just checking the books: it now shaped the definition of what constitutes "good governance" and the formation of public policy.[55]

Building on this, government legislation has often required that public agencies and civil society groups — including municipalities, NGOs, indigenous governments, universities, and hospitals — be assessed via audits to be eligible for funding. Beyond just looking at the financial records of these organizations, accounting firms have deepened the mandate of audits by developing metrics for determining productivity, establishing performance benchmarks that enable the transformation of public services into competitive markets in which different service providers were pitted against one another in a competition for scarce funding.

For instance, in the United Kingdom's university sector, the adoption of the Research Assessment Exercise (RAE) in 1992 (renamed REF in 2014) set out to achieve value for money by making university funding dependent on meeting government targets. It set out to measure and rank universities by the quality of their research activities, doling out scarce funding to institutions that performed better, thereby pitting them against one another.[56] A wide array of studies have called attention to the harmful effects of such models on higher education.[57] Such processes have fostered record-high levels of anxiety among academic ranks as they are exposed in new ways to the scrutiny of external evaluations and academic units are forced to dedicate an ever-increasing amount of time, energy, and administrative resources to performatively demonstrating their academic worth.[58] It has also contributed to a ballooning managerial class, which includes an army of consultants frequently enlisted from TPSFs to advise universities on how to improve their rankings while at the same time publicizing their own league tables as a means of exercising soft power over university administrators.[59] It is no surprise that consulting in higher education has exploded with the rise of these new forms of assessment.

Drawing from the UK model, governments in Canada have likewise moved toward an enterprise culture in government, providing lucrative contracts to TPSFs to undertake performance-based audits of countless public services. This has been especially apparent in Ontario. Beginning in the mid-1990s, under the leadership of Premier Mike Harris, the Progressive Conservative Party of Ontario mounted a self-described "Common Sense" revolution across the province in which they set out to cut costs and rationalize services in the interests of the "taxpayer."[60] Drawing inspiration from the principles of NPM and the audit explosion taking root in the UK, the provincial government pushed for performance metrics as a means of disciplining public agencies, drawing them into a hierarchical regime by which they would be pressured to compete against one another for favourable ratings. This was reflected in the 1997 Ontario Budget, which committed to "open and accountable government," requiring public-sector organizations "to identify opportunities to improve service delivery and involve the private sector in the design and delivery of those services," as well as developing and communicating "measurable performance indicators" in making services comparable across jurisdictions.[61]

Municipal governments were a central target. In 2001, Ontario became the first state or province in North America to mandate a performance measurement program for all municipalities, requiring that they publicly disclose standardized information on nine service areas on an annual basis.[62] Building on such reforms, TPSFs have racked up millions of dollars in contracts that assess municipal services. Beginning in the late 1990s, the consulting firm Chartwell, which was acquired by KPMG in 2009, initiated what came to be called municipal service delivery reviews in municipalities across Canada. Working with city managers and senior staff, consultants compiled an inventory of all the programs provided by each municipality, which were then profiled according to their outputs. Once a relatively uniform set of outputs had been created, consultants could then subject services to a series of assessments with the aim of cutting costs.

This has given KPMG consultants considerable power in defining norms for service delivery. For instance, through "Core Service Reviews," consultants set out to determine the extent to which services are necessary to the functioning of the municipality. Typically, consultants classify services in one of four categories: "mandatory" (statutorily required by government); "essential" (necessary for the functioning of the city); "traditional" (customarily provided by municipalities); and "other." Positioning services along the continuum, they are able to identify those that they consider to be "discretionary" ("nice to haves" rather than "must haves"), and hence open to cutbacks. Consultants have then advanced arguments that services like community grants, subsidized dental care, accessibility programs in public transit, and fitness centres are discretionary — compared with long-term care or storm water maintenance — and therefore "opportunities" for cost savings.[63]

KPMG consultants also assess the standard of delivery by benchmarking municipal accounts against comparable municipalities. Typically, consultants will select provincial financial data from three or four municipalities of similar size and composition to assess whether their services measure up. Along these lines, all those services that are considered to be "above standard" are deemed to be potential areas for cutbacks and restructuring. The logic is captured well by a KPMG report to the Township of Central Frontenac. The report notes that "in some instances, the Township's service levels are higher than minimum standards and those adopted by comparator municipalities with similar populations and other characteristics, allowing the Township to reduce services to an acceptable level while reducing costs as well."[64] From this perspective, the minimum and average levels are deemed to be acceptable, opening the door for municipalities to cut costs by reducing services considered to be "above standard" and eliminating services that are not common to other municipalities.

Through the application of such metrics, municipal service delivery reviews (MSDRs) have reformatted the field in which municipalities operate. Cultivating a regime of competition between municipalities, they have valorized average and mandatory services, while rendering the above-standard and uncommon outliers — such as subsidized dental care — targets for cutbacks by policymakers. Such a classificatory model has fostered a zero-sum understanding of municipal management by pitting disparate services against one another in a competition to identify the most "excessive."

In many ways, MSDRs illustrate the convergence of information technology (IT) infrastructures, cost accounting, and benchmarking discussed in Chapter 2. The framework for MSDRs was initially spearheaded as IT infrastructure. Consultants enlisted the support of municipal IT officers associated with the Municipal Information Systems Association (MISA) in developing new management information systems for municipalities. The original program was simply intended to provide a uniform data model for municipalities. In the original proposal, the Municipal Reference Model was described as a "generic municipal model which could ultimately be used as foundation for a complete and integrated municipal information system." However, it quickly became apparent that this operation was about more than just classification. As one municipal official noted:

> As that project unfolded, [the consultants] said we would really like to help you with a data model but before you can have a data model you need to have a business model. You need to define what your lines of business are and how they relate and all of that kind of stuff ... Somehow or other, we got ourselves a business model but we never did get the data model.[65]

Through developing the sociotechnical infrastructure for classifying municipal services, consultants could then position themselves as key intermediaries in deciding their degree of "essentiality" and their standard of provision, pathologizing services that are considered to be anomalous (and therefore unnecessary) and above standard (and therefore capable of cuts). Instead of increasing funding for public services through enforcing tax laws, or enhancing reporting and closing loopholes, the problem becomes one of how to effectively do more with less by developing new methods for identifying expendability.

The example illustrates several trends that speak to how these firms operate. First, these firms often generate thin second-order knowledge based on the appraisal of existing accounts, without studying the services themselves or consulting with those who use or deliver the services. As we will see in the next chapter, TPSFs have become experts at advancing these kinds of "thin analyses." Second, just as it facilitates the accumulation of accounts at the top without having to dig deeper or consult, this kind of thin approach has also facilitated the quick and easy circulation of this assessment model across jurisdictions. The project typically takes two to four weeks to complete with a team of three to four consultants. Once the data has been compiled for a jurisdiction, it can be integrated into a private database and taken up in benchmarking other jurisdictions, generating what are called *network effects* that make it easier for TPSFs to mobilize and circulate data over time. Third, it speaks to the entrenchment of consulting services in a more enduring IT infrastructure, creating path dependencies that can be taken advantage of by TPSFs in pursuit of future contracts.

At the time of writing, service reviews are being widely promoted by another provincial government. In responding to a perceived debt crisis, the right-wing populist government of Premier Doug Ford mandated service reviews for every municipality in Ontario with the aim of finding areas of cost savings. This included a $200 million funding package for small and rural municipalities in March 2019, a $7.5 million package for larger urban municipalities and school boards in May 2019, and an additional $143 million for reviews in October 2019, much of which will be funnelled to TPSFs.[66] While the outcome of these reviews is not clear, KPMG remains the dominant firm being commissioned to undertake them, with many municipalities favouring them because of their previous experience with MSDRs.

By cataloguing and appraising services in this way, TPSFs are then able to advise on organizational restructuring. As discussed earlier, this can involve cutbacks, whereby service levels are reduced. It can also involve generating internal markets for public services, whereby public agencies are pitted against one another for scarce resources and the outsourcing of "noncore" services to private sector service providers, under the auspices of optimizing service delivery and achieving cost savings. Moreover, by leveraging private capital and expertise, it is argued, governments can enhance public services while avoiding fiscal deficits. Yet, as we show in the next two sections, these cost savings seldom materialize. In fact, as restructuring can lead to deepening dependencies on the private sector, it often ends up being a costly affair for the public that enable TPSFs to extract lucrative rents from governments.

## Financialization: Risk Rentiers

In a context of austerity, TPSFs have not only spearheaded new forms of audits, they have also played a central role in transforming public services into objects of financial speculation. Indeed, they have been central protagonists in what many commentators describe as the "financialization" of the state, which is characterized by "the increasing role of financial motives, financial markets, financial actors and financial institutions" in governance and public service delivery.[67] Over the past forty years, TPSFs have been the chief architects of financial schemes and accounting methods that enable private investors to extract steep rents from the public sector.

The role and influence of TPSFs has been especially apparent in the financialization of public infrastructures. Over past two decades, they have played a central role in popularizing the narrative that governments are experiencing an infrastructure gap that can only be remedied by private partnerships. A typical example is a 2016 report by EY, *Public Private Partnerships and the Global Infrastructure Challenge*. The report estimates that the global infrastructure gap will grow to USD 50 trillion by 2030 and identifies "fiscal and political obstacles," such as revenue constraints and high levels of public scrutiny, that hinder further infrastructure development. In a context of fiscal austerity, it argues that governments have no choice but to rely on private financing for new infrastructure projects.[68]

In addressing these issues, TPSFs have positioned themselves as key brokers of information, offering "techniques to analyze, prioritize, finance, and enable greater visibility into government infrastructure projects."[69] To access the growing market, they have established separate infrastructure divisions. For example, the 2020 Capital Projects and Infrastructure practice at PwC advertises a global network of more than 1,700 professionals who include "financial, technology, project management, risk management and engineering specialists." And KPMG boasts a global network of over 3,000 "infrastructure colleagues" in "multidisciplinary teams" that are customized "depending on the unique requirements and challenges of each project."[70]

Drawing from these networks, these firms have played a central role in designing and normalizing schemes for the financialization of public infrastructures. By popularizing new models of project finance (PF) and Special Purpose Entities (SPEs), as well as financial instruments and metrics like "risk transfer" and "value for money," they have worked to interject speculative financial rationalities into the procurement process. These models create a sense that different components of a project can be broken down and traded as objects of financial speculation.[71]

We see this especially in Public–Private Partnership (PPP) schemes, which these firms have popularized as new contractual arrangements enabling private sector firms to play a larger role in financing, building, and operating public infrastructures. The Big Four firms have been central in orchestrating PPP arrangements from the very beginning. The conceptual framework for PPPs draws from financial models that these firms first refined in high-risk projects in the energy sector in the 1970s and 1980s, beginning with oil extraction in the North Sea.[72] In confronting the scale and risk of these projects, the Big Four firms helped to formalize "private partnerships" that set out to mitigate financial risks through ring-fencing investment in project-specific financing schemes, while at the same time distributing risks to various actors in complex contractual arrangements.[73] Their work involved assembling business cases, assessing deals, and gauging expected returns against the risks posed by each project.[74]

Addressing growing concerns with sovereign debt, while at the same time warding off criticisms of privatization, the Big Four firms adapted the private partnership model to the public sector in the early 1990s. They initially marketed PPPs as "alternative" financing models that governments could draw from to keep infrastructure spending off the books.[75] As with the tax avoidance industry, this involved rolling out a complex web of shell companies and financing arrangements that limited liability for private investors. Through the creation of deal-specific structures assembling a consortium of private companies — including typically a bank or institutional lender, a construction and engineering company, and property management and facilities management firms — in project-specific SPEs, investors could be paid in increments based on the performance of the asset over the course of its life.

But in selling the scheme, TPSFs faced a problem: Although they promised that PPPs would bring significant cost savings to governments, these projects were often significantly more expensive than traditional forms of public procurement. A report by the UK National Audit Office (2018) raised questions about the cost effectiveness of these schemes after finding that privately financed school building projects were 40 percent more expensive than if they had been publicly financed, and the cost of one privately financed hospital was 70 percent more expensive.[76] Alongside the significantly higher transaction fees pocketed by the TPSF consultants for their services, private firms also typically faced higher borrowing costs than governments in financing projects. The National Audit Office (NAO) report found that the cost of borrowing in PPP projects was 2 to 3.75 percent higher than government borrowing.[77] Tim Jones from the Jubilee Debt Campaign estimated that $78 billion of capital investment took place between 1990 and 2013 in the UK, and, based on average interest rates over this time period, it would have cost $140 billion for the UK government to borrow these funds publicly. Instead, they committed to repaying $420 billion via private financing. As such, he estimated, it cost the government $280 billion *more* to borrow via private financing.[78] For this reason, Scottish Finance Minister John Swinney labelled PPPs "one of the worst excesses of the age of financial irresponsibility."[79] Indeed, "rather than representing a cost saving device," political economist Heather Whiteside has argued, PPPs "are a long-run drain on public resources."[80] So, how have TPSFs been able to justify these schemes to governments? How have they succeeded in normalizing them as a model for infrastructure procurement?

TPSFs initially justified the added costs of private financing on the basis that it allowed governments to keep their debts off the books. However, in the wake of public accounting reforms, they have gone on to justify these costs through the development of new accounting schemes that have reframed the way in which infrastructure procurement is evaluated by public officials.[81] Most notably, TPSFs have created and popularized Value for Money (VfM) assessments that are now widely used by governments to decide on the best way to procure infrastructure. VfM assessments purportedly set out to compare prospective PPP projects against a hypothetical public-sector comparator (PSC) to determine whether cost savings will be achieved. At the heart of the assessment is the (much disputed) idea that the value of PPP projects lies in their ability to transfer risks from the public to the private sector. In this way, while PPPs might be dismissed for their higher base and ancillary costs, TPSFs have been able to claim that they are still better value (and thus ultimately more cost effective) because of the interjection of "risk" as an object of valuation.

The Big Four firms have played both sides of the fence, gaining the trust of governments as standard-setters through popularizing VfM as a means of impartially assessing the value of PPPs, while at the same time opening a new market for themselves as advisors to private consortia and public officials on how best to manipulate new private financing frameworks for their benefit. Besides being responsible for the creation and widespread use of VfM assessments, these firms have also assumed responsibility for rubber stamping the method. Every time a VfM analysis is conducted, a report is produced and publicized, and, for each report, one of the Big Four firms is hired to assess its validity and provide their stamp of approval. This role is ongoing and provides lucrative business for them. It also demonstrates how these firms have positioned themselves as neutral third-party auditors who, at the end, assess the value of the arrangements that they themselves have designed. As Stuart Murray has noted, these firms "make so much money on [PPP] projects, it seems unlikely they would ever speak against them."[82] So how impartial can this approval really be?

Considering the many benefits that these firms reap from PPPs, it is perhaps not surprising that VfM reports overwhelmingly find that PPPs are worth the money despite their high costs. For instance, in our survey of ninety VfM reports in Ontario between 2008 and 2020, all rubber-stamped by Big Four firms, we found that the public procurement model was cheaper in all but four of ninety cases *before* the risk transfer metric was applied.[83] In fact, in 2014, the Auditor General of Ontario noted that projects undertaken through PPPs were more expensive — by CAD 8 billion — than if they had been undertaken through traditional public procurement.[84] And this is not exceptional; in fact, it resonates with a large body of research that has found the costs of PPP projects to be higher on average in comparison with public procurement.[85]

Moreover, public auditors and accounting professionals have questioned the transparency of the methods applied by these firms in assessing value. Murray describes VfM reports as "so subjective, so susceptible to manipulation by vested interests, and so complicated that the process needs to be handed over to independent auditors to be of any legitimate use."[86] No details are provided in VfM reports as to how the numbers are arrived at in assessing risk. The Big Four firms, economist John Loxley notes, "will not allow public access to assumptions that are vital for their conclusions, such as the source of their risk calculations," which makes it "impossible to deconstruct or reproduce" their assessments. And there is "no independent verification of risk transfer assumptions being made."[87] Moreover, public auditors have found the metric is biased toward PPPs, as "often the delivery of projects by the public sector was cast in a negative light, resulting in significant differences in the assumptions used to value risks between the public sector delivering projects and the [PPP] approach."[88]

Despite such criticisms, TPSFs have managed to popularize VfM as a metric. In doing so, they have successfully worked to shift the focus of infrastructure procurement toward a speculative, market-based rationality in which potential risks can be evaluated and traded by public and private sector actors. This, in turn, reinforces the sense that these agreements exist as discrete deals to be undertaken by financial engineering specialists at a distance from the policymaking process. As a result, how (and on whom) public money is spent is in large part governed by private actors — all of whom operate with a profit motive.

And TPSFs have not stopped here. Recently, they have taken their financialization agenda even further, developing programs that directly transform public services into objects of financial speculation. We see this with the development of Social Finance and especially Social Impact Bonds (SIBs) — new financial instruments that enable private investors to fund public services with the hope of generating profits through extracting a portion of the cost savings for themselves. In these schemes, management scholar Eve Chiapello notes, "public money is used to give financial returns to providers of private capital who invest in social matters in the state's place. The investors — not the social organizations they finance — are paid on the basis of their social results (payment for success)."[89] If certain program outcomes are met, the government pays back investors for the initial program cost plus a profit. Investors of SIBs can expect to earn between 5 and 30 percent in annual returns[90] — a significant profit margin. Like PPP arrangements, the problem with SIBs is that they end up costing the public more money. Instead of investing directly in public services, a large portion of public money is used to pay investors' profits. And in the process, private investors, as well as TPSFs, are granted a significant degree of control over the ways in which services are delivered. In this sense, SIBs "represent a potentially powerful and problematic use of accounting to enact government policy."[91] Despite these types of concerns, however, SIBs have recently been taken up in public programs like preventive health, childcare, and women's shelters. In fact, according to a 2021 report by the Canadian Labour Congress, "the services being targeted for social financing are the same ones that have faced chronic underfunding and public funding cuts."[92]

Knowing that TPSFs have played a central role in advising governments on cutting public services, it is perhaps not surprising that TPSFs have served as influential actors in promoting SIBs as well. For years, McKinsey has "prepared videos, booklets, and toolkits for organizations contemplating SIBs."[93] Deloitte has been particularly active in SIBs in Canada, declaring that SIBs are the key to "solving complex societal issues" and that they represent a "coming revolution in social policy."[94] And PwC has "acted as a technical advisor to Social Finance Ltd.," one of the chief architects of the scheme.[95] Moreover, beyond providing advice on these new financial instruments, TPSFs are also investing substantial time and resources in advocating for them. EY, for instance, "made a major donation and contributed pro bono work to support the Private Equity Foundation in developing a social bond related to youth education and training in the UK." And KPMG "has been named as a supporter of SIBs in Canada."[96]

These examples call attention to the role of TPSFs in not just assessing the performance of public agencies, but also actively refashioning public infrastructures and social services in a manner that enables the extraction of rents by private investors. Through packaging and promoting PPPs and SIBs, TPSFs have actively worked to transform public infrastructures and social services into objects of financial speculation that can be bought and sold on the market. Moreover, as auditors, they have been central actors in attesting to the value of these arrangements, contributing to their legitimation, normalization, and routinization in public policymaking.[97] Such frameworks have ultimately paved the way for the privatization of services, as these firms have gone from assessing services to directly delivering them, opening new markets from which they can extract lucrative fees, and establishing more enduring and continuous relationships with governments that can be difficult for public officials to extricate themselves from.

## Privatization:
## Information Technology Oligarchs

When the COVID-19 pandemic hit, governments around the world went beyond just turning to TPSFs for advice; they also looked to them for critical IT infrastructures. In the Preface, we have already looked at Deloitte's test and trace program in the United Kingdom and vaccine tracking systems in the United States and Canada. However, more ambitiously, Deloitte has also set out to provide a whole digital platform for governing public health. The GovConnect Public Health Transformation Platform includes a range of services specifically for governments such as contact tracing, case management, call centre operations, testing process analysis, public sentiment analysis, mission support, integrated disease surveillance, an immunization registry, vaccine management, and network analysis.[98] While the firm's rapid expansion into public health has raised questions about its qualifications this has not stopped governments from procuring their services. In Alberta, the firm was hired to implement a COVID-19 tracking and tracing app in May 2020 that cost the provincial government $1 million, despite public criticism of the program's performance in the United States.[99] When it was revealed in October 2021 that just 158 people out of 306,000 had entered positive test results into the app, public officials began to question exactly why Deloitte, an accounting firm, was chosen to provide public health monitoring systems to the government. Why not hire a public health provider?

Although governments have expanded outsourcing of these types of services during the pandemic, it was also happening before. Indeed, beyond advising and auditing for governments, TPSFs have, over the past three decades, assumed responsibility for delivering a range of public services via privatized data infrastructures. As we note in Chapter 2, IT services now account for 66 percent of the spending by the Government of Canada on personnel outsourcing.[100] Over the span of seven years, spending on IT consultants more than doubled — from $605 million in 2011 to over $1.3 billion in 2018.[101] This is most apparent in personnel and payroll systems. By area, it is most common in the defence sector, with the Department of National Defence being the biggest spender on IT outsourcing, giving more than $25 billion dollars to consultants over the past four years. And while these contracts have overwhelmingly gone to IT consultancies like IBM and Microsoft, firms like Deloitte are increasingly getting their foot in the door by making heavy investments in artificial intelligence (AI), machine learning, and cloud computing.

As we saw in the previous chapter, the privatization of IT services really got going in the 1970s. While computerization initiatives had previously been undertaken in-house, neoliberal policymakers began to frame the public sector as ill-equipped for advancing technological progress. The civil service was faulted for lacking sufficient know-how to implement IT infrastructures, bolstering arguments to expand the role of private firms in providing IT services to the public.[102] Along these lines, critical IT skills and knowledge was transferred from the public to the private sector over the past four decades, as IT services were increasingly provided by independent contractors.[103] Perhaps not surprisingly, the industry became concentrated in the hands of a few large firms. This period opened a wide path for TPSFs to carve out their role as critical IT service providers and implement systems that would become entrenched in the operation of the state. Today, as e-government is becoming ubiquitous in the realm of public service delivery, more space is created for IT consultants and their supporters within government.[104] TPSFs have become increasingly entrenched in public service delivery, fostering dependencies from which it can be difficult for governments to extricate themselves.

Canada's Phoenix Pay System is an object lesson in how deeply entangled governments can get with TPSFs, and how this can foster asymmetric power relations that ultimately benefit TPSFs at the public's expense. The story begins in 2009 when the Conservative federal government introduced the Transformation of Pay Administration Initiative. Presented as a cost-savings initiative, the goal of the initiative was to update the existing 40-year-old payroll system for federal public workers. In 2011, the government hired IBM, which teamed up with Deloitte and Oracle Canada to design and implement what was dubbed the Phoenix Pay System. IBM was the only company to bid on the sole-sourced $5.7 million contract.[105]

In 2016, the first of a two-part rollout of the system was launched while 2,700 payroll clerks were laid off. After a few months, however, problems began to pile up — employees were not getting paid, staff could not keep up with all the complaints flooding in because of flaws in the system, and there were significant delays in processing benefit applications, disability claims, and parental leave requests.[106] In fact, just a few months after the first of a two-part launch, the Public Service Alliance of Canada (PSAC), the union representing the majority of federal public-sector workers, reported that up to 80,000 workers were not getting paid — and, despite a steady influx of cash, the system continued to be plagued with problems.[107]

By the time the system launched in 2016, the newly elected Liberal government estimated it would cost another $25 million to fix Phoenix. A few months later, this figure was revised to $50 million. The following year, this figure rose once again as the government committed an extra $142 million to help solve the ongoing problems with Phoenix.[108] While problems were amassing, IBM maintained that they were not responsible for the system's failures. Instead, the firm blamed the former government, arguing that their hands had been tied due to the government's decision to take charge of training and execution as well as their choice of payroll software (PeopleSoft) that had been preselected per the "Crown's specifications."[109] However, according to their original 1,700-page contract[110] (set at $5.7 million), the firm expected a "seamless integration" of the system, apparently anticipating none of the ensuing problems.

Because the integration was far from seamless, the contract was amended thirty-nine times over the following years with the contract amount rising each year. The initial $5.7 million eventually grew to $393 million by 2019.[111] As Roman Klimowics, principal analyst at the Treasury Board Secretariat put it, IBM "basically has an open bag of money to help themselves to," and each contract extension only made the project riskier.[112] The union representing professional workers in the federal government, the Professional Institute of the Public Service of Canada (PIPSC), criticized the government for giving IBM almost complete control over the implementation of Phoenix arguing that the firm now has "the keys to the kingdom."[113]

So, why did the government keep extending IBM's contract and continue paying the firm such exorbitant amounts as the problems kept piling up? As we discuss in the next chapter, such practices reflect what political scientists Marius Busemeyer and Kathleen Thelen refer to as the institutional business power of TPSFs, which "arises when policymakers invite or allow private actors to share in the delivery of public responsibilities, setting in motion feedback effects that over time enhance the power of private interests vis-à-vis publicly accountable government actors."[114] As governments come to depend on these firms for public service delivery, private firms can draw leverage from this in extorting increasing rents in service delivery. As Busemeyer and Thelen note, "these arrangements foster asymmetric dependencies of the state on the continued contribution of business actors in ways that, over time, tilt the public-private balance increasingly in favor of business interests."[115]

Along these lines, TPSFs often seek a foot in the door through offering low price or pro bono services with the aim of cultivating long-term dependencies on services that enable them to extract rents. In his book on the history of computing in government, Jon Agar argues that firms will deliberately bid too low on contracts to secure them, knowing that the cost will most likely rise afterward — a strategy he calls *penetrative pricing*. The customer (in this case the state) then has "little alternative but to pay up."[116] Penetrative pricing can, of course, end up costing the state exorbitant amounts of money. While Phoenix was originally intended to save the state $70 million per year, it may now cost taxpayers $2.2 billion to fix the system by 2023.[117] It was recently disclosed that part of that money will go to hiring yet another TPSF — McKinsey — to help improve Phoenix. In early 2020, McKinsey was awarded a $4.9-million contract and this number has since climbed to $27 million due to several amendments.[118]

Although Phoenix is an extreme case, it is symptomatic of a more longstanding problem in public-sector procurements. Drawing from their institutional business power, TPSFs have been able to foster long-term dependencies that can be difficult for governments to extricate themselves from. As with auditing and PPPs, the UK has been a centre for these practices, starting with the computerization of public administration in the 1970s and expanding to a wide array of services farmed out to outsourcing firms by the 1990s.

Beginning in the 1970s, the UK government engaged in a number of massive contracts with TPSFs in order to modernize their administrative practices. The most notable example was with the Department of Health and Social Security, which set out in 1977 to simplify the process of delivering welfare benefits through what it called the Operational Strategy. Described by historian Antonio Weiss as "the biggest and most ambitious computerization programme in Europe" at the time, the program had cost the government 2.6 billion pounds (at 1993 prices) by the end, in 1991, with 315 million going to consultancy firms, the main one being Arthur Andersen.[119] As Weiss notes, this IT infrastructure contributed to the transformation of the UK state, enabling public officials to shift away from policies of full employment to a more punitive regime, which involved carefully controlling access to welfare benefits through new means-based forms of assessment.[120] The Operational Strategy enabled "a more accurate (and larger) segmentation of the population, separating the population between those who were benefits recipients and those who were not."[121] Moreover, such technologies enabled new forms of performance reporting that could be used to discipline civil servants charged with the processing of claims.

While both the high costs of the Operational Strategy and its enrichment of consultants were widely condemned by the press, it did not stop the government from commissioning Arthur Andersen again to replace the National Insurance Recording System (NIRS2) in 1995.[122] This was done through a PPP under the Private Finance Initiative. What ensued was something akin to the Phoenix debacle — the new system was botched, and thousands of residents' pensions and welfare benefits went underpaid. Arthur Andersen was criticized for their work, with some arguing that the firm should have been better equipped considering their stature.[123]

As Agar argues, the case of the NIRS2 — and, we would argue, Phoenix — illustrates "the difficulties of managing large, complex technological projects within a hollowed-out state."[124] The story would likely have had a more positive outcome if, instead of relying on external contracts, government departments had the proper expertise in IT at the time. Yet, hollowed-out public agencies in both the United Kingdom and Canada now lack the proper expertise or resources to deliver IT infrastructures or even assess them, which has only deepened dependencies on private firms to do this work. And, as these firms land more and more contracts from the state, their expertise grows and the expertise gap widens.[125] As Horrocks argues, an enduring and self-perpetuating power loop can be created between government and IT consultants as consultants come to "occupy influential positions in government and public policy circles and then act as powerful agents in promoting the development of both e-government 'solutions' and the technology and expertise these require to 'deliver' the promised outcomes."[126] Indeed, as we discuss in Chapter 4, TPSFs have increasingly become embedded in government agencies and public institutions in both delivering and providing oversight in service delivery, leading to potential conflicts of interests.

More recently, firms have moved from simply providing IT infrastructures to governments to directly delivering back-office services. Firms such as Serco, Capita, and G4S — the giants of the outsourcing market[127] — explicitly brand themselves as experts in running services that have been outsourced by governments and public institutions. As Serco puts it, the firm "specialize[s] in the delivery of essential public services."[128] This includes prisons and detention centres in the United Kingdom as well as all of Australia's onshore detention centres. The firm was hired by the US federal government to administer aspects of Obamacare, and more recently, Serco was hired by the province of Ontario to manage part of the previously government-led job training and placement program for people on social assistance, gaining profits based on how many people they can get back to work.[129] This is despite evidence suggesting unsuccessful outcomes in similar models in the United Kingdom and Australia.

These firms work almost exclusively with governments, seeing this as a lucrative core area, which will provide growing opportunities for business in the future. As Serco notes, "we can be very confident that the world will still need prisons, will still need to manage immigration, and provide healthcare and transport, and that these services will be highly people-intensive for decades to come."[130] And, perhaps not surprisingly, these outsourcing firms — like many of the firms we have discussed so far — have also been involved in their fair share of scandals. As mentioned in Chapter 1, Serco has been repeatedly caught defrauding the UK government in scandals, which included systematically falsifying data in its contracts with the National Health Service (NHS) and with the Ministry of Justice. Nevertheless, this did not prevent the government from granting them an untendered 108-million-pound contract for COVID-19 contact tracing in 2020, while eliminating over 6,000 contact-tracer jobs from the NHS. And it did not prevent them from granting Serco another 212-million-pound contract in 2022, despite evidence of the firm's poor performance.

As governments come to depend on these firms for such large-scale management information systems and other administrative programs, TPSFs have become increasingly entrenched in governance, forming what Weiss describes as a "hybrid state."[131] This helps to explain why, despite the high-profile scandals, governments continue to rely on these firms. It also speaks to why governments turned to TPSFs to provide IT infrastructures during the pandemic even though this has often resulted in poor outcomes. As governments have become increasingly dependent on TPSFs, these firms have been able to steadily expand their mandate while delivering public services, shifting from simply providing IT infrastructures to directly delivering a wider range of services. Along these lines, TPSFs have directly benefited from the privatization of public services. Prisons, immigration detention centres, social services, and health centres are increasingly being directly administered by these firms, despite evidence of systematic cost overruns, understaffing, and poor quality. These firms have shifted from being simply advisors to serving as full partners in government. As we see in the next section, this raises significant concerns, as private-sector companies are less publicly accountable than governments, yet have access to increasing amounts of data while designing and implementing these systems.

## Hardwiring
## Neoliberalism into the State

While, on the surface, governments' use of TPSFs is supposed to bring the public innovative, efficient, and low-cost public services, we have demonstrated that that is often far from the case. On the contrary, they have facilitated increased profits for the rich and austerity for the rest. As the architects of tax avoidance schemes, these firms have starved the state of tax revenues, fundamentally restricting the government's capacity to fund and deliver public services. In the ensuing fiscal crisis, they have advised governments on where to cut costs, identifying the lowest possible service levels that can be delivered by governments while still obeying the law, and driving down the quality of public services. Moreover, through financializing and privatizing public services they have cultivated long-term dependencies that enable the private sector to extract exorbitant rents from the public, as governments lose the capacity to deliver services themselves.

Through such programs, we argue that TPSFs have contributed to hardwiring neoliberal operating systems into the state. They have provided the technologies and infrastructures through which neoliberal programs can be envisioned and enacted: new forms of audit, that make cutbacks legible at an increasingly fine-grained scale and new forms of partnership that enable the contractualization of public-private relationships, entrenching private capital in public service delivery in new ways. Moreover, we can see how their work in tax avoidance, auditing, financialization and privatization has been mutually reinforcing. As tax avoidance for the wealthy sets the stage for performance audits, these, in turn, lay the groundwork for financialization and privatization.

These programs have ultimately been to the benefit of TPSFs, who have enhanced their power in government over the past four decades while carving out lucrative markets for themselves. After years of being hollowed out and getting caught in a cycle of dependency, the state has come to rely on these firms for the provision of IT infrastructures, which has, in turn, laid the groundwork for outsourcing service delivery, leading to the establishment of a hybrid state, in which TPSFs serve increasingly as partners with governments.[132]

But *how* have these firms managed to create these types of dependencies and position themselves as necessary to public policymaking and service delivery? Why do they keep getting hired when they are frequently at the centre of public scandals? In the next chapter, we examine their strategies further to shed light on their ascent to power.

# Chapter 4

# Strategies:
# Networking, Institutionalizing,
# Commodifying, and Brokering

This book has set out to critically locate transnational professional service firms (TPSFs), exploring their rise and growing entanglement with governments. So far, we have discussed the conditions of possibility for the emergence of TPSFs, tracing their historical roots in the fields of management consulting, accounting, and information technology (IT) services. Through the course of their development, these firms have rolled out a range of services that continue to be procured by governments around the world. Their influence and reach have only grown over the past three decades, as large firms have shifted from ad hoc advice to providing more thorough data infrastructures, which, in turn, has led to more continuous and multifaceted relationships between TPSFs and governments.

In this context, we have discussed how the programs and technologies offered by TPSFs have contributed to hardwiring neoliberalism in the public sector. As we saw in Chapter 3, the Big Four firms have played a central role in starving the state of revenues through facilitating tax avoidance by the wealthy and multinational corporations. In the ensuing fiscal crisis, TPSFs have offered programs for governments to do more with less via new forms of auditing, financialization, and privatization. This includes efficiency engineering that enables governments to cut services to minimum levels and standards, off-the-books private financing for infrastructure development, and IT infrastructures that can be rented out to public agencies at exorbitant costs.

The question remains: Why are governments increasingly turning to these firms? Why did the Alberta government, for example, turn to Deloitte when the failure of their tracking and tracing app had already been well-documented in other jurisdictions? Why was KPMG hired by municipal governments to advise on austerity policies when they were embroiled in a scandal over their orchestration of tax avoidance for. the wealthy? Why did the US Food and Drug Administration turn to McKinsey to restructure their operations while they were simultaneously advising Purdue, a major manufacturer of opioids? Such examples are numerous, raising the question: Why don't governments turn to other actors, such as academics, public officials, or community organizations? How have these firms been able to get (and keep) their foot so firmly in the door?

In this chapter, we identify four strategies that TPSFs have used to gain influence and entrench themselves in public policymaking and service delivery. First, through networking, personnel from these firms actively cultivate close connections with public officials by lobbying, conferencing, circulating personnel, and establishing advocacy associations. Second, through institutionalizing relationships, firms become embedded in governance arrangements through royal commissions, regulatory committees, and new kinds of public agencies. Third, through codifying and commodifying knowledge products, managerial experience is packaged as a scarce asset, which can then be sold to governments. And fourth, through brokering access to data, firms assume responsibility for circulating information, both vertically, through their capacity to accumulate data within large data repositories, and horizontally, through their capacity to quickly deploy this data across jurisdictions. In this way, TPSFs have transformed themselves into what science and technology scholars describe as "obligatory points of passage" for those seeking access to certain kinds of professional services and data infrastructures.[1]

Through cultivating revolving-door relationships, integrating personnel into the institutional routines of public agencies, and establishing infrastructural dependencies, a vicious cycle can unfold in which governments become increasingly reliant on TPSFs for day-to-day public administration. As public agencies lose in-house infrastructure and expertise and come to rely on outsourced service delivery, they can dig themselves into a hole — a consulting trap — from which it can be difficult to escape. Moreover, this can be reinforced through interlocking levels of advice and service delivery. As the capacity for governments to assess services is hollowed out, public officials increasingly come to rely on TPSFs in not just providing services but also administering these services and assessing their quality.[2] This can lead to a self-confirming echo chamber that contributes to the growing entrenchment of TPSFs in governance over time.

## Networking

Social networks are central to the business of TPSFs. According to Thomas Armbrüster, "the quality of a network tie to a client decision-maker is the main competitive advantage of a consulting firm."[3] The capacity of firms to build a web of personal relationships spanning geographic regions, different domains, and sectors has been instrumental to their growth and influence. Insofar as they operate between different spaces, they can serve as brokers of information. In this sense, TPSFs have been described as *boundary organizations* that acquire power through their "intermediate location in the social structure."[4] By positioning themselves at the juncture between public and private enterprise and across different state jurisdictions and professional domains, they have become capable of regulating "the circulation of knowledge and personnel among these spheres" as other actors come to rely on them for the transmission of expertise, ideas, and business models.[5]

The close connections between TPSFs and political and economic elites in many countries has been well-documented in the academic literature and media.[6] Firms frequently get access to public agencies via memberships on interlocking boards and revolving-door relationships, through which their personnel circulate between the private and public sectors. Many senior politicians were former partners with TPSFs and vice versa. In the United States, for instance, Mitt Romney worked as a consultant for Boston Consulting Group and later worked at Bain, cofounding Bain Capital.[7] Pete Buttigieg, the popular presidential candidate for the Democrats in 2020, formerly worked at McKinsey.[8] In Canada, former Conservative MP of 18 years, Peter MacKay, left politics and joined Deloitte in 2020 as a strategic advisor,[9] and former Governor General of Canada, David Johnston, was hired as an executive adviser by Deloitte in 2017.[10]

Such close connections between TPSF personnel and public officials have periodically become an object of scandal. For instance, the Canadian newspaper the *Globe and Mail* has documented close ties between McKinsey and the Liberal Party of Canada through figures like Dominic Barton who was McKinsey's global managing director until 2018.[11] Hoping that he would serve as "a kind of guru of growth," Barton was appointed by the Liberals to lead the government's Advisory Council on Economic Growth in 2016 — while still working for McKinsey.[12] However, Barton's close ties to the Liberal Party raised red flags, as — while serving as a government advisor — federal agencies increasingly procured contracts with McKinsey, which grew from $2.2 million under the previous Conservative government to $32.5 million in 2021–22. This put Barton in the hot seat. During the subsequent public inquiry, he found himself compelled to affirm in a public hearing before the government operations committee of the House of Commons that he was neither a "partisan advisor" nor a "friend" of Trudeau.[13]

Similarly, in France, a senate investigation revealed close ties between McKinsey and President Emmanuel Macron. Karim Tadjeddine, the head of the firm's public-sector branch in France, worked with Macron on a government commission in 2007 and together with many other former McKinsey employees, Tadjeddine actively participated in Macron's first election campaign in 2017.[14] Notably, this was in a context where public spending on private consultants in France was rapidly increasing, doubling between 2018 and 2021– all during Macron's presidency — with much of the new spending going to McKinsey.[15]

These examples are by no means the exception. Many senior public officials are recruited from the ranks of TPSFs. In the United States, as *The Economist* has noted, President Obama had quite a "predilection for hiring McKinsey types," which marked "a distinct change from the Bush administration's apparent love of former Goldman Sachs employees" as well as President Clinton's recruitment of Rhodes scholars.[16] Two members of Obama's transition team had worked for McKinsey: Michael Warren, who coheaded the treasury team, and Roger Ferguson, who was on the economics team. He made former McKinsey Global Institute chief Diana Farrell deputy director of his National Economic Council, and McKinsey alum Karen Mills was named head of Small Business Administration. This tendency is not just specific to Democrats; Republicans have also been champions of McKinsey. When asked how he would reduce the size of government during the 2012 elections, presidential candidate Mitt Romney told the editorial board of the *Wall Street Journal*: "So I would have … at least some structure that McKinsey would guide me to put in place."[17]

In the United Kingdom as well, McKinsey is a familiar fixture in government offices. As journalist Duff McDonald notes in his book about the firm, London is perhaps "the one place where [McKinsey] has truly infiltrated government" and where the firm "has had pretty much uninterrupted access to 10 Downing Street for decades."[18] McKinsey alums include Adair Turner, the head of Britain's Financial Services Authority from 2008 to 2013, Lord Blackwell who ran Tony Blair's Policy Unity in 1995, and William Hague, who was Foreign Secretary from 2010 to 2014.[19]

Very often, consultants are framed as puppet masters in their relationships with public officials. For example, in the midst of the McKinsey scandal in Canada, Conservative MP Stephanie Kusie raised the question: "Who's actually running the show in Canada? Trudeau is the puppet and his Liberal pal Dominic Barton is busy pulling the strings."[20] However, it can be difficult to determine the direction of the influence. While some argue that consultants form a "shadow government" secretly calling the shots, others have framed these firms as simple "foot soldiers" or "hired guns" who are just following orders.[21] Rather than speculating on the directionality of the influence, we think it is more productive to explore how these networks reflect the *connectedness* of these firms to different actors and the degree to which they can serve as intermediaries between different groups. The revolving-door relationships between TPSFs and economic elites, politicians, and public officials help shed light on the firms' intermediate location in the social structure, from which they draw considerable power. Both the firms and their personnel reap considerable benefits and gain influence from their position at the intersections between public and private interests.

Often, TPSFs position themselves as hubs for elite networks through seminars, conferences, and business retreats. Here, TPSFs can foster the formation of distinctive epistemic communities through face-to-face interactions and the exchange of information, facilitating the movement of policy ideas across domains.[22] For instance, while under investigation by the Canada Revenue Agency (CRA), KPMG sponsored one of the government's post budget speeches with Elio Luongo, CEO of KPMG Canada, presenting a prize to the finance minister. And while the hearing was taking place on KPMG's role in tax avoidance, Denis Pelletier, a judge with the Federal Court of Appeal — the court that hears all tax appeals — was seen attending a KPMG-sponsored event in Madrid. Another Canadian Judge, Randall Bocock, who was managing the KPMG case day-to-day, was seen at a private party sponsored by Dentons law firm

— the firm that endorsed KPMG's tax avoidance scheme.[23] Responding to questions about whether this might raise potential conflicts of interest, a KPMG lawyer simply said, "I can't imagine that a beer and a cheese would impact their integrity."[24]

TPSFs also forge connections through advocacy organizations, which draw together public and private officials around specific policy programs. For instance, this has been a key starting point for the promotion of Public–Private Partnerships (PPPs) in Canada, the United Kingdom and the United States.[25] PwC played a central role in establishing the Canadian Council for Public–Private Partnerships (CCPPP) in 1993, and representatives from the Big Four firms have continuously served on its board since its inception.[26] Through its annual conferences and meetings, CCPPP has played an important role as an intermediary as well as a deliberative space, bringing together actors across sectors and regions. Its 2019 conference brought together over 800 people, including public officials, financial specialists, and construction and engineering firms from all over the world. The keynote speakers have included high-profile public officials, such as Doug Ford, the Premier of Ontario, provincial infrastructure ministers across the country, as well as public officials spearheading PPPs in other parts of the world, most prominently the United Kingdom, the United States, and Australia.

Through interlocking memberships on the boards of these kinds of organizations, channels can be forged through which TPSFs communicate and strategize with public and private officials in pursuit of a shared policy agenda. As sociologists J.P. Sapinski and William Carroll note, such associations provide a venue in which an inner circle of political and economic elites can come together to foster a common worldview, offering them "access to a broad resource base from which to exert their hegemony in and beyond business circles."[27] By developing networks in this way, TPSFs are able to cultivate a distinctive political-cultural community with shared normative and epistemological commitments. This goes beyond simply influencing public officials as outside movers. It can also enable what law professor James Kwak describes as *cultural capture* whereby "those in charge of the relevant state entity internalis[e], as if by osmosis, the objectives, interests and perception of reality of the vested interests they are meant to regulate."[28] As such, the lines between public and private interests fade away as influential actors in both sectors occupy the same space, fostering shared commitments and worldviews

— views and commitments closely aligned with those of TPSFs themselves. This, in turn, creates the opportunity for these firms to further
embed their interests and programs into policymaking.

These connections can also be cultivated through the circulation of
personnel between TPSFs and public agencies in revolving-door relationships.[29] Numerous scholars have noted the carefully cultivated alumni
networks fostered by these firms with former personnel occupying key
positions in public agencies and Fortune 500 companies.[30] For instance,
journalist Richard Brooks has observed a "well-oiled revolving door"
between Whitehall and the Big Four firms in the United Kingdom. As
he puts it,

> The routine exchange of senior personnel ... brings a close-
> ness that breeds a uniform, market-oriented view of the public
> realm within Whitehall. So frequently and smoothly does the
> revolving door spin that it creates a realistic hope among min-
> isters and mandarins that, subject to keeping them happy, the
> Big Four firms will present later career opportunities or some
> consulting fees to supplement their pensions. Taken with the
> closeness between those who have stepped through the revolv-
> ing door and their former colleagues, the effect is to melt away
> the healthy tension that should exist between government and
> commercial interests.[31]

While some firms have focused on building networks with political and economic elites, others have oriented themselves more toward
making connections with lower ranks of public officials. As historian
Antonio Weiss observes, different types of firms rely on different kinds of
networks.[32] During the first wave of management consulting in the early
twentieth century, he notes, efficiency engineers' networks were shaped
in part by the mutual interest of consultants and civil servants in the
"vogue concept of management efficiency," part of a "growing cultural
emphasis on managerialism."[33] In the second wave, the McKinsey generation of strategy consultants focused on building elite networks through
Ivy League business schools, establishing what anthropologist Karen
Ho describes as relations of "elite kinship,"[34] based on "personal friend-
ships of well-connected individuals."[35] Thus, in the United Kingdom,
McKinsey "tapp[ed] into Oxbridge or networks centred on gentleman's
clubs," which were based on a "everyone knows everyone culture."[36] In

contrast, in the third wave, the IT infrastructure/ accounting generation really focused on building connections with the new technical middle class — including professionals in engineering, science, and computing, as well as accounting and law.[37] In Canada, over the past 15 years, the Big Four firms have regularly hired senior CRA enforcement executives and Department of Justice tax lawyers. In their online promotional material, EY suggests that it has done the best job of all the accounting firms in hiring former public officials. "As one of Canada's leading tax practices," they boast, "we have more former senior Government of Canada tax officials than any other professional services firm in Canada."[38] This speaks to the way in which these firms broker the flow of knowledge between the public and the private by regulating the circulation of personnel across these domains. This, of course, raises questions and concerns about conflicts of interest. We can, for instance, wonder if these kinds of connections might have facilitated the deal between the CRA and KPMG surrounding the Isle of Man tax scheme, though no evidence has surfaced to corroborate that.

In some countries, networks connecting TPSFs and public agencies have been further consolidated through secondments in which the Big Four firms lend out their personnel to work pro bono or for a fee in public agencies. In 2013, for instance, lobbying watchdog Spinwatch documented that the Big Four firms had seconded at least fifty people to UK government departments over three years. As Brooks points out, most of these people "were in the Cabinet Office, the Treasury and the Department for Business, the centres of power where policies governing everything from corporate taxes and financial markets to industry and the shape of public services themselves are determined."[39] Additionally, these firms provided free assistance to "several of the Labour Party opposition teams."[40]

As accounting scholars have shown, seconded staff played a central role in developing the Private Finance Initiative (PFI) — the policy that entrenched PPPs in the United Kingdom.[41] They noted that it was the seconded staff from the private sector in the treasury and not the civil servants, "that played a key role not only in driving the policy, controlling some of the activities of other departments and of the Treasury itself, but also in changing the nexus of relationships surrounding government itself."[42] In a report from 2002, UNISON, the largest public-sector union in the United Kingdom, staunchly criticized the role of seconded personnel from the Big Four firms for helping to "devise, ne-gotiate, and drive a privatisation policy agenda," arguing that "the web of private interest that joins public policy, management consultants, ac-countants, and the privatisation industry extends across the whole of PFI and PPP."[43] Indeed, practices such as these have been criticized for insti-tutionally entrenching conflicts of interest because it is unclear whether staff are acting in the interests of their firm or the public agency. The line becomes especially murky as these relationships are institutionalized, as we show in the next section.

As intermediaries, TPSFs claim to offer a neutral third-party perspec-tive, simply communicating best practices from other jurisdictions. However, their connections with private sector firms tell another story, raising the spectre of conflicts of interest. This has periodically become the object of controversy. For instance, in Australia, a major scandal erupted in 2023 when it was revealed that PwC had shared inside infor-mation, obtained through its role as a sounding board to government on tax planning, with its corporate clients, to advise them on how to evade taxes.[44] In the United Kingdom, McKinsey has been accused of advising on reforms to National Health Service (NHS) procurement poli-cies "in ways that would benefit McKinsey's own corporate clients and then sharing those proposals with the private sector clients in advance."[45] Similarly, while working closely with the Québec government during the COVID-19 pandemic, McKinsey managed to reach an agreement with public officials whereby the firm was not obliged to reveal their private-sector clients at the time. It was then later revealed that the firm had been working with Pfizer while at the same time advising the government to reach agreements with Pfizer in order to secure vaccinations.[46]

In the United States, McKinsey consultants worked for both Purdue Pharma, a major manufacturer of opioids, as well as the Food and Drug Administration (FDA) from 2008 to 2019. During this period, McKinsey promised to "turbocharge" Purdue's opioid sales, thereby contributing to the country's deadly opioid crisis, while also advising the FDA division overseeing the development and marketing of drugs. According to a US government report:

> at least 22 McKinsey consultants, including senior partners,
> worked for both FDA and opioid manufacturers on related top-ics, including at the same time: The committee's investigation

uncovered 37 FDA contracts that were staffed by at least one McKinsey consultant who simultaneously or previously worked for Purdue. These consultants formed part of what one consultant called McKinsey's "mini 'army' here at Purdue."[47]

While TPSFs presume to stand above the fray as intermediaries, taking the "view from nowhere," a deeper examination of their affiliations demonstrates their specific allegiances. Indeed, through their role as boundary spanners, standing at the intersection of different domains and regions, they have played a central role in fostering a distinctive political-cultural community — what Brooks considers to be the breeding ground for "a uniform, market-oriented view of the public realm" — committed to deepening the entrenchment of these principles into public agencies.[48] At the same time, through spanning boundaries, they have been able to position themselves as key intermediaries in brokering access to requisite knowledge and personnel in implementing these programs.[49] These relationships can then pave the way for their entrenchment in institutional routines and procedures to which we turn next.

## Institutionalizing

Beyond building social networks that traverse domains and cross jurisdictions, TPSFs also set out to institutionalize these relationships. As Busemeyer and Thelen note, these firms exercise "institutional business power" — a distinct form of power within contemporary capitalism that essentially flows from the "entrenched position of business actors in the provision of essential public functions or services."[50] By being invited to "share in the delivery of public responsibilities," they note, a feedback effect can be set in motion that gradually enhances "the power of private interests vis-à-vis publicly accountable government actors" over time.[51] As we saw through the case of the Phoenix Pay System in the previous chapter, by assuming responsibility for delivering essential public services, governments can come to depend on these firms, making it difficult for them to exit these relationships.

This, of course, does not happen overnight. As Busemeyer and Thelen note, institutional business power "essentially represents the feedback effects of past policy choices."[52] By looking further at the processes through which TPSFs have become embedded within public institutions, we can begin to see how these dependencies are created. This entails entrenching and regularizing the authority of these firms in the everyday operations of public agencies. Through membership on advisory committees, standards-setting associations, and the boards of public institutions, firms are able to directly weigh in on policy decisions and determine regulations governing their domains. Moreover, through the establishment of new hybrid public-private forms of association, they can assume jurisdiction over whole areas of policymaking and service delivery that were previously under the control of governments.

The institutionalized power of TPSFs in policymaking is most apparent in the field of accounting, where, accounting scholar Carlos Ramirez notes, the Big Four firms "occupy a quasi-oligopolistic position on the market for accounting and auditing services to multinational companies, but also as suppliers of expertise to the standard-setting bodies."[53] The Big Four, Chiapello and Medjad note, are "the biggest donors to standard-setting, the primary contributors in terms of expertise, and the leading players when it comes to ensuring those standards are applied in practice."[54] This includes commanding majorities on the boards of national and international accounting standards boards. As Lall notes, at least eight of the fourteen original members of the International Accounting Standards Board (IASB) had been previously employed by one of the Big Six (now Big Four) firms.[55] And they are strongly represented in the IASB's auxiliary bodies, including the International Financial Reporting Interpretations Committee and the Standards Advisory Council.[56]

This has given the Big Four firms considerable power in shaping accounting standards in ways that are often self-serving.[57] Their influence has been extensively documented in the EU, where the Big Four firms played a central role in watering down proposed reforms to financial services in the wake of the 2008 economic crisis. "Despite their pretence to neutrality," Kalaitzake notes, these firms have operated as "key supporters of the financial industry, and operate as important allies in aiding financial firms to oppose and resist regulatory reform."[58] Moreover, as the architects of tax avoidance schemes for the financial sector, they have a commercial interest in the policies that they have been commissioned to assess. For instance, the Corporate Europe Observatory (2018) notes that these firms mounted a concerted campaign to resist new tax transparency measures, challenging EU proposals to implement Country-by-Country Reporting (CBCR), warning of risks to "commercial confidentiality" and "unnecessarily burdensome obligations for businesses."[59] They also played a central role in galvanizing opposition to the implementation of a Financial Transfer Tax via lobby vehicles such as the European Business Initiative for Taxation, while simultaneously being enlisted by the EU as consultants in assessing the viability of these measures.[60]

The institutional entrenchment of TPSFs in policymaking can likewise be seen in the area of PPPs, discussed in Chapter 4. The Big Four firms were central in the establishment of PPPs as a form of infrastructure procurement. Beginning in the United Kingdom, they entrenched their authority at a number of levels, starting with PPP advocacy organizations, moving to ad hoc governmental advisory committees, and eventually becoming entrenched within governmental PPP units. Building on their experiments with project finance (PF) in North Sea oil, the Big Four leveraged their networks within the Conservative Party to apply these methods to the public sector, which led to the adoption of the PFI in 1992. This initiative established PPPs as a routine form of infrastructure procurement in the United Kingdom.[61] These networks were further entrenched under the New Labour regime by Tony Blair. During this time, extensive connections were established between TPSFs and the Labour Party, including secondments to TPSFs in the treasury and other government departments.[62] And, as we saw in the previous section, positioned within these institutions, the seconded personnel served as the chief architects for a deepening PFI regime.[63] This culminated in the establishment of a new public-private agency in 2000 — Partnerships UK (PUK) — itself majority-owned by industry "shareholders" in partnership with the treasury and staffed by personnel from the Big Four firms, who assumed control over the implementation of PPPs.[64] In the process, the Big Four firms were able to standardize PPPs as a recipe for infrastructure procurement and routinize their own authority in engineering and appraising deals.

Building from their adoption in the United Kingdom, the Big Four firms then strove to package PPPs as a product that could be sold to other jurisdictions. This involved exporting British expertise in deal-making via lobbying organizations such as International Financial Services London — which was led by senior personnel from TPSFs — acting in partnership with PUK, as well as establishing PPP advocacy organizations in other parts of the world.[65] In Canada, PwC played a central role in establishing the CCPPP in 1993, with each of the Big Four firms regularly sitting on its board since its inception.[66] From here, TPSFs could generate national coalitions in support of PPPs, building networks with political and economic elites. As in the example of the United Kingdom, the Big Four firms used these advocacy groups to push for the establishment of standalone governmental PPP units, including Partnerships BC (from 2002), Infrastructure Ontario (from 2005), Agence des partenariats public-privé du Québec (from 2004), PPP Canada (from 2009), and the Canada Infrastructure Bank under Dominic Barton's recommendation (from 2017). These units were largely populated by personnel from the Big Four firms, while simultaneously employing the Big Four firms as auditors to attest to the value generated by PPPs through VfM assessments, as we saw in the previous chapter. Finally, in rubberstamping the validity of these methods, personnel from the Big Four firms sit on the Public Sector Accounting Standards Boards charged with developing frameworks for assessing PPPs.[67]

Building from the networking strategies discussed in the previous section, the institutionalization of business power involves the entrenchment of TPSF power in public agencies. This involves creating new public agencies such as governmental PPP units, populating these agencies with staff from TPSFs, and translating their ideas into routinized governmental practices that are often outsourced back to themselves.[68] Thus, while TPSFs have been actively advocating for PPPs and assembling the institutions through which they are implemented, they are also commissioned as neutral third-party experts in assessing their relative value, as discussed in the previous chapter. This creates a self-perpetuating cycle enabling them to become more deeply entrenched in public service delivery.

It can also lead to the outright privatization of public services through contractual delegation of public power to private agencies. A good example of this is in India, where private consulting firms have assumed control over the core functions of urban planning via recent urban reform initiatives.[69] Under the Jawaharlal Nehru Urban Renewal Mission, Neha Sami and Shriya Anand, from the Indian Institute for Human Settlements, note that the central government has incentivized cities to use external consultants to develop urban master plans and city development plans. For instance, in the case of Bangalore, they note that the city's master plans "were drawn up by international consulting firms with little familiarity or local knowledge of the particular challenges and constraints the city faced."[70] Moreover, they involved little input from the public and have been held up in a series of lawsuits. More recently, the Indian government's Smart Cities Mission has required cities to consult with Bloomberg Philanthropies and work with TPSFs like IBM and Accenture to implement the plans. The projects were organized under Special Purpose Vehicles (SPVs) — legal entities that are often a key feature of PPP arrangements — under the control of consultants with very little accountability to the public. Indeed, as Sami and Anand note, the plans suffered from "minimal public participation" and the level of accountability of the SPVs has been called into question as public and democratic representation were not mandatory parts of the program.[71] The consultants used by city officials, Ghosh and Arora argue, often played the role of gatekeepers who cherry-picked and translated only "some ideas out of a wide range of concerns and solutions offered by participating citizens."[72] The selected ideas, they further note, "are attached to, or are consistent with, technology-centred 'global' visions of smart urbanism" — visions that poorer and marginalized groups of residents don't often fit into. Consequently, those voices are often "filtered out" of the ostensibly participatory process.[73]

Through these programs, TPSFs have come to share numerous core public functions and responsibilities with the state. As Busemeyer and Thelen note, while in some cases the state consciously decides to share certain public functions with business actors through delegation, or completely cede some functions to private actors through deregulation, institutional business power is also manifested when "private actors acquire power by taking the initiative to move into a policy arena previously dominated by the state, or into an emerging arena where the role of the state is still limited, and gradually assume a central intermediating role."[74] While TPSFs have gained influence through these avenues, their role in creating and regularizing PPP programs — programs that in many places have become the default way of delivering public infrastructures — provides a good example of their ability and craftiness in identifying exactly where they can create a need for themselves, then swoop in and take over certain public functions.

While these programs have led to significant changes in government, they have also been taken up as new products that can be lifted out of their specific institutional contexts, commodified and sold to governments around the world. As we show in the next section, these firms present these values and principles as prepackaged recipes that can be applied to any geographical, political, and cultural context.

## Codifying and Commodifying

While institutional business power is premised on the entrenchment of firms in the institutional routines of government, these firms are also able to exercise power through their capacity to lift knowledge out of these contexts, which they then package as a product that can be sold across different institutional settings. As our discussion of the scientific management movement in Chapter 2 showed, this involves processes of codification through which management experience is converted into "something that can be stored, moved and reused."[75] Management scholars describe it as a "people to documents approach" whereby experience is "extracted from the person who developed it, made independent of that person, and reused for various purposes."[76] This approach also involves processes of commodification, through which this experience is converted into a "reified, commercially valuable form."[77] In this way, management experience is made valuable through its enclosure, converting it into a scarce resource that is owned by the firm as intellectual property.

The aim is to generate a generic product in which the labour of the firm can be objectified. Management consultants have often referred to this as the *million-dollar slide* — "a single image that captured and conveyed so much information ... that by itself, it was worth a million dollars in consulting fees."[78] Strategy consultants working in the private sector initially framed such figures as a means of showing companies where they were positioned in the wider market. For instance, in his history of strategy consulting, Walter Kiechel notes that the central product offered by Boston Consulting Group was the "growth-share matrix," which charted a firm's relative market share in different product areas (on the x-axis) alongside projected market growth rate (on the y-axis) to identify the best areas for investment, with each product area represented by a circle whose size was proportional to its sales.[79] The matrix was divided into four quadrants. In the upper left quadrant were the product areas with high market share of a fast growing market (the "stars"); in the lower left quadrant were those with high market share in a slow-growing market (the "cash cows"); in lower right quadrant were low share and low growth product areas (the "dogs"); and in the upper right

**Figure 4.1 Boston Consulting Group's Growth-Share Matrix**

MARKET SHARE

|  |  | HIGH | LOW |
|---|---|---|---|
| GROWTH | HIGH | Stars | Question Marks |
|  | LOW | Cash Cows | Dogs |

quadrant were those with high market growth but low market share (the "question marks"). Such an image, Kiechel notes, enabled the Boston Consulting Group (BCG) to package their advice as a clear product that could be easily reproduced across contexts. At the same time, it gave senior management the capacity to make sense of their different product lines quickly and easily without requiring a comprehensive knowledge of their circumstances, thus, strengthening their decision-making authority in their organizations.

Such models have been adapted by management consultants to the public sector. For instance, KPMG's Municipal Service Delivery Review, which we explored in the previous chapter, is also framed around a million-dollar slide.[80] A three-by-four matrix quite similar in appearance to the growth-share matrix instantly allows municipal officials to see the status of their services and how they measure up against comparable jurisdictions along the axes of standard for delivery and essentiality.[81] (Note 81 gives several websites where examples of KPMG's matrix may be viewed.) The matrix plots the relative position of each of the city's services according to the necessity of the service (as mandatory, essential, traditional, or other) on the y-axis, and the standard of delivery (below, above or at standard) on the x-axis, with the size and colour of the point displaying the degree and source of the funding for each service.

The information is graphically presented in such a way that any service considered to be mandatory/below standard fall on the top left of the matrix, and any services deemed discretionary/above standard fall on the bottom right. As we discussed in the previous chapter, such an image packs a rhetorical punch in public deliberations as it creates the impression that such services can be known and compared from a distance. Policymakers, public officials and members of the public can swiftly sort through the slides, identifying areas to cut based on their location in the matrix without requiring a comprehensive knowledge of the social, cultural, or geographical milieux in which services are provided. In order to establish such a model as a *boundary object* that can be taken up and applied across institutional settings, it is detached both from its creator and from the context of its creation.[82] The knowledge it ostensibly conveys is generalized and, based on this generalization, it is argued that these models can be applied to *any* context.

Codifying policy-knowledge in this way is convenient and lucrative for TPSFs as they can quickly and easily translate these models for different jurisdictions, though its simplicity and lack of contextual grounding also makes it vulnerable to critique.[83] Indeed, such "PowerPoint policymaking," as former UK Prime Minister David Cameron described it, is often criticized as lazy, simplistic, and out of touch.[84] For instance, challenging McKinsey's outputs in restructuring Canadian immigration department, public officials noted: "We had a few presentations on very generic, completely vapid stuff. They arrived with nice colours, nice presentations and said they would revolutionize everything." Another noted, that "in the end, we don't have any idea what they did." It was "nice marketing" that "isn't science."[85]

Perhaps not surprisingly, TPSFs protect their exclusive right to profit from these models. They enforce the ownership of these products through intellectual property regimes. Hence, the million-dollar slide is copyrighted by KPMG. This, in turn, reinforces the status of these firms as *obligatory points of passage* who broker access to specific kinds of knowledge that they then can sell to governments at high costs. It also has important implications for transparency, as these firms often do not disclose the formulae or calculations that went into the production of these images, which they retain for reasons of "commercial sensitivity" (see Chapter 4). As Mazzucato and Collington note, clients are often provided with very little information about the services provided by these firms.[86] Thus, they do not know "how likely it is that the dataset the consultancy is drawing on contains flaws, or that the consultants working directly on the project do not possess the expertise their firm's bid promised. They don't have access to that information." [87] This may enable consultants to hide the self-confirming selection of data, including the selective use of comparators and interviews with senior officials who share their views (for instance, see KPMG's *The Wolf Is at the Door* report discussed in the previous chapter) — though, of course, this cannot be proven, because the data itself is not available.

Over the past twenty years, TPSFs have set out to expand their ownership of intellectual property via mergers and acquisitions, identifying smaller consultancies with social networks and intellectual property that can be appropriated and transformed into knowledge products that can be branded and sold all over the world. The Municipal Service Delivery Review discussed in the previous chapter is a good example of this. The program was not originally devised by KPMG but was initially developed by Chartwell Information Resource Management (IRM) — a small Canadian consultancy specializing in public-sector IT services — in partnership with Municipal Information Systems Association (MISA) of Canada. But when KPMG acquired Chartwell IRM in 2009, they seized the opportunity to commodify the model and set out to develop municipal benchmarking services as part of their global product line. Making former Chartwell consultant, Alan Mitchell head of the firms' Cities Global Center of Excellence in 2012, KPMG promptly began promoting MSDRs to other parts of the world.

The commodification of knowledge has only accelerated with the growing investment by TPSFs in IT infrastructures. In 2020, it was reported that the Big Four had made commitments to invest over $9 billion in technology over the next three to five years.[88] By 2026, PWC planned to spend $12 billion, hiring 100,000 new people in areas such as artificial intelligence and cybersecurity. Beyond million-dollar slides, these firms now claim proprietary rights over a wide array of administrative software, databases, and platforms.[89] This has included new technologies that have automated the gathering and processing of contracts and legal documents,[90] and new cloud-based software through which governments can subscribe to various programs for administering and managing personnel and data. Deloitte has made it its mission to be an "end-to-end cloud provider," managing cloud software for both public and private enterprises. In 2012, the firm partnered with cloud-based software company Salesforce to develop a range of new apps and programs that governments can subscribe to for the day-to-day management of services.

The degree of investment in new IT infrastructures only intensified during the COVID-19 pandemic, as TPSFs quickly brokered deals with IT firms to assume ownership over tracking and tracing apps and other technologies that could then be sold to governments. For instance, as we mentioned in the previous chapter, building from their alliance with Salesforce, Deloitte launched its GovConnect Public Health Transformation Platform in 2020. The platform offers a "suite of case management and analytics solutions, built on Salesforce, that help government leaders and public health officials make better real-time decisions about complex and rapidly changing public health crises."[91] This includes tracking and monitoring of vaccine performance, clinic monitoring, population sequencing, logistics and inventory management, call centre coordination, public sentiment and trust campaigns, integrated disease surveillance, network analysis, and higher education, among other things. This is quite a departure from either ad hoc consultancy work or bookkeeping, and it reflects the direction that these firms are taking today.

Through the commodification of knowledge in this way, TPSFs have been able to further entrench themselves in government, going beyond just social networks and institutional affiliations to establishing control over technologies that public agencies rely on to do their day-to-day work. This can foster deepening dependencies as governments become invested in technological infrastructures that are difficult to extricate themselves from in the long run. The case of the Phoenix Pay System that we discussed in Chapter 3 provides a good example of this kind of relationship — once a TPSF has its foot in the door to provide critical IT infrastructure to the public, they tend to stick around for a long time, continuing to acquire lucrative contracts regardless of their performance. The government is left with little choice but to keep hiring and paying these firms, as they own much of the knowledge, expertise, and infrastructure necessary for its day-to-day operations.

# Brokering

While these firms are concerned with lifting management ideas out of specific contexts, codifying them, and packaging them as commodities, they also seek to position themselves as brokers that others must rely on for access to these commodities. Political economist Rasmus Christensen describes the *infrastructural power* of these firms, which involves control over expertise and management information systems that other actors must rely on to be able to act.[92] This involves generating power through standing as intermediaries responsible for gathering and circulating ideas, information, personnel, and infrastructures across jurisdictions. Sociologist Leonard Seabrooke's concept of epistemic arbitrage is useful in describing the process.[93] Arbitrage typically refers to the practice of taking advantage of price differences between markets in order to bring in a guaranteed return — buying an asset for cheap in one market and selling it for dear in another. Seabrooke extends this notion to the brokering of professional knowledge. As he notes, epistemic arbitrage "provides an understanding of how particular professionals are able to exploit differences in professional knowledge pools for strategic advantage by positioning particular forms of knowledge as the most appropriate to deal with particular problems."[94]

Along these lines, TPSFs position themselves as the brokers of ideas, described by Christensen as "cognitive infrastructure." They are able to achieve a degree of power through their capacity to provide governments with knowledge, frameworks, and models taken from other sectors and regions. Through their capacity to selectively pick and choose these ideas, taken from specific sectors and regions, and representing specific interests, they exercise power as curators. As Eckl and Hanrieder note, "the consultants gain an information advantage in comparison to the other players in the reform process. While consultants serve as a nodal point towards which knowledge flows (as they review internal documents and interview people), they can determine which knowledge is shared with others."[95] In their case study of the World Health Organization (WHO), which we will discuss shortly, they show how consultants take advantage of this information asymmetry to "overload decision makers with hard-to-dispute information in short periods of time."[96] In their interviews with WHO officials, they describe how McKinsey consultants overwhelmed public officials with massive decks of slides presented at the last minute, and often without any outside references. This gave the consultants leverage to push their ideas through despite the opposition of public officials.

Along with brokering access to ideas, TPSFs also act as brokers of human capital. In their capacity as "career hubs," Christensen notes, "global Professional Service Firms control the 'production of producers,'" providing much of the requisite expertise that other institutions rely on to get things done.[97] Along these lines, firms provide access to so-called professionals in possession of what is believed to be scarce knowledge that can be quickly parachuted in by public agencies in times of crisis. Indeed, public officials often justify their use of outside consultants on the basis that they lack the in-house knowledge to perform these duties themselves. A common strategy for these firms is to poach senior-level officials from public agencies and then rent them back to governments, often at exorbitant rates. Likewise, more human capital–centred firms like McKinsey serve as brokers to personnel from Ivy League institutions. Their power, in part, comes from their capacity to recruit from the most reputable universities around the world, promising much higher pay than public institutions. In their investigations of consulting during the COVID-19 pandemic, ProPublica notes that "[a] single junior consultant at McKinsey will cost governments $67,500 per week [USD], or $3.5 million annually. For $160,000 per week, you get two consultants, the second one mid-level."[98] Of course, the degree to which these firms offer services that cannot be provided by governments themselves is often up for debate. For instance, after revelations that spending on McKinsey by the Government of Canada had increased nearly twentyfold under the Liberals, rising from $1.8 million in 2016–17 to $32.5 million in 2021–22, critics challenged the value for money from contracts by calling attention to how the same services could be provided much cheaper in-house. As Matthew Green, the New Democratic Party's ethics critic noted, "Canada has a strong public service who can do this work at a fraction of the cost, so there's no reason for [Prime Minister Justin Trudeau] to choose to hand buckets of money to his billionaire CEO friends instead."[99]

Much of the literature focuses on the human capital of these firms — and indeed frame them chiefly as human capital–based operations — but the immense physical infrastructure of these firms is also instrumental in brokering access to knowledge and expertise. Beyond just looking at personnel, it is also important to take into consideration the offices, databases, servers, and cloud computing networks through which firms are able to quickly mobilize information across jurisdictions. Indeed, the data infrastructures commanded by these firms has, in some areas, supplanted professional expertise to become their chief commodity. By engineering digital platforms, TPSFs have been able to both accumulate and circulate data in new ways, developing channels that accelerate the flow of information while establishing public-sector dependencies on their data infrastructures. This reflects a distinctive way of creating and capturing value. As Rahman and Thelen note, firms generate value through "their capacity to extract and harness immense amounts of data in ways that allow them to operate as critical intermediaries and market makers."[100]

The power of these firms as data brokers can be traced vertically through examining their capacity to aggregate information in centralized archives.[101] By virtue of their service to so many jurisdictions, these firms position themselves as centres of calculation, brokering access to data that governments would not otherwise be able to access. As we saw in the previous section, firms have invested heavily in new data infrastructures that can rapidly gather and analyze information (though this data is often thin, selective and open to contestation, as we discuss in the next chapter). As Mazzucato and Collington note, companies now have "sophisticated systems for collating and distributing information about previous contracts. Work with a previous client is usually recorded internally and stored digitally so that other consultants are able to access them."[102] These databases have become increasingly automated with the development of new technologies. For instance, in 2014, Deloitte developed a document-review platform that has "automated the process of reviewing and extracting all the relevant information from contracts."[103] Through such technologies, the company has been able to reduce the amount of time spent in "reviewing legal contract documents, invoices, financial statements and board meeting minutes by up to 50 percent or more."[104] Likewise, EY has begun to automate its auditing processes, developing new artificial intelligence (AI), technologies that enable the quick management and analysis of leases and contracts. They have even acquired airborne drones for monitoring inventory. PwC has invested heavily in Natural Language Processing to make sense of complex contracts. And KPMG has taken up AI to develop an Anomalous Event

Predicting Tool, with the aim of predicting future business events. These kinds of technologies have enabled these firms to gather a vast amount of information, which can then be analyzed and transformed into products that can be bought and sold to public agencies as a scarce commodity.

In addition to looking at the vertical accumulation of information, the mobilization of data by TPSFs can also be traced horizontally in terms of the flow of information across jurisdictions. Along these lines, these firms have accelerated the flow of policy knowledge across jurisdictions — facilitating what Jamie Peck and Nik Theodore describe as "fast policy," or a policymaking condition that is characterized by "the intensified and instantaneous connectivity of sites, channels, arenas, and nodes of policy development, evolution, and reproduction."[105] Their capacity to quickly circulate these kinds of ideas is made possible, in part, through the scale of their operations. As of 2022, the Big Four firms employed more than 1,464,000 people in 150 countries. And McKinsey employs 30,000 consultants in 130 offices in sixty-five countries. At this scale, they command a significant degree of power as they are capable of quickly mobilizing personnel and data from around the world.

This is reinforced through the scale advantages that can be generated through their capacity to marshal big data. As these firms mobilize these products across jurisdictions, they can build up robust infrastructures through which they can gather and circulate information, creating a network effect that can be deepened over time.[106] As more and more users, for instance, take up and format their services using KPMG's Municipal Reference Model, the model is further validated as the standard. In seeking to emulate best practices in other jurisdictions, public officials become more likely to take up this model as it becomes more widely diffused, and less likely to adopt alternative forms of benchmarking and classification.[107] The first company to consolidate support around a specific benchmark is often able to retain primacy, establishing it as the principal norm for assessing an industry or sector. Operating at this scale often gives TPSFs leverage in gaining market share against small and more boutique consulting firms, widening market dominance over time.

Thus, McKinsey's tremendous organizational footprint gave it a leg up in getting untendered contracts from governments during the pandemic. With the onset of the crisis, journalist Ian Macdougall from ProPublica documents how the firm "sprang into sales mode," to deploy "its partners across the country to seek contracts with federal agencies, state governments and city halls."[108] In addition to leveraging social networks, this included cold calls to government offices across Canada, including Ontario, where the firm was put in charge of setting up the provincial government's pandemic command structure — at a price of $1.6 million. The government justified hiring the firm for an untendered and admittedly exorbitant contract by pointing to the firm's presence in other jurisdictions. According to the government's Procurement Business Case from March 2020, which we gained access to through a Freedom of Information request:

> Though the anticipated value for this procurement is higher than standard industry rates, McKinsey has been selected to do this work as they are already supporting other jurisdictions in Europe and Asia where the COVID-19 pandemic exists. McKinsey is currently advising other jurisdictions with data analytics and reporting, and understands the framework and strategies to assist the Ontario government to identify opportunities, identify pain points, and areas of focus daily.

In other words, because McKinsey already had their foot in the door on pandemic management in other jurisdictions, they were deemed to be qualified to work in Ontario. And, it was reasoned, because the firm had "pre-existing models on epidemiological evolution, supply chain networks and real estate availability that can be quickly and easily adapted for Ontario," hiring McKinsey would indeed allow the province to get "ahead of the curve" to "protect lives of Ontarians and the economy."

Such power is also augmented through the institutional entrenchment of TPSFs in national and supranational organizations. For instance, McKinsey and BCG have embedded themselves in the WHO and have been involved in major international disease outbreaks in recent years, including the Mers outbreak in Saudi Arabia, Zika in Brazil, and Ebola in West Africa. In 2017, the WHO decided to increase its use of management consultants as part of a new agency initiative to restructure their operations. The reasoning behind the call for more consultants was that they lacked in-house expertise in certain areas. McKinsey, Bain, BCG, Deloitte, and Accenture are all on the list of hires, with McKinsey and BCG being the most prominent. According to an investigation by American news site Vox, WHO staffers have continually complained that the agency is now "crawling with outside consultants,"[109] and that "it was like a beehive on the seventh and eighth floors.... there were many people in suits, but they don't talk to us directly.... It's now been two years [the reform] has been going on. We have no idea what is happening."[110] One senior official in particular lamented the "McKinsey type of reform" which meant "musical chairs," "cost cutting," and "debunked management fads," [111] During the COVID-19 pandemic, McKinsey was able to draw on their entrenchment in WHO to generate credibility and access clients, mobilizing data across jurisdictions.

The circulation of policy ideas across jurisdictions in this way — beginning from TPSFs headquartered in the Anglo-American heartland and embedded in supranational organizations like WHO — can consequently reinforce colonial relationships, as it elevates the status of expertise located the Global North while marginalizing other sources of knowledge. As epidemiologist Madhukar Pai notes, the consulting industry (along with nongovernmental organizations [NGOs] and donor agencies) send "'experts' to low- and middle-income countries to offer 'technical assistance' when they might know little about the countries they are advising or the problems they are trying to fix."[112] He calls this "consulting malpractice." Management scholar Mehdi Boussebaa argues that these firms have played a central role in universalizing a distinctively Anglo-American mode of professional practice.[113] They "do not merely provide a 'neutral' set of services on a worldwide basis; they also (re)produce core-periphery relations in the modern world economy." As we noted earlier, the commodified and codified ideas, models, and data applied by these firms are often prepackaged and divorced from local contexts, and often do not actually respond to local needs. This has real and tangible consequences for those who are at the receiving end. Thus, Boussebaa contends that "the process not only serves to diffuse Anglo-American standards globally and facilitate cross-national service delivery but also leads to the gradual exclusion of local forms of knowledge and issues of importance to local business communities."[114]

But transnational firms are not always able to get access to local consulting markets. While economies of scale and scope may give these firms a competitive advantage in accessing personnel and data, social networks still make a difference. For instance, in Russia, Daria Volkova notes that boutique consultancy firms have remained prominent in advising city governments due to the importance of social networks linking

local consultants with powerful insiders.[115] "Before becoming consultants," she notes, "the majority [of consultants] had already established
a wide web of contacts with the Moscow authorities and federal government and gained a reputation through different pathways: business,
economics, architecture, and the university sphere."[116] This has given
them a leg up in accessing local elites versus transnational firms. Thus,
the power of TPSFs as knowledge brokers is not a foregone conclusion;
it is conditioned, in part, by the degree to which they have established
social networks with political and economic elites in a given jurisdiction, as well as their degree of institutionalization in its public agencies.
Ultimately, social networking can feed the institutionalization, codification, and commodification of policy ideas, and vice versa. As ideas
become more robust as they are objectified and commodified in specific
knowledge products, it can be easier to move them across jurisdictions
without heavy investments in human capital, but social networks remain
important in mediating these relationships.

## A Self-Perpetuating Cycle

We have discussed four strategies by which TPSFs set out to influence
governments. By pursuing these strategies together, TPSFs have often
expanded their influence in public policymaking and service delivery
in a self-perpetuating cycle. By leveraging social networks with public
officials, TPSFs get their foot in the door to secure lucrative contracts.
Through membership on the boards of standards-setting organizations
and public agencies, they entrench themselves in the delivery of public
services. Through commodifying knowledge products that are routinely
used in service delivery, they foster public-sector dependencies on their
infrastructures. And finally, through brokering access to ideas, information, personnel, and infrastructures as scarce commodities across jurisdictions, they position themselves as obligatory points of passage, which
governments must procure to get access to requisite knowledge.

Operating at these different levels can set in motion feedback effects
that lead to the entrenchment of TPSFs in government over time. For
instance, in his analysis of the implementation of e-government in the
UK, Ivan Horrocks observes that consultants have been able to leverage
influential positions in government and public policy circles to advocate
for deepening outsourcing arrangements, extending further contracts to
TPSFs, which, in turn, further entrenches their power and expertise in

service delivery.[117] As public officials become dependent on these firms as brokers of knowledge about service delivery, the firms are then able to deepen their role in assessing and advising on these same systems. "The ongoing and expanding exchange process," he notes, "builds increasingly widespread interpersonal alliances and networks."[118] Thus, power loops are established that entrench the power of TPSFs in government over time.

Moreover, such power loops can foster dependency relationships, creating a consulting trap from which it can be difficult for governments to extricate themselves. As Busemeyer and Thelen note, "once private actors are established and involved in the provision of crucial public goods and services" they are likely to stick around and "influence future policymaking processes."[119] In some areas, the degree of control over professional services is alarming. In the area of accounting, for example, the Big Four firms have been described as "too big to fail." As one KPMG director notes, "KPMG simply can't be allowed to fail — there just isn't capacity in the market for others to take up the slack." Thus, he expects that "everybody will bust a gut to make sure that they turn it around."[120] This gives firms considerable leverage in defining the norms that govern their conduct.

The state of things might seem disheartening as TPSFs expand and deepen their influence in public policymaking and service delivery, posing significant threats to democratic accountability. Yet, as we show in the next chapter, there are opportunities for resistance. Often, the same strategies that TPSFs use to entrench themselves in government can also be taken up to challenge their authority. By exposing their social networks, confronting the opacity of their knowledge products, and challenging their thin knowledge of social policy, the producers and users of public services can contest the power of these firms in government. This provides some hope in overcoming the consulting trap.

# Chapter 5

# Resistance:
# Challenging Transnational
# Professional Service Firms

The previous chapter explored the strategies that TPSFs employ to generate influence in public policymaking. Through their capacity to both span jurisdictions and embed themselves in institutions, these firms are able to position themselves as masters of code, acting as standard-setters for some, while assisting others with gaming the system. Through building networks with public officials, TPSFs are able to get their foot in the door to access contracts. By seeking affiliation with the boards of public agencies, they can embed themselves in institutional routines, further entrenching their authority in government. Through extracting knowledge of public services from local contexts, codifying it, and transforming it into a commodity, they are able to package generic policy programs that can be quickly mobilized across jurisdictions. And through brokering access to data infrastructures, they can make themselves obligatory points of passage relied on by public officials to assess and deliver public services.

The growing reliance of governments on these firms has serious implications for democracy, as TPSFs are increasingly positioned at the core of public service delivery but with very little accountability or transparency. Their entrenchment inside government has contributed to the privatization of public administration, as whole areas of policymaking and service delivery are cordoned off as commercial property beyond the purview of public scrutiny. As these firms seek to enhance their own profits as well as the profits of those they serve, this also raises potential conflicts of interest, as these firms may (and often do) prioritize their own interests over public interest. Such conflicts only grow as these firms expand through mergers and acquisitions. The procurement of such large firms for a range of services on an ongoing basis can foster long-term dependencies, setting in motion "feedback effects that enhance and entrench the influence of business over time."[1]

In this context, contesting the power of these firms might seem like a daunting task. Indeed, much of the literature has tended to frame the power of the consultocracy as monolithic and irreversible. There is seldom any discussion of how people can work, or have worked, to actively challenge or restrain their influence. In this chapter, we consider how the power of TPSFs can be contested, discussing some of the strategies that have been taken up to resist the incursion of these firms into public policymaking. As we show, the strategies that TPSFs employ to entrench their power can also be flipped back on them. Where TPSFs rely on social networks to generate influence, critical researchers can track their affiliations, mapping the web of interests in which they are entangled. Where TPSFs deny public access to their models and formulae under the auspices of commercial sensitivity, critical researchers can expose and contest the boundaries of intellectual property regimes, demanding greater transparency and access to information. Where TPSFs depend on their reputation to attract and maintain clients, critical researchers can call attention to their toxic business practices, putting them at risk of losing their brand value.

Ultimately, all of this creates the potential foundations for another way of knowing public services that builds greater connections between the producers and users of public services. In the process of mobilizing against these privatized knowledge networks, communities of public service producers and users can foster other ways of understanding and engaging with the public sector that are built on collective learning, community archives, and public deliberation.

## Challenging Managerial Knowledge

In the previous chapters, we have explored how TPSFs set out to transform management information into intellectual property. Often, this involves codifying existing records to extract second-order data, which can then be commodified and sold back to governments. Drawing on the legacy of F.W. Taylor and scientific management, such practices are notable in segmenting the production of knowledge — excluding those at the frontlines from the conversation — and concentrating it in the hands of senior managers and consultants. In this context, it is vital for those who produce or use public services to demand a seat at the table, developing their own accounts in ways that can talk back to official accounts produced by these firms.

A notable example of this was the 2011 struggle against the KPMG Municipal Service Delivery Review in the city of Toronto.[2] After the election of right-wing populist Rob Ford as mayor in 2010, whose campaign was built on a mandate to "stop the gravy train," a coalition of right-wing councillors hoped that management consultants could be used to identify areas for cutbacks and cost savings, legitimizing a neoliberal program of austerity. As Ford noted at the time: "For years, our city has spent more money than it brings in. Instead of fixing the problem, we've kept passing the buck to 'next year.' Well, next year has arrived. It's time we fixed the problem."[3]

Confronting a projected $774 million budget deficit, the KPMG review framed the policy debate around questions of essentiality (are services must have or nice to have?) and standards of delivery (are services above, at, or below standard?). As Ford argued:

> If we are going to reduce spending ... and ladies and gentlemen, we must reduce our spending ... it only makes sense to take the time to figure out which things are "must haves" and which things are "nice to haves." Because it makes sense to look at "nice to haves" first. That's what this process is about.

In response, a broad coalition mobilized — including progressive city councillors, community groups, neighbourhood associations, anti-poverty activists, student associations, and labour unions — to both contest the claims of KPMG and generate their own knowledge of public services. As one city councillor recounts:

> It was a pretty hard grind for four years. Once the gravy train mantra took over and once the promise we could do it for less took hold, you had to watch every single file to make sure they weren't slipping one past you and weren't using bad data to try and justify poor decisions.[4]

A central aspect of the coalition's work involved conducting research to counter the claims of KPMG consultants. Along these lines, activists established a division of labour, delegating community expertise to specific areas. As one city councillor noted: "When the reports came down, we looked at it and we parcelled up the work and we all sunk into our areas of expertise and did different things on different files."[5]

Central to this project was the inclusion of city workers and local residents with tacit knowledge about the services in contesting KPMG's claims. After gathering data, local residents used both demonstrations and public consultations as a theatre where they could mobilize counter-narratives that challenged the consultants' positions. Public deliberations on KPMG's final report were scant and the mayor attempted to ram through in-person consultations in a single meeting. In response, over 300 people turned out, culminating in a 25-hour deputation process, the longest meeting in the history of the municipality and a powerful rebuke to the consultants. As one activist noted, "You bottle things up, they tend to explode more, and I think that was an example of that." In their allotted three minutes, each deputant spoke back to the KPMG report. Against the disembodied metrics ranking so-called core services, they appealed to their direct experiences of service delivery. As one activist noted, "People coming from all corners of the city talking about their personal experiences and how this was going to affect them helped a lot in reframing the conversation."[6]

In the end, the project was widely delegitimized, with even the major newspapers condemning it as a fruitless exercise. The *Toronto Star* noted that the city's administration had delivered "a process that is rushed, incoherent, poorly thought out, heavy on political dogma."[7] Moreover, the project galvanized a broader movement in opposition to the mayor's austerity policies. An activist recounts that "people started to hold budget town halls all across the city that were generated to a large extent by community groups rather than by the councillor or by the community groups asking the councillor to hold them, and those were huge meetings."[8]

Such coalitions can be a powerful starting place for opposing the programs of TPSFs. Conducting grassroots research and gathering popular accounts provides a means of drawing people together, providing grounds for organizing political opposition.[9] Moreover, actively confronting public officials through public mobilizations provides a means through which critical researchers can gain access to information about these firms and their relationships with government. Taking inspiration from these struggles, we identify four strategies that can be taken up in challenging the power of TPSFs in government. First, through following paper trails, tracking contractual arrangements, and interrogating their terms and conditions, the nature and extent of TPSF involvement in service delivery can be critically unpacked. Second, through tracing the biographies of TPSF personnel and their social networks with public and private officials, their allegiances can be gauged, and potential conflicts of interest can be identified. Third, through Freedom of Information requests, activists can identify and contest the privatization of policy information under the auspices of commercial sensitivity and cabinet confidence. Finally, through gathering accounts from public service producers and users themselves and presenting them in public meetings, other ways of knowing public services can be fostered, rooted in people's everyday experiences.

## People's Audits: Track Paper Trails

How can we gauge the extent to which TPSFs are entrenched in government? A tried and tested strategy for challenging the power of consultancies has been to follow paper trails. By using government procurement databases to track down contracts, critical researchers can determine spending levels, identify key players, and interrogate terms and conditions. Further, they can expose inconsistencies, institutional blind spots, and areas where liability and ownership are unclear, opening the doors to contestation.

Such strategies are well-established, taken up by activists since at least the mid-1960s as a means of interrogating the relationships between governments and contractors. In the United States, Ralph Nader's Centre for the Study of Responsive Law served as an important hub for this kind of research, spearheaded by two attorneys, Donald Guttman and Barry Willner (1976) who documented the rise of consultocracy in the United States. A central aspect of their work involved the comprehensive investigation of government procurement records. In an interview, Guttman recounts walking into a contracts office at the Health, Education, and Welfare (HEW) Department in search of a report: "'Help yourself,' said the man at the desk, and, over the next few weeks, he did. Poring over contract files, he discovered that most HEW contracts went to a few well-connected firms, often without competition."[10] Through the course of his research, Guttman made friends with the HEW staff, joining them for coffee breaks, and even answering the phone when they went to lunch.

Out of such research, Guttman and Willner published a damning book in 1976, *Shadow Government*, which exposed the degree of

government reliance on outside contractors, often with very little accountability.[11] They noted that, while the number of full-time civil
servants had remained relatively stable over two decades, the federal
budget had ballooned from $70 billion to $370 billion, with a significant amount ($110 billion) going to management consultants, experts
and think tanks. In the book, Guttman and Willner carefully trace the
institutional arrangements through which such contracts are brokered.
Beginning from the contracts they dug up at the HEW, they went on to
follow the paper trails, including the letters, memoranda, and internal
documents through which decisions are made. Through this research
they identified conflicts of interest. For instance, in studying the contract logs, they noted a letter justifying the selection of the consultant
based on his friendship with the Secretary: "as you perhaps know, Mr.
Green was a personal adviser to the Secretary for about three months
during the transition period and accompanied the Secretary on his
trip to Israel."[12]

Moreover, they interrogated all the roadblocks and jurisdictional
fragmentation that they confronted, demonstrating both the lack of
transparency in procurement as well as the state's own incapacity to effectively manage such relationships. In the absence of formal, centralized
record-keeping, they showed that public officials were not able to make
sense of contracts or share information across jurisdictions. The book
spurred government oversight hearings into public-sector procurement
through the 1970s, making the power of consultants a public issue.

For many decades, critical researchers and investigative journalists
have drawn from such methods as a means of determining the degree of
involvement by TPSFs in government.[13] Of course, these days one cannot
simply walk into a contracts office and start leafing through the files. The
regime brokering access to information is more sophisticated and TPSFs
have become more deeply entrenched in service delivery. At the same
time, new Freedom of Information (FOI) and e-government laws and
regulations have provided a useful resource for those who are seeking to
contest their power. An example of this is Barnet, an outer borough of
London in the United Kingdom where — based on the advice of PwC —
over 70 percent of local government services were outsourced to a single
firm, Capita, in 2012 in three enormous contracts (see Chapter 3).[14] The
local council adopted the moniker easyCouncil, likening their project to
the discount airline company, easyJet. "We are looking at how [easyJet's]

relentless drive for keeping costs down has worked for them," Mike Freer, the model's champion noted, "and we are looking at doing the same."[15]

In this context, the Barnet Alliance for Public Services (BAPS) took up FOI requests and "People's Audits" in investigating both the nature and degree of outsourcing arrangements between local governments and TPSFs. Drawing from new legislation granting citizens access to government financial records, folks with financial expertise were able to scour the documents and identify inconsistencies, ambiguities, and errors. As one activist notes:

> once a year, you're allowed [under the Audit Commission Act] to inspect invoices and anything that contributes to the accounts. So, I requested every single Capita invoice, which they provided me but I then noticed ... all the paperwork that went behind it, which we had to have a fight over... all the supporting documentation. So, they give me an invoice which says, "miscellaneous payments £29,769.00," so I say, "well what is it?"[16]

Since the contracts were awarded, activists have diligently followed the paper trails in documenting the steady inflation of outsourcing costs, which have cost £257.73 million more than the contracted value over the course of nine years, as well as the ambiguities and inconsistencies in oversight.

Moreover, activists have also transformed public demonstrations and encounters with public officials into opportunities for research, identifying areas for further investigation. For instance, at a council town hall meeting, activists encountered heavy-handed private security guards who were hired by the council to monitor their activities. In the wake of the event, several local bloggers and activists submitted FOI requests asking for the borough's contracts with private security. Out of this process, it was revealed that the council had no formal contract with the security firm, MetPro, that had been used to monitor the residents. After five months, the FOI requests for MetPro culminated in an internal audit that revealed the £1.36-million-pound contract had been awarded without a tendering exercise, without a written contract, and no proper invoicing. According to the borough's own official report, the agreement "failed to comply with ... Financial Regulations, exposing the council to significant financial and reputational risks."[17] More broadly, there were "serious deficiencies in current procurement arrangements," and there

were no guarantees against a repeat of such practices.[18] The confronta-
tion widely delegitimized the council's larger outsourcing project. Given
that they could not even adequately manage private security services
through small-scale contracts, how would they be able to manage large,
complex multimillion pound contracts?

A central aspect of the activism in Barnet has focused on identifying and politicizing such institutional blind spots. By posing questions
at council meetings, digging through the archives and submitting FOI
requests, local residents have become adept at negotiating the documentary practices of the council. The information gathered by local bloggers
and by labour and community activists was then disseminated through
various media, initially through local blogs and newspapers, then public
meetings, eventually culminating in two documentary films that were
shown in the local cinema in the spring and fall of 2012. These screen-
ings served as opportunities to raise awareness and mobilize community
members even further.[19]

## Social Network Analysis: Identify Allegiances

Beyond following paper trails, critical researchers can also investigate
the allegiances of these firms and their personnel. As we noted in the
previous chapter, TPSFs extensively rely on social networks with political and economic elites to generate influence.[20] Through advocacy
coalitions, memberships on the boards of public agencies, and revolving-door relationships, these firms entrench themselves in public policymaking. And yet, while this may give these firms considerable leverage in winning contracts, their posture as neutral third parties can
also be challenged through exposing these same allegiances. Revealing
how TPSFs are bound to political and economic elites helps locate the
kinds of knowledge that they produce, and demonstrates how it might
be used to advance commercial prerogatives that are at odds with the
public interest.

In the area of TPSFs, such research is often left to investigative journalists. Indeed, some of the most damning stories about TPSFs have come
from journalists tracing the links between politicians and consultants.
For instance, investigative journalists looking at McKinsey have fore-
grounded the firm's close ties with President Barack Obama in the United
States,[21] President Emmanuel Macron in France,[22] Prime Minister David
Cameron in the United Kingdom,[23] President Jacob Zuma in South

Africa, and Prime Minister Justin Trudeau in Canada.[24] These relationships are most thoroughly documented in *When McKinsey Comes to
Town*, the 2022 book by *New York Times* journalists Walt Bogdanich and
Michael Forsythe, who note they were able get their foot in the door
thanks to the work of an aggressive group of investigative journalists in
South Africa. "McKinsey consultants were feeling the heat," they note,
"and they began to talk."[25]

   However, while investigative journalists have spearheaded this kind of
analysis, the allegiances of TPSFs, their memberships on boards of public
agencies and advocacy groups, and the biographies of their personnel
are often anecdotal and not systematically documented. This can be ac-
complished through power structure research, which sets out to map
the networks linking TPSFs with public officials. Inspired by C. Wright
Mills' (1956) book on *The Power Elite* and William Domhoff's *Who
Rules America?* (1967), such research has been undertaken by activists
and academics since the mid-1960s to trace the connections linking political and economic elites.[26] More recently, sociologist William Carroll
has refined these methods as part of the Corporate Mapping Project, investigating the influence of oil and gas companies over Canadian policymaking.[27] Tom Juravich has promoted these tools for labour organizers
in investigating the composition of companies — including their boards
of directors, shareholders, clients, and memberships in advocacy groups
and lobbying organizations.[28] Jane McAlevey has adopted a similar approach, which she describes as Power Mapping that extends the analysis
beyond tracing the networks of the powerful to investigating the capacities of community groups themselves.[29]

   A central method deployed in mapping power structures is social network analysis (SNA). SNA provides a means for investigating the scope of
social relationships extensively across numerous sites.[30] Rather than focusing on the internal structure and organization of TPSFs, it enables us
to shed light on the extensive relationships connecting TPSFs with other
organizations and individuals that have facilitated their integration in
different ways and to different degrees with other actors. In a number
of countries, critics — including investigative journalists and critical researchers — have exposed the allegiances of these firms by tracking the
close connections between TPSF personnel and political and economic
elites, documenting the boards that they sit on, tracking their movement
between organizations, and identifying potential conflicts of interest.[31]

SNA can be deployed in at least two ways. First, it can be taken up in investigating the interorganizational links connecting TPSFs with other institutions. For instance, we can look at how the personnel of TPSFs and public officials come together on the boards of public agencies and advocacy organizations. As we saw in the previous chapter, TPSFs have played a central role in establishing advocacy organizations promoting Public–Private Partnerships (PPPs) in many countries around the world, including Canada, the United States and the United Kingdom.[32] With members sitting on the boards of these organizations alongside public officials and private contractors, these firms have actively worked to establish a political-cultural community around the promotion of PPPs as a method of financializing infrastructure, while simultaneously presenting themselves as neutral third parties in gauging their value. By exposing their role in orchestrating these networks, critical researchers can begin to question just how impartial they are in their assessments.[33]

There are numerous resources that can help track TPSF memberships on boards of public agencies and advocacy organizations. Very often, this information is publicly available on the websites of these organizations, in public lobbying registries, or via access to information requests. Moreover, activists have developed tools to help map these relationships. For instance, LittleSis — "a free database of who-knows-who at the heights of business and government" — provides a tool to map the structure of TPSFs as well as their leadership and staff, donations, memberships, and interlocks with other organizations.[34] The database enables activists to document how TPSFs are connected with other organizations via the boards of advocacy organizations, such as the United Kingdom's Oil and Gas Industry Direct Forum, where the Big Four firms have come together with oil and gas companies to lobby for government subsidies and tax cuts (see Figure 5.1). Critical researchers have drawn from such methods to unearth the networks through which TPSFs have lobbied the UK government for £6 billion in subsidies per year to the fossil fuel sector.[35]

Second, SNA can be taken up to investigate the circulation of individuals across organizations. Drawing on publicly available data on social networking websites, we can track revolving doors, following the movement of personnel from TPSFs to public agencies and vice versa. For instance, critical researchers have taken up Powerbase — a "free encyclopedia of people, issues, and groups shaping the public agenda" — to trace the allegiances of senior officials responsible for reforming the

National Health Service (NHS) in the United Kingdom. Drawing on this database, a 2015 Spinwatch report documents the revolving doors between government and TPSFs advising NHS reforms, with at least sixteen senior officials moving between TPSFs and NHS.[36] For instance, David Bennett, the director of the Monitor, the NHS regulator, was previously a senior partner with McKinsey for eighteen years. David Milburn, who was Secretary of State and Health Minister under Tony Blair went on to serve as an adviser to PwC, which boasts to have "acted on more privatisations than any other financial advisor," and has been actively advising NHS on how to reform health services.[37] And Mark Britnell, who had been a senior official at NHS and Director General of the Department of Health, went on to serve as the chair of KPMG's Global Health Practice. Powerbase profiles these figures, which enables users to track the movement of personnel between the public and private sector over time.

Likewise, in our research on the Province of Ontario's PPP sector, we drew on official reports, official websites, and social networking

**Figure 5.1 Social Network Analysis:**
**Big Four connections with the Oil and Gas Lobby**

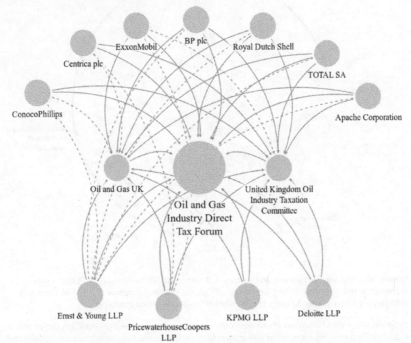

Source: "North Sea Oil Network Costing UK Taxpayers Billions," littlesis.org/oligrapher/2059-north-sea-oil-network-costing-uk-taxpayers-billions.

platforms to document the circulation of personnel between the private sector and public agencies.[38] Having identified instances when personnel moved from the public to the private sector or vice versa, we created an organizational network that revealed a high degree of movement between sectors, with 42 percent of total career changes being from public to private or from private to public (see Figure 5.2). In our research, we found that staff members working as transaction advisors with the Big Four firms tended to move around the most in comparison with personnel from other sectors. This includes high-level personnel moving from government to TPSFs, such as Michael Jordan, who served as the chief of infrastructure development before moving on to serve as a partner for PwC. It also includes personnel from TPSFs to government, such as John Casola, the Chief Investment Officer of the Canada Infrastructure

**Figure 5.2 The PPP Enabling Field: Tracking the Circulation of Personnel between Public and Private Agencies in Ontario**

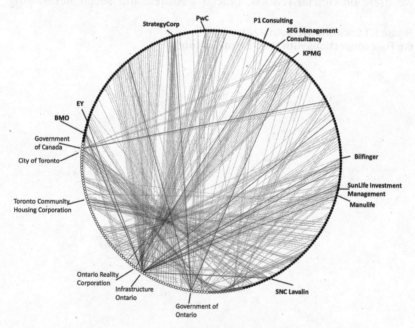

Source: Chris Hurl, Valerie l'Heureux, and Susanne A. Kraemer, 2022, "Elite Networks in Public Private Partnerships: Mapping the Enabling Field in Ontario," *Studies in Political Economy* 103, 1, p. 46. Reprinted with permission from Taylor & Francis Ltd on behalf of Studies in Political Economy.

Note: The figure shows a network of revolving door employment ties between private (black circles) and public (white circles) organizations, as well as ngos (grey circles). Connections were treated as non-directed and thicker lines indicate more than one employee moving between two organizations. Organizations with more than ten ties to other organizations are labelled.

Bank, who was previously the managing partner for Infrastructure and Government Services with PwC.

Exposing these allegiances, critical researchers can challenge the credibility of TPSFs by calling attention to a core paradox in their work — that is, while these firms present themselves as detached observers, standing apart from the fray, their core business model is fundamentally premised on their capacity to forge alliances, entangling themselves with the same interests that they purportedly set out to impartially assess. By tracing the memberships of TPSF staff in lobbying organizations, critical researchers can get a better sense of the policies that these firms advocate. By investigating secondments in public agencies, they can investigate the extent to which they are embedded in the institutional regimes of government. And by tracing revolving doors, they can get a sense of the political-cultural community in which they circulate. All of this helps to critically locate the kinds of knowledge that they produce as well as identifying potential conflicts of interest that may arise through their connections.

## Access to Information: Make Things Public

While People's Audits and SNA provide a good starting point to confront the power and influence of TPSFs, vital information is not always disclosed to the public. In fact, as we saw in the previous chapter, the core business model of TPSFs is based on their capacity to commodify information, brokering access to programs, technologies, methodologies, and datasets as intellectual property. In this context, the disclosure of information itself can become an arena of struggle and a starting place from which to renegotiate the boundaries between the private and the public.

TPSFs often frame themselves as bastions of transparency. Indeed, transparency is one of the products they sell to their clients. The Big Four firms each offer "Trust and Transparency Solutions,"[39] while McKinsey and Bain advise clients on how to achieve "transparency across value chains."[40] This is ironic considering how little information these firms publicly disclose themselves. In a 2018 study by Transparency International, the Big Four firms received an average score of 35 percent for their transparency. According to Transparency International's Corporate Political Engagement Index, which ranks companies according to their relations with government — including political contributions, lobbying, revolving doors, and transparency — EY received the grade of F, Deloitte and PwC received a D, and KPMG received a C.[41] The report noted that firms in this bracket did not publish any details on secondments and did not have publicly available procedures for implementing cooling-off periods for new employees who were formerly public officials, leaving the public sector open to "potential widespread conflicts of interest." McKinsey is even more secretive, refusing to disclose the names of its clients, which makes it very difficult to identify potential conflicts of interest. As Boganich and Foresyth note, there is a "culture of secrecy" at the firm: "Consultants in their first days at the firm are programmed to say nothing publicly about clients or their advice." This, they argue, makes reporting on the consultancy "akin to chasing shadows."[42]

As we saw in the previous chapter, the business model of TPSFs is premised on strategically withholding access to information. And yet, while these firms hold their cards close to their chests, they must also be public-facing, reaching out, fostering trust in their methods. This makes them vulnerable as they tend to leave traces of what they hide in their public statements. Starting from the line that firms draw between opacity and transparency, the pretensions of TPSFs to cast a clear light can be challenged. When access to information is denied, community activists can use it as a basis for mobilization. Interrogating the relationship between governments and TPSFs can run in two directions: Activists can either pressure TPSFs to release information about their operations themselves — pushing firms to disclose their revenues, their employees, their contracts, and so on; or they can push governments to disclose contracts and deliverables through FOI legislation.

The trickier route is pushing for the disclosure of information from TPSFs themselves. While some TPSFs — especially in the areas of IT consulting and outsourcing — are listed as publicly traded companies legally required to disclose information to their shareholders on an annual basis, many have the status of Limited Liability Partnerships (LLPs), under the ownership of private partners and not required to publicly disclose any information about their clients, their revenue or their personnel. As of 2021, Mazzucato and Collington note, twelve of the fifty largest consulting companies (measured by consulting revenue), including the Big Four and the Elite Three, are registered as a form of partnership.[43] Indeed, many TPSFs are organizations in name only, "bound by contractual arrangements to operate common standards under a common name," but "are actually made up of numerous separate legal entities that are not under common ownership."[44] This means that assets and liabilities are legally ringfenced, and the disclosure of information is restricted across jurisdictions, making it more difficult to make sense of how they operate cross-nationally.[45]

Although their opaque structures and reporting practices have enabled these firms to escape public scrutiny for years, they are now being challenged by a growing movement for public transparency and accountability. This is most apparent in the area of tax avoidance, where the Tax Justice Network (TJN), an independent international network launched in 2003, has been actively pushing for new reporting standards that would compel these firms to release more information about their clients. In the wake of the 2008 economic crisis, the TJN led a push to reform company reporting standards. Challenging the efforts by multinational corporations to take advantage of tax loopholes by divvying up profits and losses across a multitude of discrete shell companies, there were efforts to re-compose the corporation, conceptualizing it as a "unitary entity, operating as a singular, global whole."[46] Along these lines, the TJN has spearheaded a campaign for Country-By-Country Reporting (CBCR), requiring that multinational corporations report their profits and losses for every jurisdiction where they trade. By marshalling technical expertise in a transnational network to support this initiative, Christensen and Seabrooke note, TJN has been able to "change the game 'from the inside,'" contributing to the adoption of limited CBCR regimes in Europe as well as under the Dodd-Frank Act in the United States, and finally to an Organisation for Economic Co-operation and Development (OECD) standard requiring companies to report country-by-country information in 2014, albeit in watered down form.[47] Out of the public campaign for such standards, Christensen and Seabrooke document how the "Big 4's grip on established frames and practices on multinational corporate tax transparency were effectively challenged, leading to an expanded range of actors involved in contesting field practices."[48]

While an important victory, the OECD reforms were limited to the extent that they did not require the public disclosure of CBCR records. In response, critical researchers have also actively worked to produce their own databases featuring information on these firms and their clients.[49] For instance, drawing on the limited data produced in annual reports,

Open Data for Tax Justice (ODTJ) has attempted to piece together a broader picture of their operations from the bottom up. According to UK tax justice activist and accountant, Franki Hackett, the aim was to assemble a database of CBCR information and other financial information with the hope of "extrapolat[ing] the tax behavior of multinational entities from their general generic financial statements."[50] This was part of a broader process that aimed to democratize access and engagement with such information. As the ODTJ *White Paper* notes, activists hoped to foster

> a shift beyond a narrow conception of accounting for the activities of multinationals as a niche activity for professional specialists, and towards a vision which sees a broader range of actors involved in witnessing the tax arrangements of multinationals and engaging in a range of activities to hold them to account.[51]

This involved assembling "data publics" that would facilitate "democratic deliberation and public engagement around how the global economy is organised."[52] However, in practice, this has been challenging as the information is spotty, collected intermittently using different reporting standards and accounting principles, making it very difficult for even certified accountants to make sense of the data. Ultimately, it is difficult to assemble a clear picture of these firms and their operations in the absence of uniform accounting standards across jurisdictions.

While TPSFs can appeal to their LLP status in resisting the disclosure of information, a more promising direction can be to go through government. Activists can often request access to TPSF documents and deliverables procured by governments using FOI legislation. Indeed, this has been a central means through which critical researchers and investigative journalists have gained access to contracts. However, here a critical researcher can also encounter obstacles. TPSFs can have confidentiality clauses written into their contracts. For instance, the Canadian public broadcaster, CBC, revealed that the Canada Development Investment Corporation signed contracts with Credit Suisse and PwC to offer advice on the possible sale of Canadian airports, which "contain[ed] clauses that give the firms vetoes over the public release of any information, including the cost of the work."[53] Likewise, in their investigations of COVID-19 contracts, ProPublica discovered that McKinsey forbade clients from disclosing that they had hired them. Where public officials pushed back and demanded the right to disclosure, the firm, at times, allowed public agencies to share their work with "special entities," but they required that they be given the power "to define those entities and ... attach guardrails to such disclosure."[54] Through such tactics, the firm has restricted what governments are able to say about their work and to whom.

The problem becomes even more pronounced when governments enter long-term contracts with these firms, as TPSFs contracted to perform public services are often not subjected to the same kinds of accountability standards as governments. This has been flagged as an issue by government information officers for many years. In a 2015 report, the Information Commissioner of Canada noted that, while "quasi-commercial entities, special operating agencies and public-private sector partnerships have become increasingly common modes for governments to carry out their business ... many of these bodies are not covered by the [Access to Information] Act," making "information about public functions and services ... difficult to obtain or unavailable to the public through access to information requests."[55] In this context, reformers have been pushing to extend FOI laws to private firms operating with substantial public funds or carrying out public functions or services.[56]

A central area of struggle has been over disclosure of information regarding PPPs. As we show in Chapter 3, it has been difficult to gain access to the VfM formulae and calculations used to decide the procurement of PPPs. In their reports, TPSFs never disclose the calculations that went into determining the degree of risk transferred from the public to the private sector. Auditors General in numerous Canadian provinces have subsequently taken this up to challenge the credibility of VfM as a way of assessing value.[57] For instance, the Auditor General of Ontario noted that "there is no empirical data supporting the key assumptions used ... to assign costs to specific risks." The metrics relied on "the professional judgement and experience of external advisors ... making them difficult to verify." Moreover, it warned of potential bias toward PPPs, as "often the delivery of projects by the public sector was cast in a negative light, resulting in significant differences in the assumptions used to value risks between the public sector delivering projects and the AFP [alternative financing and procurement] approach."[58]

Access to information is often denied under the auspices of "cabinet confidence." For instance, in 2009, a case went before British Columbia's Information Commissioner in which the Canadian Union of Public Employees (CUPE) had sought records relating to a "business case" for

PPPs as well as for VfM reports. The commissioner ruled that because the documents had gone before the provincial cabinet or treasury board, or a committee of cabinet, these documents were cabinet secrets and could not be released.[59]

Nevertheless, while access to information is limited, FOI requests can be used to probe the limits of the access regime, while also providing a site for contestation through which activists can more broadly challenge the privatization of policy information. The denial of access to information can be a starting point for public campaigns and larger legal challenges against the secrecy of these firms. For instance, in Canada, the Ontario Health Coalition spearheaded a campaign to push for the disclosure of financial information on Brampton's William Osler hospital, a PPP that had been initiated in 2001. After seven years of struggle, they were eventually able to secure a court order that forced the province and private consortium to disclose their records pertaining to the deal. The documents revealed that the provincial government knew the deal with the private consortium could cost as much as $300 million more than if the project was publicly financed and administered, but nevertheless went ahead with it. By fighting for access to these records, critical researchers unearthed an important source of data discrediting the claims of governments that PPPs add value for money, and established a precedent in gaining access to records from future PPP projects.

Ultimately, there can be significant roadblocks to getting access to information on TPSFs and their relationships with governments. FOI requests can only go so far when information is protected for reasons of cabinet confidence or commercial sensitivity. However, by identifying the boundary lines, exposing the regime that demarcates public from private knowledge, activists can also create opportunities for contestation. They can expose just how much information remains undisclosed to the public as well as mount campaigns and legal challenges that seek to extend the boundaries of disclosure in new and innovative ways. And if they get stonewalled, they can use public consultations as opportunities to confront barriers to access. In this context, access to information itself becomes an object of mobilization.

## Public Consultations:
## Testify to Experience

The final area where TPSFs can be challenged is through mobilizing the knowledge and experience of public service producers and users themselves. This challenges the distance that TPSFs set out to achieve in their advice to governments. As Peter Fleming argues, TPSFs can promise "overidealized 'solutions' that elide real-world implications" in part *because* they are remote from everyday service delivery and insulated from public scrutiny.[60] Through their arm's length position, they are seldom answerable to the public for their advice. Even if citizens are consulted, Anne Vogelpohl notes that they are often turned into "passive passengers ... whose opinions, identifications, and maybe even commitments may be referred to if necessary, but who, in any event, are never seen as a decisive factor."[61]

By convening grassroots fora made up of affected publics with the power and capacity to talk back to these ideas, these firms can be held to account. The aim here is to counter the "thin" knowledge claims of TPSFs with "thick" knowledge rooted in the experiences of service providers and users themselves. In engaging with workers and citizens about their experiences with public service delivery, such methods can contribute to establishing an open archive for knowing public services, while also contributing to the establishment of a community of practice through which to understand and confront the privatization of public policymaking.

Along these lines, even when participation is restricted, public consultations can provide opportunities for scrutinizing the ideas of TPSFs and contesting barriers to access. As we saw at the beginning of this chapter, activists in Toronto took advantage of the very limited opportunities for public consultation afforded to them by the city government to challenge the thin analysis of KPMG's Core Service Review. Speaking within the tight constraints of a three-minute window, over 160 community members creatively framed and presented testimony that talked back to the KPMG report. Some accounts were more conventional, including a brief biography, claims to represent a wider community of interest, and drawing from stories and statistics; others included songs, poems and even a puppet show that contested the process. Testimonies often called attention to the ideological circularity of the KPMG account, interrogating its methods and questioning the credibility of its comparisons. For instance, in challenging KPMG's suggestion that the city look into privatizing transit services, Councillor Adam Vaughan questioned consultants on the experience in Melbourne, which was introduced as a key comparator in their report:

> *Councillor*: Is KPMG familiar with the Melbourne experience of privatizing service in that city, of its streetcar lines?
>
> [...]
>
> *Consultant*: Not particularly streetcar lines, but we certainly recognize that a lot of services — buses, trains, subways — in Melbourne have been privatized, and according to reports that system is working fairly efficiently.
>
> *Councillor*: Okay. So, in 1999, they privatized them. In 2001, are you familiar with why the subsidy had to be increased by $100 million dollars per company that was operating the transit lines?
>
> *Consultant*: Obviously that level of detail would be beyond the scope of the Core Service Review.
>
> *Councillor*: Right. Are you familiar with why the firms pulled out and went into receivership in 2002?
>
> *Consultant*: Nope. Did not go into that level of detail... Again...
>
> *Councillor*: In 2004, are you familiar with why the subsidies to private companies operating the tram lines in Melbourne [...] increased by a billion dollars?
>
> *Consultant*: I would probably advise that if that information is relevant to the Council in making its decision that you make it available in your debates, in terms of making decisions on these examples.
>
> *Councillor*: But you are suggesting that we explore the possibility of privatizing certain of our services, including I would expect tram lines, streetcar lines...
>
> *Consultant*: I think that it would be incumbent on the Council to at least consider the possibility and develop a business case on whether that makes sense in the city or not.
>
> *Councillor*: So, do you know why within a ten-year period, the subsidy went from $3 to $5 billion dollars, a billion dollars over

the estimated cost, and why tram fares — which originally were contracted at being no greater than the rate of inflation — that was removed, to an extra cost to tram riders of a hundred million dollars a year. Are you familiar with what caused those pressures?

*Consultant*: I believe we've answered that question.

*Councillor*: Okay. So, I guess the next question would be: In 2010, when the contracts went to be expired, recommendations were made to the state government and to the transportation system to increase the amount of privatization despite the fact that the cost was now 30 percent more than originally projected, which was an additional cost to taxpayers of $2.1 billion dollars, but the service levels — because of night-time cuts, another recommendation you're making — [were] 30 percent less. Do you know why that happened in Melbourne?

*Consultant*: This was not a detailed review of the Melbourne transportation service, Councillor.

*Councillor*: So, the question is this: KPMG was the consultant that recommended the privatization of the tram lines in Melbourne. Why, with that in-house experience from 161 and 159 Collins Street in Melbourne... why with that experience, would you replicate the proposal here in Toronto, knowing that you were 30 percent off on cost, 30 percent off on service, and you generated $100 million dollars above and beyond inflation annually?

*Mayor*: Thank you. That's your three minutes.[62]

Through the process of cross-examination, the city councillor challenges the credibility of KPMG by exposing the report's methodological blind spots. In this case, the consultant demonstrates a lack of knowledge about a key comparator, which incurred significant cost overruns, calling into question whether Melbourne should have really served as a benchmark for Toronto. More fundamentally, it reveals the limited internal communication within KPMG as an organization, as KPMG consultants located at "161 and 159 Collins Street" in Melbourne were themselves involved in advising the city government on the privatization of its transit services — an important source of information of which the consultant appears to be unaware. While these firms command substantial economies of scale that enable them to mobilize and circulate information from around the world, very often the knowledge that is gathered is thin. Through these kinds of cross examinations, the fragility of consultants' data can be exposed, opening it up to critique.

Beyond challenging the credibility of consultants' reports, public consultations can also provide opportunities where community members can testify to their own experience of public services and speak to how service cuts would negatively affect them. In Toronto, hundreds of deputants attested to their own experiences using late-night transit, recreation centres, animal services, and the meals-on-wheels program. In responding to KPMG's suggestions to cut back on library services, dozens of people testified to the role of libraries as not simply "warehouses for books" but as important sites for educating young children, welcoming newcomers, helping the unhoused access social services, and providing those without air conditioning a place to cool off in the summer — serving as "a small heart in the neighbourhood." By accounting for libraries as sites for these kinds of services, such testimonies provided an alternative framework for assessing the essentiality of services, one that was centred on the experiences of the users themselves.

Activists in South Africa have also made good use of public testimonies. Here, several firms — including KPMG, McKinsey, and Bain & Co — were embroiled in the largest corruption scandal in the country's history since the apartheid era, as it was revealed that they facilitated the looting of public contracts under the presidency of Jacob Zuma. In response, the government was pushed to convene a commission on state capture (the Zondo Commission) looking at the degree to which private individuals and companies had "[taken] over state agencies to redirect public resources into their own hands, while weakening the institutions for ferreting out that corruption."[63] In a context of widespread corruption, activists were concerned that the official commission would be toothless. So, they responded by convening their own Civil Society Working Group on State Capture in 2019.

A coalition of twenty-three civil society organizations,[64] the Working Group operated in parallel to the Zondo Commission, enabling popular participation in the process while holding the government's commission accountable for its investigation. Activist Mamello Mosiana notes that "we wanted to act as both a watchdog and support to the State Capture

Commission." The Working Group set out to provide what Mosiana describes as "the hardcore facts," including fifteen evidence-based submissions to the commission documenting the role of TPSFs in enabling state capture. But it also set out to gather what she describes as "the softer facts of the lived experiences." This included creative forms of advocacy, such as a #DearJudgeZondo social media campaign in which South Africans provided videos and voice notes on their experiences with government corruption and a one-day People's Hearing on State Capture which invited members of the public to testify to how state capture had impacted their lives. According to human rights lawyer, Yasmin Sooka, the aim was to "begin to document people's experiences so that we can preserve them for future accountability processes."[65] The campaign also played an important role in educating people about state capture. As Mosiana notes, many people were unfamiliar with state capture as a concept but were able to begin making connections to it via their experiences of "normalized everyday corruption." Moreover, the campaign made the commission publicly accountable for its work. Mosiana argues that "it made Judge Zondo responsive to civil society. I think it really kept him on his toes. I think several times during the commission's commission, he had to respond directly to civil society because we were writing statements, writing letters."

Through these sorts of campaigns, activists have fostered public fora for the discussion of policy ideas. Rather than leaving things to consultants, they have established alternative spaces for understanding and assessing public services that begin from the experiences of those affected. Recentring knowledge production in this way has provided affected publics with opportunities to cross-examine the ideas and programs of TPSFs. It has enabled them to assess the degree to which knowledge-making has been privatized and challenge the constitutive exclusions through which the policymaking process is codified and commodified. Against these arrangements, they have been able to foreground the rich and multivarious experiences of public service producers and users themselves to develop a thick knowledge of service delivery.

## Conclusion: Knowing Otherwise

Assembling popular coalitions to oppose government outsourcing to TPSFs can create the foundations for other ways of knowing public services. By following paper trails, tracking social networks, negotiating access regimes, and testifying to experience, activists and critical researchers can foster collective learning and develop capacities for understanding and confronting complex public-private governance arrangements.[66] Moreover, they can establish a different basis for understanding public services rooted in direct experiences with public service delivery, one that is based in a public rather than proprietary archive. In this sense, such struggles can foster the formation of what sociologist and activist Alan Sears calls "infrastructures of dissent"[67] that establish "a range of formal and informal organizations through which people develop their capacities to analyze and map the system, communicate using official and alternative media, and take strategic action in solidarity with others."[68]

The networks can be thin in the beginning, relying on the forensic accounting of one or two critical researchers, investigative journals, or bloggers. However, over time, a community of practice can be cultivated. For instance, in Barnet, resistance to the easyCouncil was initially organized by the public-sector union, who were joined by a group of bloggers in critically investigating the terms and conditions of the council's contracts with Capita. However, through establishing a coalition — the Barnet Alliance for Public Services (BAPS) — they were able to gradually expand their capacities, training people on how to submit FOI requests, track and analyze documents, and pose questions at council meetings. After attending a documentary on the easyCouncil hosted by BAPS at the local cinema, local resident Barbara Jacobson says that she "just started going to meetings." She notes:

> By this time, I had retired, so I actually thought to myself, well I have time to be informed and to do these things. Then they [BAPS] asked me if I would go to a committee meeting and speak about a particular [issue]. I'd never been to a council meeting, I'd never been to a committee meeting. So, I read the papers ... I put in the required request and I read the papers that we were talking about.[69]

At the peak of their activity, from 2011 to 2013, local activists reported submitting upward of 150 questions every council meeting.[70] Information gathered at meetings was supplemented by regular FOI requests as local residents came to know the regime through which access to information was brokered.

By developing collective capacities to track and interrogate the relations between TPSFs and governments in this sort of way, new forms of public knowledge can be established. This involves collective learning through which people become proficient in identifying and tracking. It involves establishing community-based archives where knowledge of these relationships can be publicly accessed. And it involves opening new forms of public deliberation through which knowledge and services produced by TPSFs can be exposed to public scrutiny, and knowledge of public services rooted in the experiences of producers and users can be generated. Against the privatization of public administration, it fosters new methods of making things public.

# Chapter 6

# Escaping the
# Consulting Trap

We are at a crossroads. One road leads in the direction of further privatizing public administration. Over the past thirty years, transnational professional service firms (TPSFs) have assumed jurisdiction over a growing number of areas in government. In a context of economic globalization, they have come to serve as powerful intermediaries in brokering the flow of financial and managerial information across borders. And with the rise of digital platforms and big data, they have assumed control over the administrative infrastructures of governance like never before.

Critical researchers have often diagnosed this as a problem of consultocracy, by which consultants are thought to increasingly colonize the public sector.[1] From this perspective, the focus is on social networks, as consultants take advantage of their inside connections to get access to public officials and gain the ears of government. However, beyond McKinsey alumni cozying up to one another at cocktail parties, the consulting trap goes much deeper. In our book, we have set out to show that this is, in part, a structural problem. TPSFs have set out to restructure the state in a manner that hooks governments, fostering growing reliance on their services. In response to fiscal crises generated partly by their role in the global tax avoidance industry, these firms have played a powerful role in advising governments to outsource and marketize services. Beyond providing guidance, they have rolled out the sociotechnical infrastructures that make such programs actionable. This has involved establishing new auditing frameworks through which to assess performance and identify service cuts, new financial arrangements through which investors can extract regular dividends from public services, and new platforms through which to outsource services.

Through a range of strategies, TPSFs have been able to hardwire a policy program built around neoliberal principles inside the state, effectively fostering the establishment of hybrid governance arrangements in which they serve not simply as consultants but as partners to governments. Through institutionalization, these firms have been able to entrench their programs in the everyday routines and procedures of public agencies. Through codification and commodification, they have been able to lift these programs out of their respective contexts and make them modular, capable of being bought and sold across jurisdictions. And through brokerage, they have positioned themselves as obligatory points of passage that governments must rely on to get access to requisite ideas, expertise, and infrastructures.

The problem of dependency has only grown in recent years as TPS-Fs have invested in expansive data infrastructures, rebranding themselves as tech companies that provide the basic hardware of governance. Beyond just providing advice, they now supply governments with whole platforms through which to administer services, from taking service requests and managing case files to enterprise risk management and disease surveillance. Billions of dollars are being invested in cloud computing technologies, artificial intelligence (AI), data analytics, and tech training. Consequently, there has been a shift from ad hoc advice to more continuous and multifaceted relationships between TPSFs and governments.

The growing reliance of governments on these firms for a range of services that now more closely resemble administration than consulting can make it very difficult for public officials to extricate themselves from these arrangements. However, while TPSFs have become increasingly embedded in government, establishing path dependencies that have deepened their position in policymaking and service delivery over time, these processes have not gone uncontested. Cutting across the road to privatization, there is another road. Its contours become visible in the resistance that is being mounted against these firms. In the wake of the COVID-19 pandemic, the immense power of these firms has been widely aired as a public problem. In France, the United Kingdom, the United States, Canada, South Africa, India, Germany, and many other countries, people are questioning why exactly we are delegating powers of government to these firms and at what price.

We discussed strategies for contesting the power of these firms in the previous chapter, but we have not yet addressed long-term solutions. How can we end the cycle of dependency that keeps governments hooked on these firms and, instead, cultivate new public-sector capacities? How can we escape the consulting trap? To conclude, we examine different policy programs that have been rolled out to confront the growing power of TPSFs, discussing efforts to better regulate the industry, break up the monopolies, and bring consulting services back in-house. Then, we put these policies in context, setting out next steps for critical research and organizing. Beyond challenging the power of TPSFs in privatizing public administration, we argue that it is vital to build collective capacities that enable us to know and value public services differently. This provides the starting point for a different orientation toward public administration — one that is premised on making things public.

## Searching for Solutions

### Increasing Regulation, Improving Reporting, Banning Bad Apples

Perhaps the most common response to the growing power of TPSFs has been to demand greater regulation of the industry and its relationships with governments. From this perspective, the problem is that these firms are given a blank cheque in terms of the kinds of advice that they can provide. There is often very little oversight or assessment of their services. How, then, can public officials more carefully delimit and manage the work that they do?

On the one hand, public officials have advocated for increasing regulatory oversight of TPSFs themselves. As we discuss in Chapter 2, these firms find their roots in occupations where professional governance frameworks have been very weak. While professional associations have been established in the consulting field in some countries, consultants are not required to join these associations or obtain professional credentials to ply their trade. Anyone can choose to be a consultant, without registration or qualifications. Consequently, it has been very difficult to assess their work since "malpractice cannot be defined against a set of determined norms" that would be entrenched in a professional code of conduct.[2] This has led some critics to describe consulting as a "failed," "hollow," or "corporate" profession.[3]

Likewise, in the liberal market economies of the Anglo-American heartland, accounting firms have typically operated quite autonomously from government oversight, with members from the major firms dominating the major accounting standards boards, as we saw in Chapter 4. The problem has become even more pronounced with the globalization of their operations. As these firms have expanded to operate across jurisdictions and at the transnational scale, management scholars note that they have "outgrown" the capacities of governments to oversee their work.[4] This gives them considerable leeway in setting their own standards and methods of appraisal that are often more closely aligned with the commercial interests of their clients than the public interest.

Consequently, there have been efforts to regulate these professional areas more rigorously, making firms more accountable for the services that they provide. For instance, in the context of consulting, management scholar Christopher McKenna notes that recurrent scandals have presented an opportunity "to press the leading ... firms to accept liability for their professional advice or to abandon this area of professional practice in the face of substantial fines and adverse legal judgement."[5] Likewise, in the wake of the 2008 crisis, there have been greater efforts on the parts of government to provide oversight in assuring the quality of audits and auditors. This is reflected in escalating government fines for shoddy work. For instance, in 2022, the US Securities and Exchange Commission (SEC) charged EY a $100 million penalty — the largest penalty it has ever imposed on an auditing firm — after uncovering widespread evidence of cheating by its personnel on exams required to obtain Certified Public Accountant licences, and discovering that the firm withheld evidence of this misconduct from the SEC during their investigations.[6] This prompted calls for governments to more thoroughly oversee certification processes, as well as to pressure firms to overhaul their internal controls. Such scandals have been cropping up in many countries around the world, leading to demands for greater government oversight.

On the other hand, there are efforts to increase government oversight over public procurement processes to more carefully regulate the relationship *between* government clients and TPSFs. Since the 1990s, many jurisdictions have introduced a third-party public "purchaser" or government intermediary that sets out to ensure that procurements are necessary, clearly elaborated and cost effective.[7] As management professor Andrew Sturdy notes, this has involved "a shift away from traditional 'relational' or collaborative contracting, based on informal mechanisms and trust within a client-consultant dyad, to a more formalized transactional, 'openly' competitive approach around a client-consultant-purchaser triad."[8] Drawing on the guidance of supranational agencies such as the Organisation for Economic Co-operation and Development (OECD) and the recommendations of public audit offices and government commissions, governments have set out to establish clear protocol to more rigorously formalize the procurement process. This has included adding requirements that clients submit business cases for projects above a certain financial value, as well as clearly delimiting the project's scope and outcomes. It has also involved requirements for public officials to justify why internal resources are not being used.

To ensure the transparency of government procurements, public officials have also set out to improve public reporting practices. While many governments provide public access to tendering websites documenting all contract procurements over a specified amount, very often the information that they provide is limited. For instance, it can be difficult to make sense of the grab bag of activities that are listed under "professional and special services" in the annually released Public Accounts of Canada.[9] Moreover, these categories are not commensurable across jurisdictions, making it very difficult to compare the degree and nature of government spending on TPSFs cross-nationally.[10]

Tendering websites can also be very limited in the kinds of information that they publicly disclose. While many countries provide a list of contracts, they do not disclose contract outputs or deliverables, which can only be obtained through Freedom of Information (FOI) requests provided they are not subject to cabinet confidence or commercial sensitivity rules, as they often are. In response, critics have advocated for increasing access to information. For instance, a recent report from the Australia Institute (2021) proposes that the senate issue a continuing order requiring ministers to disclose "details about requests for tender/ contracts with consultancies, covering the purpose, scope and anticipated elements of the consultancy's report or advice" as well as "the final reports and/or written advice received from a consultancy." The order "would identify major consultancies by name, as well as consultancy work more generally, since the 'consultancy flag' on AusTender is used so inconsistently."[11]

There are also efforts to open the work of TPSFs to outside assessment. Considering how instrumental these firms have been to establishing benchmarks for other professions, it is ironic how seldom they are subjected to public ranking or assessment themselves, and, indeed, how resistant their structures and programs are to outside assessment. Along these lines, we might consider different avenues through which affected publics might be able to provide feedback on their advice and services. For instance, in the context of consulting in higher education, Fleming proposes creating public websites that "identify the consulting firm and the nature of the project," and encourage feedback from public service producers and users.[12] He suggests that consulting reports should be required to include critical feedback sections, where responses from affected publics are included for consideration, and even suggests a "star rating system" through which firms could be rated for their services.

In addition to public reporting on contracts and deliverables, there are also efforts to track and regulate the circulation of personnel between the public and private sectors. To confront the problem of revolving doors, a common government policy has involved cooling-off periods, restricting public officials or politicians from taking up positions with TPSFs working with governments for a specified period of time after they have left office. However, while many countries have adopted such policies, Sturdy notes, such regulations are often weakly enforced. In many countries, he observes, "personal or network contacts ... still dominate selection preferences," and it can be difficult to enforce boundaries in the context of informal and indirect relationships.[13]

Finally, when TPSFs are caught behaving badly, public officials have pushed to ban them from bidding on government contracts altogether. For instance, in the wake of the state capture scandal in South Africa, the South African and UK governments banned Bain from bidding on public-sector contracts for several years. Likewise, the Cabinet Office in the United Kingdom has threatened KPMG with a ban on government contracts, leading the firm to briefly withdraw from bidding on new contracts. In India, PwC was banned from practising as chartered accountants for two years in the wake of a major auditing scandal.[14] However, while such measures aim to discipline actors for their misconduct, they often fail to address the wider field within which these firms are acting. The capacity of TPSFs for misconduct arises, in part, from the scale of their operations and their capacity to cross jurisdictional boundaries, taking advantage of loopholes and regulatory gaps as a way of opening new markets. In this context, rather than targeting bad apples, it may also be a matter of addressing what management scholars refer to as "bad barrels."[15]

*Breaking up Monopolies, Disaggregating Services*

Enhanced regulations aim to make TPSFs more accountable in their relationship with governments. However, such policies can be limited to the extent that they remain narrowly focused on regulating the consultant-client relationship without fully considering the context in which policy ideas are produced. This can lead to the reification of the public sector and private sector as discrete actors, ignoring the degree to which state power is already entangled with the infrastructures provided by these firms and vice versa. Beyond taking aim at a few bad apples, it is necessary to put these cases in the context of a structural trend toward privatization of public goods and how this trend has reconfigured the relationship between the public and private more broadly.[16] The state's capacity for regulation remains limited to the extent that governments are dependent on these firms for their services. In the context of oligopoly, a limited number of suppliers can call the shots. In response, going beyond enhanced regulations, reformers have also called for breaking up monopolies in professional services, diversifying contracts and disaggregating services.[17]

An important first step is to assess the reliance of governments on these firms. The growing concentration of professional services in the hands of a few large firms has spurred policymakers to gauge government dependencies. For instance, assessing spending levels by the European Commission in 2022, the European Court of Auditors noted that the commission had become overdependent on a few professional service firms, contracting over 240 million euros to the top three suppliers. In response, it has recommended "periodically analysing the risks of concentration and overdependence" of the commission on these firms.[18] This includes calls to monitor competitiveness of the procurement process as well as to analyze market concentration "to show the degree of competition among ... contractors and to limit the risk of competitive advantage."[19] Moreover, there have been calls to make the procurement process more competitive by prioritizing new bidders over incumbents, enabling bids from smaller firms, and disaggregating big contracts into smaller contracts.

There have also been efforts in many countries to break up the monopolies of these firms in certain lines of service delivery. For instance, in the area of accounting, critics have often argued that the Big Four firms are "too big to fail" and should be broken up.[20] The idea started

building steam in the United Kingdom after the collapse of the outsourcing firm Carillion in 2018, which was attributed in part to the auditing
failures of KPMG. Spearheaded by John McDonnell, the Labour Party's
shadow chancellor at the time, it was argued that these firms formed
an anti-competitive 'cartel'. In response, McDonnell floated ideas such
as capping the Big Four's share of the audit market at 50 percent of the
largest companies, limiting the number of companies that each firm was
allowed to audit, and banning companies from auditing and consulting
for the same client.

While such proposals prompted a public inquiry on the monopoly
power of these firms, the solutions have been watered down and technocratic, shying away from restricting market share and instead pursuing
the internal disaggregation of services. Part of the problem, it is argued,
is that these firms have taken on a range of services, which fosters interdependencies and potential conflicts of interest. Since Enron's collapse,
ers have problematized the role of the Big Four accounting firms in both
auditing and advising clients, calling attention to potential conflicts of
interest that may arise as they provide a range of value-added services
to clients whose books they are also responsible for impartially assessing (see Chapter 2). This has provoked a wave of legislation, such as the
Sarbanes Oxley Act in the United States, prohibiting firms from consulting with the companies they audit with the aim of minimizing such
conflicts.

There is evidence demonstrating that such legislation has had an impact. For instance, Sturdy notes that the 2013 Dutch Audit Profession
Act, one of the stricter pieces of legislation prohibiting auditors from
serving as consultants for the same client, "led to significant restrictions
or 'collateral damage' on consultancy work when firms had to move to
new audit clients where consultancy work had been underway."[21] This
has prompted firms to either disaggregate their consulting and auditing
arms, making them separate organizations, or sell off their consultancy
wings altogether. As we discuss in Chapter 2, such legislation initially
led to the Big Four firms divesting their consultancy operations in the
early 2000s, selling them to Big Tech companies. More recently, in 2022,
EY decided to split its auditing and consulting services, separating them
into two distinct multidisciplinary organizations. Though this decision
was later reversed after a revolt by EY partners, it reflected frustrations
within the firm about its inability to get contracts due to conflict of

interest rules. As one source within the firm complained: "There's work we can't do."[22]

However, while such legislation may address specific conflicts of interest, it often does not address the wider field across which these firms operate. A firm may refrain from advising a company while they serve as its auditor, but they can continue to pursue value-added relationships with these companies in the future, incentivizing them to stay in their good books. Brooks reports a Big Four partner telling him that "'the conflict of interest [in providing both audit and non-audit services] has just moved along a time period,' to when the auditor is preparing to surrender the audit contract and teeing up the client as a major consultancy client."[23] Moreover, this does not resolve the problem of revolving doors, with personnel moving between auditors and clients, as auditors often aim for future jobs with their clients. Nor does it fully address the degree of market concentration, as these firms may remain too big to fail in their respective domains and, while they are internally disaggregated, they may maintain de facto connections between auditing and consulting. Though legislation may prompt firms to divest, they have been quick to reestablish market dominance, as we saw in the wake of the Enron scandal. After selling off their consulting wings, the Big Four were able to recapture the market within several years, raising the same problems of market concentration.

## Diversifying Providers, Bringing Services Back In-House

Beyond breaking up these firms, critics have questioned whether governments should be procuring such services from private firms in the first place. Perhaps advice should be coming from other places. For instance, public or nonprofit organizations might be better suited to deliver advice on certain issues. Or priority could be placed on developing in-house capacities. Why not turn to other actors?

Following trends in the corporate world,[24] there have been efforts to bring consulting services in-house, creating public-sector consulting units to advise on public policy and government restructuring. For instance, the German government set out to curtail dependency on outside consultants by establishing an in-house public-sector consulting firm in 2016, and the UK government established their own internal consulting hub in 2020 unofficially named Crown Consultancy. The initiative was spearheaded by Conservative Cabinet Office minister Lord Agnew who complained that the use of external consultants was "providing poor value for money" and "infantilis[ing] the civil service by depriving our brightest people of opportunities to work on some of the most challenging, fulfilling and crunchy issues."[25] Staffed by sixty specialist civil servants, the hub set out to provide strategic advice across government and build in-house consulting capacities.[26] Following the UK example, the Australian government also moved to establish its own internal consulting hub in 2022 with the aim of reducing consultant spending and building capacities, tapping into the deep expertise that already exists in the public sector.[27] Nevertheless, there are questions of whether these in-house operations can compete with the scale and scope of TPSFs. Thus, after a two-year trial, the UK consulting hub was abruptly scrapped in 2023 as it was argued that "departments did not use the hub because it didn't have the range of external consultants."[28]

Alongside the establishment of in-house consultancies, there are also efforts to move from for-profit TPSFs to smaller scale and community-based civil society and not-for-profit providers. For example, the UK-based Corporate Reform Collective has advocated for "alternative, socially and publicly accountable corporate forms of ownership and governance."[29] For instance, we can look at the role of nonprofit and democratic civil society organizations in developing their own metrics for gauging the quality of services, rooted in the knowledge and experience of workers and users, as well as developing tools for assessing the work of consultants and senior managers themselves.[30] By removing the profit motive from the equation, and rooting advice in community-based accountability networks, professional service providers may not be as easily incentivized to advance commercial interests over the public interest.

Finally, rather than relying on the expertise of accountants and MBAs in responding to complex social and ecological crises, critics have suggested recruiting experts from other backgrounds. We might also look to universities as fora where different forms of expertise can be enlisted and proposals for responding to social problems and reforming governance arrangements can be publicly developed and debated. Over the past decade, many universities have instituted policy labs assembling experts from government, academia, and community organizations to collaborate on research with the aim of informing policy decisions and public-sector "innovation."[31]

## From Challenging Consultocracy to Making Things Public

Each of the above strategies aim to make government relationships with consultants more accountable and transparent. Adopting more rigorous regulations and reporting standards, there are efforts to give TPSFs and public officials less wiggle room in negotiating contracts and delivering services. Through breaking up service providers, there are efforts to open the market to greater competition and address conflicts of interest in service delivery. Through establishing in-house consultancy operations, there are efforts to bring the business model of TPSFs in-house in order to cut down costs and increase public-sector capacities.

Such strategies have tended to frame the problem as structural. If we just better regulate the market for consultancy or establish these same capacities in-house, then we can resolve these issues. However, these kinds of approaches can be limited to the extent that they remain focused on the *form* of consulting while neglecting the *content* of the services provided. Changing procurement arrangements does not necessarily change the character of the ideas proposed. As we have seen, the core business model of TPSFs has been premised on advancing a particular program for governance: As the architects of the Wealth Defense Industry, they have designed programs to minimize tax liabilities for corporations and the one percent, significantly curtailing the revenues of governments. As auditors, they have developed technologies that direct public attention to austerity, seeking to cut services and minimize public spending. As financial engineers, they have designed programs that transform public services into objects of financial speculation. As privatizers, they have transformed public services into vehicles for rent extraction.

Far from serving as impartial advisors, TPSFs are the professional managerial cadre at the centre of the program to hardwire neoliberalism into the state over the past 40 years. From this perspective, the hollowing out of the state is not just a byproduct of poor regulation; it is not a matter of getting better management consultants. Rather, the hollowing out of the state is a deliberate outcome of these programs. Consultants have served as chief architects in the design and implementation of the contractor state, entrenching the idea that governments should "steer" rather than "row," and rolling out a proprietary regime for service delivery that is based on governance by contract. Following this normative agenda, the business model of TPSFs is based on enclosing knowledge in ways that make it proprietary, enabling the ongoing extraction of rents through outsourcing a growing number of areas for service delivery. Such an approach has contributed to the privatization of whole areas of policymaking and public administration that have decreased the transparency and responsiveness of the state to its citizens, as the technologies and policy models that went into decision-making are hidden from public scrutiny or deliberation under the auspices of "commercial sensitivity."

Beyond problematizing the arrangements through which TPSFs are procured, then, it is also necessary to challenge their core business ideas that are premised on deepening austerity, financialization, and privatization. How might we counterpose programs of privatization with our own programs to make things public? As we show in Chapter 5, struggles against the enclosure of public administration provide opportunities for establishing new publics and new ways of imagining public interest, public service, and public futures. Disassembling the management information systems of TPSFs can also present opportunities for public service producers and users to actively valourize alternative forms of knowledge production.

Similarly, challenging the capacity of firms to enclose public administrative functions and transform them into private property can be paralleled by efforts to open public administration to more inclusive and democratic forms of ownership and control. For instance, public administration specialists Amanda Clarke and Sean Boots have proposed reversing government policies that prioritize private ownership of IT infrastructures to emphasize public ownership of custom software code and advancing greater use of open-source software. They advocate for a "services, not software" approach, "procuring the services of a software development team to build a software product, rather than procuring the complete product itself."[32] The separation of the service from the product in this way could contribute to challenging the enclosure of data and services by these firms, making it easier for public officials to exit underperforming contracts and transfer infrastructures to other actors or bring them in-house.

We might imagine extending such protocol to professional services procured from TPSFs more broadly. For instance, what if we treated consultancy reports as public property or open-source software to be freely shared and adapted by affected publics? Such initiatives could challenge the right of consultants to freely and unaccountably expropriate knowledge about public services, reversing information asymmetries and challenging the hierarchization of knowledge production in ways that inhibit public accountability. In this sense, they could contribute to upending the enduring principles of scientific management in public administration, premised on the notion that information is something to be expropriated from producers and users and transformed into the property of a management/consultancy class, which we discuss in Chapter 2.

Against the expropriative view of public knowledge, such programs might foster alternative visions of what public services could be. According to Fleming this involves "creat[ing] our own utopian image to counter the one being proffered by the consulting industry."[33] Advancing the notion of open-source public administration in which policy knowledge is treated as a commons, and service users and producers can contribute to collectively defining needs and norms provides a means of countering the libertarian market utopias advanced by consultants, premised on the private ownership and circulation of information in a market-like arena.

## Next Steps

As we have shown, the seeds of an alternate public administration can be sown through public opposition to the enclosure of public policy information. By fostering collective capacities to map and confront the privatization of public administration, common knowledge of the public sector can be developed. The production of policy information can be publicly situated though tracking paper trails, locating the key actors involved through social network analysis, challenging the private ownership of data through Freedom of Information struggles, and exposing such practices to critical scrutiny via public hearings. Rather than leaving it to governments, we can thus assemble affected publics into collective vehicles for deliberation and decision-making.

It is in this spirit that we have attempted to provide a citizen's guide for understanding and confronting these firms. Very often, the problems discussed in this book — tax avoidance, austerity, financialization, privatization — are treated as disembodied policy programs advanced by governments without considering the political economy of knowledge production through which they are made actionable. By providing an overview of these firms and their dominant role in the production of public administration today, this book has aimed to situate these ideas, exposing the market in which they are located and the different strategies through which they become operationalized. By situating the work of private firms in public administration in this way, we hope that the book will enhance public debates on the role of these firms in government as well as provide people with tools that they can use to challenge their influence. Moreover, we hope that it will provide people with a greater sense of possibility in terms of how knowledge of public services could be produced and what public services could be.

Nevertheless, this can only be a rough cut. As two researchers, it has been impossible for us to provide a comprehensive account of these firms and their operations, as they are dispersed across hundreds of offices located in dozens of countries around the world. There are necessary limitations to our study that should be noted in laying the groundwork for a fuller investigation of how these firms operate around the world. Most notably, beginning from our standpoint in the Anglo-American heartland of consulting, many of our examples and case studies are located in Canada, the United Kingdom, and the United States. While we have called attention to how these firms operate in other places, such as India and South Africa, and explored how they are implicated in colonialism in Chapter 4, we have not been able to provide a comprehensive account of how these firms operate in the Global South.[34] Nor have we accounted for the variable power and influence of these firms across jurisdictions. As Saint Martin notes, it is important to attend to the distinctive institutional contexts in which these firms operate to understand their degree of influence.[35] While they are powerful actors that shape the policy agenda in the anglosphere, they can be more peripheral in other parts of the world — though, as anthropologist Kimberly Chong demonstrates in her study on the financialization of state-owned enterprises in China, their influence has been growing even in postsocialist countries.[36] Likewise, while these firms may be more influential in some professional domains — such as IT services, accounting, and consulting — they do not have as much clout in other areas such as education or health, where teachers and medical practitioners may be able to challenge their claims to expertise. More research is needed to investigate the extent to which these firms are able to set down roots in other professional areas, as well as investigate the capacity of professionals to resist their incursions.

Ultimately, part of the problem is that these firms are just too big for any single actor to be able to account for everything. Their overwhelming scope and scale give them protection, as they thrive on information asymmetries. Substantial investments in time and energy are required to get a sense of where they are located and what they do. Access to information requests take time and are often denied under the auspices of cabinet confidence or commercial sensitivity. And then a legal battle is required if communities want to pursue it further. These asymmetries are further exacerbated by the ephemeral natures of their work. They often parachute into jurisdictions for a short period of time, making it difficult for citizens and policymakers to get ahead of the curve in understanding their operations, let alone challenging them.

In confronting these information asymmetries, we contend that collaboration is necessary. There are many researchers — including investigative journalists, academics, community activists, and civil society organizations — conducting research on these firms. However, as they are looking at these firms in different domains (accounting, consulting, IT services) and geographical regions (Canada, India, South Africa), they don't often find themselves in the same conversations. The research process can be solitary and disconnected, leading to a situation where critical researchers must start from scratch to learn how these firms operate in their communities.

Just as the scope and scale of these firms is transnational, so also must be the critical research networks and movements that set out to resist them. We hope that this book will contribute to an emerging transnational body of research through which the activities of these firms can be documented and compared across jurisdictions, and lessons from struggles taking place in different parts of the world can be shared. Moreover, we hope that this book can be used to enhance further collaborations, drawing connections between researchers and community groups working in different domains and across geographical regions. Be it as users or producers of public services, we all have a stake in the decisions made by these firms. We hope that we have given our readers some tools to understand and interject in the process.

# Notes

## Preface

1. Robert Booth, "Deloitte Selling Contact Tracing Services to Local UK Health Officials," *The Guardian*, September 30, 2020. www.theguardian.com/uk-news/2020/sep/30/deloitte-selling-contact-tracing-services-to-local-uk-health-officials.
2. Booth, "Deloitte Selling Contact Tracing Services."
3. Jessica Hill, "Exclusive: Deloitte Accused of 'Profiteering' After Attempt to Sell 'Local Test and Trace Solution," *Local Government Chronicle*, September 30, 2020. www.lgcplus.com/politics/coronavirus/exclusive-deloitte-accused-of-profiteering-after-attempt-to-sell-local-test-and-trace-solution-30-09-2020/.
4. Andrew Woodcock, "Coronavirus: Hancock Defends Private Firm Marketing Test and Trace Package to Councils," *Independent*, October 1, 2020. www.independent.co.uk/news/uk/politics/deloitte-matt-hancock-test-trace-coronavirus-b738822.html.
5. Samuel Osborne, "Management Consultancy McKinsey Brought in to Review NHS Test and Trace Programme," July 15, 2020. www.independent.co.uk/news/health/nhs-test-and-trace-mckinsey-management-consultancy-review-a9621351.html.
6. Booth, "Deloitte Selling Contact Tracing Services."
7. Andrew Downey, "McKinsey Bags £560K Deciding 'Vision' for New NHS Test and Trace Body," *Digital Health*, August 26, 2020. www.digitalhealth.net/2020/08/mckinsey-bags-560k-deciding-vision-for-new-nhs-test-and-trace-body/.
8. Helen Pied and Juliette Garside. "'We Have Had Zero Information': GPS in the Dark Over Covid-19 Tests," *The Guardian*, May 6, 2020. www.theguardian.com/world/2020/may/06/we-have-had-zero-information-gps-in-the-dark-over-covid-19-tests.
9. Pied and Garside, "We Have Had Zero Information."
10. British Medical Association, "The Role of Private Outsourcing in the COVID-19 Response," July 2020. www.bma.org.uk/media/2885/the-role-of-private-outsourcing-in-the-covid-19-response.pdf.
11. Peter Geoghegan, Russell Scott, and Caroline Molloy, "Revealed: 'Failing' Serco Won Another £57m COVID Contract Without Competition," openDemocracy, October 16, 2020. www.opendemocracy.net/en/dark-money-investigations/revealed-failing-serco-won-another-57m-covid-contract-without-competition/.
12. Geoghegan et al., "Revealed: 'Failing' Serco Won Another £57m COVID Contract."
13. Ed Conway, "Coronavirus: More Than 1,000 Consultants from Deloitte on Test and Trace Programme," *Sky News*, October 9, 2020. news.sky.com/story/coronavirus-more-than-1-000-consultants-from-deloitte-on-test-and-trace-programme-12099127.
14. House of Commons Committee of Public Accounts, "Test and Trace Update," October 27, 2021. committees.parliament.uk/publications/7651/documents/79945/default/.

15. Consultancy.uk, "Test and Trace Spends £1 Million Per Day on Deloitte Consultants," Consultancy.uk (blog), July 02, 2021. www.consultancy.uk/news/28374/test-and-trace-spends-1-million-per-day-on-deloitte-consultants.
16. Andrew Gregory, "England's COVID Test and Trace Spending over £1m a Day on Consultants," *The Guardian*, November 21, 2021. www.theguardian.com/world/2021/nov/21/england-covid-test-and-trace-spending-over-1m-a-day-on-consultants.
17. House of Commons Committee of Public Accounts, "Test and Trace Update."
18. National Audit Office, "Test and Trace in England — Progress Update," Department of Health and Social Care, by the Comptroller and Auditor General, Session 2021–22, June 25, 2021. www.nao.org.uk/wp-content/uploads/2021/06/Test-and-trace-in-England-progress-update.pdf; House of Commons Committee of Public Accounts, "Test and Trace update."
19. National Audit Office, "Test and Trace in England."
20. Caroline Molloy, "Deloitte's COVID 'Bonanza': This Is How Much the British Public Has Paid So Far," openDemocracy, November 12, 2020. www.opendemocracy.net/en/ournhs/deloittes-test-and-trace-bonanza-this-is-how-much-the-british-public-has-paid-them-so-far/
21. CBC News Online, "Mobile Contact-Tracing App Can Help Alberta Slow Spread of COVID-19, Top Doctor Says," May 01, 2020. www.cbc.ca/news/canada/edmonton/deena-hinshaw-abtracetogether-covid-19-coronavirus-1.5552413.
22. Taylor Lambert, "Why Is Alberta Clinging to Its Failed COVID-19 App?" *The Sprawl*, November 20, 2020. www.sprawlcalgary.com/alberta-covid-tracing-app-failure.
23. Howard Solomon, "Privacy Expert Says Flawed Alberta COVID-19 Contact Tracking App Shouldn't Have Been Released," ITWorld Canada, May 04, 2020. www.itworldcanada.com/article/privacy-expert-says-flawed-alberta-covid-19-contact-tracking-app-shouldnt-have-been-released/430252.
24. James Keller, "Alberta to Adopt National COVID-19 Exposure App," *Globe and Mail*, August 08, 2020. www.theglobeandmail.com/canada/alberta/article-alberta-to-adopt-national-covid-19-exposure-app/.
25. Darius Tahir and Rachel Roubein, "Trump Officials Rush to Introduce Untested Vaccine Tracking System," Politico, September 13, 2020. www.politico.com/news/2020/09/12/trump-vaccine-tracking-system-412968.
26. Cat Ferguson, "What Went Wrong with America's $44 Million Vaccine Data System?" MIT *Technology Review*, January 30, 2021. www.technologyreview.com/2021/01/30/1017086/cdc-44-million-vaccine-data-vams-problems/.
27. Ferguson, "What Went Wrong."
28. Ferguson, "What Went Wrong."
29. Aria Bendix, "The US Paid Deloitte $44 Million for a Vaccine Appointment System Laden with Glitches. Some States Are Scrambling for an Alternative." *Business Insider*, February 06, 2021. www.businessinsider.com/cdc-deloitte-flawed-coronavirus-vaccine-appointment-system-2021-2?r=US&IR=T.
30. Sheryl Gay Stolberg, "Immunization Expert Accuses C.D.C. and Deloitte of Stealing Her Idea," *New York Times*, February 06, 2021. www.nytimes.com/2021/02/06/us/politics/coronavirus-vaccines.html.
31. Stolberg, "Immunization Expert Accuses C.D.C."
32. Stolberg, "Immunization Expert Accuses C.D.C." According to Newman Law Offices, representing Tate, the CDC awarded Deloitte a one-year contract for $15,891,816.74. This amount was around 0.6 million more than what MSPP offered to sell CDC for a national license. int.nyt.com/data/documenttools/cease-and-desist-letter/8f6900be59536352/full.pdf.

## Chapter 1

1. David Macdonald, "The Shadow Public Service: The Swelling Ranks of Federal Government Outsourced Workers," Canadian Centre for Policy Alternatives (2011). policyalternatives.ca/publications/reports/shadow-public-service.

2. Naomi Klein, *The Shock Doctrine: The Rise of Disaster Capitalism* (Toronto: Vintage, 2008).

3. David Craig and Richard Brooks, *Plundering the Public Sector* (London: Constable, 2006).

4. Bessma Momani, "Management Consultants and the United States' Public Sector," *Business and Politics* 15, 3 (2013): 381–99.

5. Larence Dunhill and Rajeev Syal, "Whitehall 'Infantilised' by Reliance of Consultants, Minister Claims," *The Guardian,* September 29, 2020. www.theguardian.com/politics/2020/sep/29/whitehall-infantilised-by-reliance-on-consultants-minister-claims.

6. Elisa Braun, "'McKinseygate' Dogs Macron's Reelection Campaign," *Politico,* March 31, 2022. www.politico.eu/article/mckinsey-gate-emmanuel-macron-campaign-france/.

7. Walt Bogdanich and Michael Forsythe, *When McKinsey Comes to Town: The Hidden Influence of the World's Most Powerful Consulting Firm* (New York: Random House. 2022), 533.

8. Walt Bogdanich and Michael Forsythe "How McKinsey Lost Its Way in South Africa," *New York Times,* June 26, 2018. www.nytimes.com/2018/06/26/world/africa/mckinsey-south-africa-eskom.html.

9. Julia Kollewe, "Bain and Co Barred from UK Government Contracts over 'Grave Misconduct' in South Africa," *The Guardian,* August 3, 2022. www.theguardian.com/business/2022/aug/03/bain-and-co-barred-from-uk-government-contracts-over-grave-misconduct-in-south-africa.

10. Bogdanich and Forsythe, *When McKinsey Comes to Town.*

11. Harvey Cashore, Kimberly Ivany, Katie Pedersen, "Canada Revenue Agency's Case against KPMG over Offshore 'Sham' Delayed — Again," CBC News, April 10, 2016. www.cbc.ca/news/canada/canada-revenue-agency-kpmg-court-case-delayed-1.3529363#:~:text=A%20judge%20first%20ordered%20KPMG,intended%20to%20deceive%22%20the%20treasury.

12. SFO (Serious Fraud Office, United Kingdom), "SFO Announces DPA in Principle with Serco Geografix Ltd.," July 3, 2019. www.sfo.gov.uk/2019/07/03/sfo-announces-dpa-in-principle-with-serco-geografix-ltd/#:~:text=The%20Director%20of%20the%20Serious,they%20are%20held%20to%20account.

13. Industry Report L6712-GL Global Management Consultants (IbisWorld, 2023). www.ibisworld.com/global/market-research-reports/global-management-consultants-industry/.

14. Janet French, "158 Albertans with COVID-19 Reported Their Illness to Province's Multimillion-Dollar App," CBC News, October 07, 2021. www.cbc.ca/news/canada/edmonton/158-albertans-with-covid-19-reported-their-illness-to-province-s-multimillion-dollar-app-1.6202636.

15. Iain Sherriff-Scott, "McKinsey Won $1,6-million Contract after 'Cold Call' to Premier's Office," *ipolitics,* February 09, 2021. ipolitics.ca/2021/02/09/mckinsey-won-1-6-million-contract-after-cold-call-to-premiers-office/.

16. Public Services and Procurement Canada, buyandsell.gc.ca, accessed on 01 September 2021. buyandsell.gc.ca/procurement-data/tender-notice/PW-20-00915494.

17. Conor O'Reilly, "The Transnational Security Consultancy Industry: A Case of State-Corporate Symbiosis," *Theoretical Criminology* 14, 2 (2010): 183–210.
18. Mariana Mazzucato and Rosie Collington, *The Big Con: How the Consulting Industry Weakens Our Businesses, Infantilizes Our Governments, and Warps our Economies* (Penguin Random House, 2023), 26.
19. Antonio E. Weiss, *Management Consultancy and the British State* (London: Palgrave Macmillan, 2019).
20. Denis Saint Martin, "Governments and Management Consultants: Supply, Demand, and Effectiveness," in *The Oxford Handbook of Management Consulting,* eds. Mathias Kipping and Timothy Clark (Oxford, New York: Oxford University Press, 2012), 447–64.
21. Denis Saint Martin, *Building the New Managerialist State: Consultants and the Politics of Bureaucratic Reform in Britain, Canada, and France* (Oxford, New York: Oxford University Press, 2000); Graeme Hodge and Diana Bowman, "The 'Consultocracy': The Business of Reforming Government," In *Privatization and Market Development,* ed. Graeme Hodge (Northampton, MA: Edward Elgar 2006); Mathias Kipping and Christopher Wright, "Consultants in Context: Global Dominance, Societal Effect, and the Capitalist System," in *The Oxford Handbook of Management Consulting,* eds. M. Kipping and T. Clark (Oxford, New York: Oxford University Press, 2012): 165–185; Daniel Guttman and Barry Willner, *The Shadow Government* (New York: Pantheon Books, 1976).
22. Saint Martin, "Governments and Management Consultants."
23. Christopher McKenna, *The World's Newest Profession: Management Consulting in the Twentieth Century* (Cambridge: Cambridge University Press, 2006).
24. Lucy Sherriff, "Ernst & Young Removes University Degree Classification from Entry Criteria as There's 'No Evidence' It Equals Success," *Huffington Post,* April 08, 2015. www.huffingtonpost.co.uk/2016/01/07/ernst-and-young-removes-degree-classification-entry-criteria_n_7932590.html.
25. Weiss, *Management Consultancy and the British State.*
26. Matthias Kipping and Ian Kirkpatrick, "Alternative Pathways of Change in Professional Services Firms: The Case of Management Consulting," *Journal of Management Studies* 50, 5 (2013): 777–807; Matthias Kipping, "Trapped in their Wave: The Evolution of Management Consultancies," in *Critical Consulting: New Perspectives on the Management Advice Industry,* eds. T. Clark and T. Fincham (Oxford: Blackwell, 2002); Lars Engwall, Matthias Kipping, and Behlül Üsdiken, *Defining Management: Business Schools, Consultants, Media* (London: Routledge, 2016); Matthias Kipping, "America First: How Consultants Got into the Public Sector," in *Professional Service Firms in a Global Era,* eds. C. Hurl and A. Vogelpohl (London: Palgrave Macmillan, 2021).
27. Louise Amoore, *The Politics of Possibility: Risk and Security Beyond Probability* (Duke University Press, 2013).
28. Colin Ellis, "Why Deloitte Canada Won Ottawa's Lucrative Vaccine Platform Contract," *Canadian Accountant,* January 12, 2021. www.canadian-accountant.com/content/technology/why-deloitte-canada-won-ottawa-s-lucrative-vaccine-platform-contract.
29. Leonard Seabrooke, "Epistemic Arbitrage: Transnational Professional Knowledge in Action," *Journal of Professions and Organization* 1, 1 (2014): 2.
30. Marion Fourcade and Jeffrey Gordon, "Learning Like a State: Statecraft in the Digital Age," *Journal of Law and Political Economy* 1, 1 (2020): 94; Mike Raco, *State-Led*

*Privatisation and the Demise of the Democratic State: Welfare Reform and Localism in an Era of Regulatory Capitalism* (London: Routledge, 2006).

31. Kipping, "Trapped in their Wave"; Denis Saint Martin, *Building the New Managerialist State: Consultants and the Politics of Public Sector Reform in Comparative Perspective* (Oxford: Oxford University Press, 2000); Kees van der Pijl, *The Making of an Atlantic Ruling Class* (London: Verso Books, 2014).

32. Statista, "Size of the Global Consulting Market 2019, by Country," July 6, 2022. www. statista.com/statistics/1065188/management-consulting-market-size-country/.

33. Mehdi Boussebaa, "Professional Service Firms, Globalisation and the New Imperialism," *Accounting, Auditing & Accountability Journal* 28, 8 (2015): 1217–33.

34. McKenna, *The World's Newest Profession.*

35. Saint Martin, "Governments and Management Consultants."

36. Boussebaa, "Professional Service Firms."

37. Mazzucato and Collington, *The Big Con*; Leonard Seabrooke and Ole Jacob Sending, "Contracting Development: Managerialism and Consultants in Intergovernmental Organizations," *Review of International Political Economy* 27, 4 (2020): 802–27; Julian Eckl and Tine Hanrieder, "The Political Economy of Consulting Firms in Reform Processes: The Case of the World Health Organization," *Review of International Political Economy* (2022): 1–24.

38. Boussebaa, "Professional Service Firms."

39. Katharina Pistor, "The Rise of Autonomous Financial Power," in *Capital Claims: Power and Global Finance,* eds. Benjamin Braun and Kai Koddenbrock (London: Routledge, 2022), 258.

40. Alain Deneault touches on their role in his discussion of tax havens in *Legalizing Theft* (Halifax: Fernwood Publishing, 2018). Internationally, this has been taken up by Richard Brooks in *Bean Counters* (London: Atlantic Books, 2018) and by Ian D. Gow and Stuart Kells in *The Big Four* (Berrett-Koehler, 2018).

41. Mike Raco, "Hegemonic Privatization and Its Discontents: Reflections on the Rise and Limitations of the Parastate and Local Governance Reform in England," in *Professional Service Firms and Politics in a Global Era: Public Policy, Private Expertise,* eds. C. Hurl and A. Vogelpohl (London: Palgrave Macmillan, 2021); House of Commons, "After Carillion: Public Sector Outsourcing and Contracting," Public Administration and Constitutional Affairs Committee, July 9, 2018. publications.parliament.uk/pa/cm201719/cmselect/cmpubadm/748/748.pdf; Office for Budget Responsibility, obr.uk/forecasts-in-depth/brief-guides-and-explainers/public-finances/.

42. Matti Ylönen and Hanna Kuusela, "Consultocracy and Its Discontents: A Critical Typology and a Call for a Research Agenda," *Governance* 32, 2 (2019): 242.

43. Marius R. Busemeyer and Kathleen Thelen, "Institutional Sources of Business Power," *World Politics* 72, 3 (2020): 448–80.

44. Ivan Horrocks, "'Experts and e-Government': Power, Influence and the Capture of a Policy Domain in the UK," *Information, Communication & Society* 12, 1 (2009): 110–27.

45. Sociologist William Carroll has refined these methods as part of the Corporate Mapping Project, investing the influence of the oil and gas sector in Canadian policymaking: www.corporatemapping.ca/. Tom Juravich has promoted these tools in labour organization: strategiccorporateresearch.org/strategic-corporate-research/. Jane McAlevey has adopted a similar approach, which she describes as Power Mapping: janemcalevey.com/.

46. Marriage, Madison, "Big Four Accounting Firms Accused of 'Anti-Competitive' Behaviour," *Financial Times,* April 2, 2019. www.ft.com/content/3343b274-5559-11e9-91f9-b6515a54c5b1.

## Chapter 2

1. David Grayson Allen and Kathleen McDermott, *Accounting for Success: A History of Price Waterhouse in America, 1890–1990* (Cambridge, MA: Harvard Business Review Press, 1993), 233.
2. Antonio Weiss, *Management Consultancy and the British State* (London: Palgrave Macmillan, 2019); Matthias Kipping and Ian Kirkpatrick, "Alternative Pathways of Change in Professional Services Firms: The Case of Management Consulting," *Journal of Management Studies* 50, 5 (2013): 777–807; Lars Engwall, Matthias Kipping, and Behlül Üsdiken, *Defining Management: Business Schools, Consultants, Media* (London: Routledge, 2016).
3. Saint Martin, *Building the New Managerialist State*; Weiss, *Management Consultancy*; Thomas Armbrüster and Matthias Kipping, "Strategy Consulting at the Crossroads: Technical Change and Shifting Market Conditions for Top-Level Advice," *International Studies of Management & Organization* 32, 4 (2002): 19–42.
4. Amoore, *The Politics of Possibility.*
5. Weiss, *Management Consultancy.*
6. John Stoner and Maia Hansen, "A Leaner Public Sector," McKinsey & Company, August 1, 2009. www.mckinsey.com/industries/public-and-social-sector/our-insights/a-leaner-public-sector.
7. William Eggers, Amrita Data, David Parent, Jenn Gustetic, "A Step-by-Step Guide to Optimizing Human-Machine Collaboration in the Public Sector," *Deloitte Insights,* August 05, 2019. www2.deloitte.com/xe/en/insights/industry/public-sector/job-automation-future-of-work-in-government.html.
8. KPMG, "Why KPMG?" n.d. home.kpmg/xx/en/home/industries/government-public-sector/human-social-services/why-kpmg.html.
9. Armbrüster and Kipping, "Strategy Consulting at the Crossroads."
10. "Frederick Taylor, Early Century Management Consultant," *The Wall Street Journal,* June 13, 1997, A1.
11. Harry Braverman, *Labor and Monopoly Capital* (New York: Monthly Review Press, 1974).
12. Braverman, *Labor and Monopoly Capital,* 86.
13. Braverman, *Labor and Monopoly Capital,* 86.
14. Frederick Winslow Taylor, *The Principles of Scientific Management* (NuVision Publications, LLC, 1911).
15. Magali Sarfatti Larson, *The Rise of Professionalism: A Sociological Analysis* (Berkeley: University of California Press, 1977): 141.
16. Martin J. Schiesl, *The Politics of Efficiency: Municipal Administration and Reform in America, 1800–1920* (Berkeley: University of California Press, 1977), 113.
17. Cited in H.L. Schacter, "Public Productivity in the Classical Age of Public Administration," in *Public Productivity Handbook,* second edition, eds. M. Holzer and S.H. Lee (New York: Marcel Dekker, 2004): 23.
18. For instance, the City of Toronto hired consulting engineers from New York in 1911 to make waste collection more efficient, utilizing "scientific" methods, which included measuring the total amount of refuse produced, appraising the process of

waste collection in detail, and advising on methods to maximize efficiency. This was followed by a consulting contract with the New York Bureau of Municipal Research to conduct a comprehensive survey of the treasury, assessment, works, fire, and property departments in 1913. It was thought that the survey would decrease expenditures and increase productivity and efficiency in the delivery of municipal services by applying the principles of scientific management. See Chris Hurl. "From Scavengers to Sanitation Workers: Practices of Purification and the Making of Civic Employees in Toronto, 1890–1920." *Labour* 79 (2017): 81-104.

19. Cited in Alasdair Scott Roberts, *So-Called Experts: How American Consultants Remade the Canadian Civil Service, 1918–21* (Toronto: Institute of Public Administration of Canada, 1996): 46.
20. Cited in Roberts, *So-Called Experts*, 49.
21. John Clarke and Janet Newman, *The Managerial State: Power, Politics and Ideology in the Remaking of Social Welfare* (London: Sage, 1997).
22. Wendy Brown, *Undoing the Demos: Neoliberalism's Stealth Revolution* (New York: Zone Books, 2015), 117.
23. Schacter, "Public Productivity," 14.
24. Braverman, *Labor and Monopoly Capital,* 119.
25. Thomas Armbrüster, *The Economics and Sociology of Management Consulting* (Cambridge University Press, 2006), 41.
26. Walter Kiechel, *Lords of Strategy: The Secret Intellectual History of the New Corporate World* (Harvard Business Press, 2010), 35.
27. Alfred Chandler, *Strategy and Structure: Chapters in the History of the American Industrial Enterprise* (Cambridge, MA: MIT Press, 1969).
28. Matthias Kipping, "American Management Consulting Companies in Western Europe, 1920 to 1990: Products, Reputation, and Relationships," *Business History Review* 73, 2 (1999): 210.
29. On how mobilizing for war contributed to the formation of the welfare state, see: David Edgerton, *Warfare State: Britain, 1920-1970* (Cambridge: Cambridge University Press, 2006); Jytte Klausen, *War and Welfare: Europe and the United States, 1945 to the Present* (London: Palgrave Macmillan, 1998).
30. Price Waterhouse, *Ontario Hospital Services Commission, Survey of Organizations and Operations,* November 1962, 2. RG 10-222-0-86, Archives of Ontario, Toronto.
31. Price Waterhouse, *Ontario Hospital Services Commission,* 109.
32. Saint Martin, *Building the New Managerialist State,* 119–20.
33. Saint Martin, *Building the New Managerialist State,* 123.
34. P.A. DonVito, *The Essentials of a Planning-Programming-Budgeting System* (Santa Monica, CA: RAND Corporation, 1969), 2.
35. Sonja Michelle Amadae, *Rationalizing Capitalist Democracy: The Cold War Origins of Rational Choice Liberalism* (Chicago: University of Chicago Press, 2003), 63.
36. Cited in Amadae, *Rationalizing Capitalist Democracy,* 69; original emphasis.
37. Amadae, *Rationalizing Capitalist Democracy.*
38. Amadae, *Rationalizing Capitalist Democracy,* 69.
39. DonVito, *The Essentials of a Planning-Programming-Budgeting System.*
40. Saint Martin, "Governments and Management Consultants," 118; See also: Clinton Free, V.S. Radcliffe, C. Spence, and M. J. Stein, "Auditing and the Development of the Modern State," *Contemporary Accounting Research,* 37, 1 (2020): 485–513; Clinton Free, V.S. Radcliffe, and B. White, "Crisis, Committees and Consultants: The Rise of Value-for-Money Auditing in the Federal Public Sector in Canada," *Journal of Business Ethics* 113 (2013): 441–59.

41. Saint Martin, *Building the New Managerialist State*, 139.

42. Cited in Saint Martin, *Building the New Managerialist State*, 131.

43. Saint Martin, *Building the New Managerialist State*.

44. Kiechel, *Lords of Strategy*.

45. Karen Ho, *Liquidated: An Anthropology of Wall Street* (Durham, NC: Duke University Press, 2009).

46. McKenna, *The World's Newest Profession*.

47. Kiechel, *Lords of Strategy*, 4.

48. William Davies, *The Limits of Neoliberalism: Authority, Sovereignty and the Logic of Competition* (Los Angeles: Sage, 2014), 114.

49. Davies, *The Limits of Neoliberalism*, 114.

50. Davies, *The Limits of Neoliberalism*, 113

51. Isabelle Bruno, "The 'Indefinite Discipline' of Competitiveness Benchmarking as a Neoliberal Technology of Government," *Minerva* 47, 3 (2009): 261; Isabelle Bruno and Emmanuel Didier, *Benchmarking: L'État sous pression statistique* (Paris: Zone, 2013).

52. McKinsey, "Customer Experience in the Public Sector," November 16, 2022. www.mckinsey.com/industries/public-sector/our-insights/Customer-Experience-in-the-Public-Sector.

53. Deloitte Insights, "Student Success Benchmarking in Higher Education," n.d. www2.deloitte.com/us/en/insights/industry/public-sector/interactive-benchmarking-in-higher-education.html.

54. IBM, "Performance Data and Benchmarking," n.d. www.ibm.com/thought-leadership/institute-business-value/benchmarking.

55. KPMG, "The Value of Benchmarking Cities," September 27, 2017. kpmg.com/be/en/home/insights/2017/09/the-value-of-benchmarking-cities.html.

56. Martin Kornberger and Chris Carter, "Manufacturing Competition: How Accounting Practices Shape Strategy Making in Cities," *Accounting, Auditing & Accountability Journal* 23, 3 (2010): 325–49: 329.

57. Peter Triantafillou, "Benchmarking in the Public Sector: A Critical Conceptual Framework," *Public Administration* 85, 3 (2007): 829–46: 844.

58. André Broome, "Gaming Country Rankings: Consultancies as Knowledge Brokers for Global Benchmarks," *Public Administration* 100, 3 (2022), 557.

59. Bruno Isabelle, Didier Emmanuel and Vitale Tommaso (2014), "Statactivism: forms of action between disclosure and affirmation", in *Partecipazione e conflitto. The Open Journal of Sociopolitical Studies* 7.2 (2014): 198-220: 207 As Bruno et al. note, power resides in "appropriating the rules for production of data serving in one's self-evaluation in a way … so as to adapt them to one's own interests."

60. Tom Peters, "Professional Service Firms as Innovators," tompeters! blog, n.d. tompeters.com/columns/professional-service-firms-as-innovators/.

61. Horrocks, "'Experts and E-Government'"; Ylönen and Kuusela, "Consultocracy and its Discontents"; Busemeyer, and Thelen, "Institutional Sources of Business Power."

62. Mathias Kipping, "Trapped in Their Wave: The Evolution of Management Consultancies," in *Critical Consulting: New Perspectives on the Management Advice Industry*, eds. T. Clark and R. Fincham (Oxford: Blackwell, 2002), 34.

63. Kipping, "Trapped in their Wave," 34.

64. Roncagliolo noted at the time that "financial organizations [have] become increasingly dependent on the availability of data banks which are capable of providing instantly complete and up-to-date files of world-wide information related to in-

vestment alternatives. These computerized systems not only take into consideration classical economic variables, but also information relating to political stability,
socio-economic policies of governments, characteristics of opposition and general
cultural aspects on a day-to-day basis" (cited in Hamelink, 1983: xix). Rafael Ronga-
gliolo. "Preface," In Cees. J. Hamelink, *Finance and Information: A Study of Converging Interests* (Norwood, NJ: Ablex, 1983), xix.
65. Armbrüster, *The Economics and Sociology of Management Consulting.*
66. David J. Cooper, Royston Greenwood, Bob Hinings, and John L. Brown, "Globalization and Nationalism in a Multinational Accounting Firm: The Case of Opening New Markets in Eastern Europe," *Accounting, Organizations and Society* 23, 5/6
(1998), 540.
67. Richard Brooks, *Bean Counters: The Triumph of the Accountants and How They
Broke Capitalism* (London: Atlantic Books, 2018), 18.
68. Statista, "Number of Employees of the Big Four Accounting/Audit Firms Worldwide in 2022," November 2022, www.statista.com/statistics/250503/big-four-ac-
counting-firms-number-of-employees/.
69. Brooks, *Bean Counters,* 30.
70. Saint Martin, "Governments and Management Consultants."
71. Prem Sikka, Colin Haslam, Christine Cooper, et al. *Reforming the Auditing Industry.*
Report commissioned by the Shadow Chancellor of the Exchequer, John McDonnell MP, 2018; McKenna, *The World's Newest Profession,* https://betterfinance.eu/
wp-content/uploads/LabourPolicymaking-AuditingReformsDec2018.pdf.
72. Roy Suddaby, David J. Cooper, and Royston Greenwood, "Transnational Regulation of Professional Services: Governance Dynamics of Field Level Organizational
Change," *Accounting, Organizations and Society* 32, 4–5 (2007), 337.
73. Corporate Europe Observatory. *Accounting for Influence: How the Big Four Are Embedded in EU Policymaking on Tax Avoidance,* July 2018. corporateeurope.org/sites/
default/files/tax-avoidance-industry-lobby-low-res.pdf.
74. Derek Matthews, Malcolm Anderson, and John Richard Edwards, *The Priesthood
of Industry: The Rise of the Professional Accountant in British Management* (Oxford:
Oxford University Press, 1998), 104-105. See also Kipping, "Trapped in their Wave."
75. Kipping, "Trapped in their Wave."
76. Armbrüster, *The Economics and Sociology of Management Consulting,* 121.
77. Weiss, *Management Consultancy and the British State,* 85.
78. Weiss, *Management Consultancy and the British State,* 151
79. Armbrüster, *The Economics and Sociology of Management Consulting,* 122.
80. Hall, cited in Armbrüster, *The Economics and Sociology of Management Consulting,*
122.
81. Before they became the Big Four, there were eight large accounting firms: Price
Waterhouse, Deloitte, Young and Co, Ernst and Whitney, Peat Marwick Mitchell,
Touche Ross, Coopers & Lybrand, and Arthur Andersen.
82. Brooks, *Bean Counters,* 137.
83. Saint Martin, "Governments and Management Consultants"; Brooks, *Bean Counters,* 31.
84. Weiss, *Management Consultancy and the British State,* 157.
85. Suddaby, Cooper and Greenwood, "Transnational Regulation of Professional Services," 334.
86. Cited in Brooks, *Bean Counters,* 179.
87. McKenna, *The World's Newest Profession*; Saint Martin, "Governments and Manage-

ment Consultants," 216; Colin W. Boyd, "The Structural Origins of Conflicts of Interest in the Accounting Profession," *Business Ethics Quarterly* 14, 3 (2004): 377–98.

88. Don van Natta Jr., John Schwartz and Jim Yardley, "In Houston, the Lines Dividing Politics, Business, and Society Are Especially Blurry," *New York Times,* January 20, 2002: 25, cited in Colin W. Boyd, "The Structural Origins of Conflicts of Interest in the Accounting Profession," *Business Ethics Quarterly* 14, 3 (2004): 377–98.

89. Oshin Olafimihan, "SEC Probing Big Four Accounting Firms over Conflict-of-Interest Concerns: Report," *The Hill,* March 15, 2022. thehill.com/regulation/finance/598342-sec-probing-big-four-accounting-firms-over-conflict-of-interest-concerns/.

90. McKenna, *The World's Newest Profession,* 107.

91. Jon Agar, *The Government Machine: A Revolutionary History of the Computer* (Cambridge, MA: MIT Press, 2003), 372.

92. Agar, *The Government Machine,* 372.

93. Microsoft, "The History of Microsoft — 1990," May 21, 2009. learn.microsoft.com/en-us/shows/history/history-of-microsoft-1990.

94. For details, see Chapters 17 and 18 in James W. Cortada, *IBM: The Rise and Fall and Reinvention of a Global Icon* (Cambridge, MA: MIT Press, 2019).

95. Kipping, "Trapped in their Wave," 35.

96. Agar, *The Government Machine,* 372.

97. Agar, *The Government Machine,* 373

98. Weiss, *Management Consultancy and the British State,* 32.

99. Weiss, *Management Consultancy and the British State,* 213.

100. Joel Benjamin, "Capita Don't Just Provide a Few Services, They Seem Practically to Run Entire Councils," *Independent,* January 31, 2018. www.independent.co.uk/voices/capita-carillion-outsourcing-local-authorities-councils-barnet-northamtonpshire-a8188006.html.

101. Reema Patel, "The One Barnet Case Heralds Local Government's Disappearing Act," *New Statesman,* 2013. www.newstatesman.com/politics/2013/05/one-barnet-case-heralds-local-governments-disappearing-act.

102. NUPGE (National Union of Public and General Employees), "Fraud Investigation of Privatization Firms Gets Little Response," Online Archive of Nudge, December 06, 2013. nupge.ca/content/fraud-investigation-privatization-firms-gets-little-response.

103. Weiss, *Management Consultancy and the British State,* 217.

104. Weiss, *Management Consultancy and the British State,* 218.

105. Kipping, "Trapped in their Wave."

106. Armbrüster, *The Economics and Sociology of Management Consulting,* 71.

107. Ola Söderstrom, Till Paasche, and Fransisco Klauser, "Smart Cities as Corporate Storytelling," *City* 18, 3 (2014): 307–20.

108. Armbrüster, *The Economics and Sociology of Management Consulting*; Mariana Mazzucato, *The Value of Everything: Making and Taking in the Global Economy* (London: Hachette, 2018); Pepper D. Culpepper and Kathleen Thelen, "Are We All Amazon Primed? Consumers and the Politics of Platform Power," *Comparative Political Studies* 53, 2 (2020), 288–318.

109. Armbrüster, *The Economics and Sociology of Management Consulting,* 129.

110. Ellis, Colin, "Big Four Accounting Firms Lead Canadian Consulting Market," *Canadian Accountant,* June 24, 2019. www.canadian-accountant.com/content/profession/big-four-accounting-firms-lead-canadian-consulting-market.

111. Busemeyer and Thelen, "Institutional sources of business power"; Ylönen and Kuusela, "Consultocracy and its discontents."

112. Walt Bogdanich and Michael Forsythe, *When McKinsey Comes to Town: The Hidden Influence of the World's Most Powerful Consulting Firm* (New York: Random House. 2022), Chapter 7.

113. https://www.reuters.com/business/australia-announces-tax-adviser-crackdown-after-pwc-tax-leak-scandal-2023-08-06/.

## Chapter 3

1. Kean Birch and Matti Siemiatycki, "Neoliberalism and the Geographies of Marketization: The Entangling of State and Markets," *Progress in Human Geography* 40, 2 (2016): 177–98; David Harvey, *A Brief History of Neoliberalism* (Oxford: Oxford University Press; 2007); Margaret R. Somers, "Dedemocratizing Citizenship: How Neoliberalism Used Market Justice to Move from Welfare Queening to Authoritarianism in 25 Short Years," *Citizenship Studies* 26, 4–5 (2022): 661–74.

2. Friedrich Hayek (1945). "The use of knowledge in society," *The American Economic Review* 35, 4 (1945): 519-530; see also Mirowski. Phillip Mirowski and Edward Nik-Khah, *The Knowledge We Have Lost in Information: The History of Information in Modern Economics* (Oxford: Oxford University Press, 2017); William Davies, "Elite Power under Advanced Neoliberalism," *Theory, Culture and Society* 34, 5–6 (2017): 227–50.

3. Somers, "Dedemocratizing Citizenship," 664.

4. Somers, "Dedemocratizing Citizenship," 664.

5. Greta R. Krippner, *Capitalizing on Crisis: The Political Origins of the Rise of Finance* (Harvard University Press, 2011); Wolfgang Streeck, *Buying Time: The Delayed Crisis of Democratic Capitalism* (London: Verso Books, 2014).

6. Donald J. Savoie, *Breaking the Bargain: Public Servants, Ministers, and Parliament* (University of Toronto Press, 2003), 337.

7. David Osborne and Ted Gaebler, *Reinventing Government: How the Entrepreneurial Spirit Is Transforming the Public Sector* (Reading, MA: Addison Wesley, 1992).

8. Aaron Shapiro, "Dynamic Exploits: Calculative Asymmetries in the On-Demand Economy," *New Technology, Work and Employment* 35, 2 (2020): 162–77.

9. Seabrooke, "Epistemic Arbitrage."

10. Nick Couldry and Ulises A. Mejias, "Data Colonialism: Rethinking Big Data's Relation to the Contemporary Subject," *Television & New Media* 20, 4 (2019): 336–49; Nick Srnicek, *Platform Capitalism* (Cambridge, UK: Polity Press, 2017); Shoshana Zuboff, *The Age of Surveillance Capitalism,* New York: PublicAffairs, 2019).

11. Srnicek, *Platform Capitalism,* 47.

12. Aaron Shapiro, "Between Autonomy and Control: Strategies of Arbitrage in the 'On-Demand' Economy," *New Media & Society* 20, 8 (2018): 2954–71; Shapiro, "Dynamic Exploits;" Alex Rosenblat and Luke Stark, "Algorithmic Labor and Information Asymmetries: A Case Study of Uber's Drivers," *International Journal of Communication* 10 (2016): 27; Jamie Woodcock, "The Algorithmic Panopticon at Deliveroo: Measurement, Precarity, and the Illusion of Control," *Ephemera: Theory & Politics in Organizations* 20, 3 (2020): 67–95.

13. Srnicek, *Platform Capitalism,* 51.

14. Julie Eckl and Tine Hanrieder, "The Political Economy of Consulting Firms in Reform Processes: The Case of the World Health Organization," *Review of International Political Economy* 1, 24 (2022): 11.

15. Armbrüster, *The Economics and Sociology of Management Consulting,* 47.

16. Pistor, "The Rise of Autonomous Financial Power," 334.

17. Wendy Nelson Espeland and Mitchell L. Stevens, "A Sociology of Quantification," *European Journal of Sociology/Archives européennes de sociologie* 49, 3 (2008): 416.

18. Tax Justice Network, "The State of Tax Justice in 2021," November 16, 2021. taxjustice.net/reports/the-state-of-tax-justice-2021/.

19. CTV News, "Ottawa Lost Average of $22 Billion a Year in Unpaid Tax From 2014–2018: CRA Report," CTV Online News, June 28, 2022. https://www.ctvnews.ca/politics/ottawa-lost-average-of-22-billion-a-year-in-unpaid-tax-from-2014-2018-cra-report-1.5966639.

20. Eve Chiapello and Karim Medjad, "An Unprecedented Privatisation of Mandatory Standard-Setting: The Case of European Accounting Policy," *Critical Perspectives on Accounting* 20, 4 (2009): 448–68; Carlos Ramirez, "How Big Four Audit Firms Control Standard-Setting in Accounting and Auditing," in *Finance: the Discreet Regulator: How Financial Activities Shape and Transform the World,* eds. I. Huault and C. Richards (London: Palgrave Macmillan, 2012).

21. Lena Ajdacic, Eelke M. Heemskerk, and Javier Garcia-Bernardo, "The Wealth Defence Industry: A Large-Scale Study on Accountancy Firms as Profit Shifting Facilitators," *New Political Economy* 26, 4 (2021): 693.

22. Michael Hudson, Sasha Chavkin, Bart Mos, "Big 4 Audit Firms Play Big Role in Offshore Murk," International Consortium of Investigative Journalism, November 5, 2014. www.icij.org/project/luxembourg-leaks/big-4-audit-firms-play-big-role-offshore-murk/.

23. Austin Mitchell and Prem Sikka, *The Pin-Striped Mafia—How Accountancy Firms Destroy Societies* (Basildon, Essex: Association for Accountancy and Business Affairs, 2011).

24. Brooks, *Bean Counters,* 161; see also Prem Sikka, "Big Four Accounting Firms: Addicted to Tax Avoidance," in *Pioneers of Critical Accounting: A Celebration of the life of Tony Lowe,* eds. J. Haslam and P. Sikka (London: Palgrave Macmillan, 2016), 259-274.

25. US Senate Permanent Subcommittee on Investigations, *The Role of Professional Firms in the US Tax Shelter Industry* (Washington, DC: USGPO, 2005): 9.

26. Statista, "Revenue of the Big Four Accounting/Audit Firms Worldwide in 2022, by Function, April 2023. www.statista.com/statistics/250935/big-four-accounting-firms-breakdown-of-revenues/.

27. "UK House of Commons Report on Tax 2013," cited in Lena Ajdacic, Eelke M. Heemskerk, and Javier Garcia-Bernardo. "The Wealth Defence Industry: A Large-Scale Study on Accountancy Firms as Profit Shifting Facilitators," *New Political Economy* 26.4 (2021): 690-706, 691.

28. Brooks, *Bean Counters*; HMRC UK (HM Revenue and Customs, UK), "Estimation of Tax Gap of Direct Taxes," 2017. assets.publishing.service.gov.uk/government/uploads/system/uploads/attachment_data/file/329278/direct-tax-gaps.pdf.

29. Mitchell and Sikka, "The Pin-Striped Mafia," 19.

30 Harvey Cashore and Frédéric Zalac, "Wealthy KPMG Clients Continued to Dodge Taxes for Years after CRA Detected Offshore '1Sham,'" CBC Politics, June 04, 2021. www.cbc.ca/news/politics/kpmg-isle-of-man-taxes-house-commons-finance-committee-1.6047111.

31. CBC, "The Untouchables," *The Fifth Estate,* CBC, March 03, 2017. www.cbc.ca/player/play/889846851694.

32. CBC, "The Untouchables."

33. John Guyton, Patrick Langetieg, Daniel Reck et al., "Tax Evasion at the Top of the Income Distribution: Theory and Evidence," NBER Working Paper Series, National Bureau of Economic Research (2021). gabriel-zucman.eu/files/GLRRZ2021.pdf; Christopher Ingraham, "The Richest 1 Percent Dodge Taxes on More Than One Fifth of Their Income Study Shows," *Washington Post*, March 26, 2021. www.washingtonpost.com/business/2021/03/26/wealthy-tax-evasion/.

34. James S. Henry, "The Price of Offshore Revisited," Tax Justice Network, July 2012. www.taxjustice.net/cms/upload/pdf/Price_of_Offshore_Revisited_120722.pdf.

35. John Guyton, Patrick Langetieg, Daniel Reck et al., "Tax Evasion at the Top."

36. Nick Davies, "Cosy Relationships Keeps Corporates Happy but Could Cost £20bn in Taxes," *The Guardian*, July 23, 2022. www.theguardian.com/politics/2002/jul/23/uk.economy.

37. Chris Jones, Yama Temouri, and Alex Cobham, "Tax Haven Networks and the Role of the Big 4 Accountancy Firms," *Journal of World Business* 53, 2 (2018): 177–93.

38. Jones et al, "Tax Haven Networks," 178.

39. Lena Ajdacic et al., "The Wealth Defence Industry."

40. Sikka, "Big Four Accounting Firms," 7.

41. Brooks, *Bean Counters*; Simon Bowers, "Former PWC Employees Face Trial Over Role in LuxLeaks Scandal," *The Guardian*, April 24, 2016. www.theguardian.com/world/2016/apr/24/luxleaks-antoine-deltour-luxembourg-tax-avoidance-pricewaterhousecoopers-trial.

42. Michael O'Dwyer, "Widespread Distrust Among Tax Officials of Big Four, Says OECD Survey," *Financial Times*, September 5, 2022. www.ft.com/content/5299ca4bade0-4054-a039-161671f7f2f6.

43. O'Dwyer, "Widespread Distrust Among Tax Officials"; OECD (Organization for Economic Co-operation and Development), "Tax Morale II: Building Trust between Tax Administrations and Large Business," OECD Library, September 05, 2022. www.oecd-ilibrary.org/taxation/tax-morale-ii_7587f25c-en.

44. Brooks, *Bean Counters*, 295.

45. Sikka, "Big Four Accounting Firms," 261

46. UK House of Commons Committee of Public Accounts, 2013a: 5 — cited in Sikka, "Big Four Accounting Firms," 261.

47. UK House of Commons Committee of Public Accounts, 2013a: 5 — cited in Sikka, "Big Four Accounting Firms," 261.

48. Sikka, "Big Four Accounting Firms"; Brooks, *Bean Counters*.

49. Sikka et al., *Reforming the Auditing Industry*, 9.

50. KPMG International, *The Wolf Is at the Door: The Global Economic Crisis and the Public Sector*, 2009: 8.

51. KPMG International, *The Wolf Is at the Door*: 15, 8.

52. Michael Power, "Evaluating the Audit Explosion," *Law & Policy* 25, 3 (2003):185–202, 187.

53. Michael Power, *The Audit Society: Rituals of Verification* (Oxford: Oxford University Press, 1997); Marilyn Strathern, "Introduction: New Accountabilities," in *Audit Cultures*, ed. M. Strathern (London: Routledge, 2000); Cris Shore and Susan Wright, "Audit Culture Revisited: Rankings, Ratings, and the Reassembling of Society," *Current Anthropology* 56, 3 (2015): 431–32.

54. Cris Shore, "Audit Culture and Illiberal Governance," *Anthropological Theory* 8 (2008) 278–89.

55. Shore, "Audit Culture and Illiberal Governance," 288.

56. Zeena Feldman and Marisol Sandoval, "Metric Power and the Academic Self: Neoliberalism, Knowledge and Resistance in the British University," *tripleC: Communication, Capitalism & Critique. Open Access Journal for a Global Sustainable Information Society* 16, 1 (2018): 214–33.

57. Strathern, "Introduction: New Accountabilities"; Shore, "Audit Culture and Illiberal Governance"; Shore and Wright, "Audit Culture Revisited."

58. Wendy Nelson Espeland and Michael Sauder, *Engines of Anxiety: Academic Rankings, Reputation, and Accountability* (New York: Russell Sage Foundation, 2016).

59. Broome, "Gaming Country Rankings."

60. Conservative Party of Ontario, *The Common Sense Revolution* (Toronto: Party 1994).

61. Government of Ontario, *1997 Ontario Budget: Investing in the Future* (Toronto: Queen's Printer of Ontario, 1997) 42.

62. Alicia Schatteman, "The State of Ontario's Municipal Performance Reports: A Critical Analysis," *Canadian Public Administration* 53, 4 (2010): 531–50.

63. For instance, see KPMG, 2020, *The City of Greater Sudbury Core Service Review.* www.greatersudbury.ca/city-hall/pdfs/kpmg-final-report-of-core-service-review/, accessed 10 June 2020.

64. KPMG, 2013, Corporation of the Township of Central Frontenac Service Delivery Review Final Report, accessed 8 September 2019, 2.

65. Personal Interview, 2020.

66. Government of Ontario, "Ontario Invests in Small and Rural Municipalities to Improve Service Delivery and Efficiency," (2019). news.ontario.ca/mma/en/2019/03/ontario-invests-in-small-and-rural-municipalities-to-improve-service-delivery-and-efficiency.html, accessed 16 May 2019; Government of Ontario, "Premier Ford Asks Partners to Find Four Per Cent Savings and Help Front-Line Services," (2019). news.ontario.ca/opo/en/2019/05/premier-ford-asks-partners-to-find-four-per-cent-savings-and-help-protect-front-line-services.html, accessed 21 May 2019.

67. Gerald A. Epstein, "Introduction: Financialization and the World Economy," in *Financialization and the World Economy,* ed. G.A. Epstein (Cheltenham: Edward Elgar, 2005) 3; see also Eve Chiapello, "Financialisation of Valuation," *Human Studies* 38, 1 (2015): 13–35; Eve Chiapello and Lisa Knoll, "Social Finance and Impact Investing: Governing Welfare in the Era of Financialization," *Historical Social Research/Historische Sozialforschung* 45, 3 (2020): 7–30.

68. EY, "Public Private Partnerships and the Global Infrastructure Challenge," 2016.

69. Deloitte, "Public Infrastructure and Capital Projects." www2.deloitte.com/us/en/pages/public-sector/solutions/government-infrastructure-services.html.

70. KPMG, "Infrastructure," https://kpmg.com/ca/en/home/industries/infrastructure.html; see also Chris Hurl and Anne Vogelpohl, "Transnational Professional Service Firms and the Corporatization of Infrastructure Procurement," in *Pervasive Powers: The Politics of Corporate Authority,* eds. S. Aguiton, M Deplaude, N. Jas, E. Henry, and V. Thomas (London: Routledge, 2021).

71. Fleur Johns, "Financing as Governance," *Oxford Journal of Legal Studies* 31, 2 (2011) 391–415.

72. Christian Bordeleau, "Building State Infrastructure Privately: The Emergence and Diffusion of Public Private Partnerships in Canada, the United Kingdom and the United States of America," PhD diss., Carleton University (2014); Edward R. Yescombe, *Public–Private Partnerships: Principles of Policy and Finance* (New York: Elsevier, 2011).

73. Stefanie Kleimeier, and William L. Megginson, "A Comparison of Project Finance

in Asia and the West," in *Project Finance in Asia,* ed. Larry H.P. Lan (New York: Elsevier, 1998) 57–90.

74. Bordeleau, "Building State Infrastructure Privately," 50.

75. Bordeleau, "Building State Infrastructure Privately"; Heather Whiteside, "P3s and the Value for Money Illusion," in *Orchestrating Austerity,* ed. Donna Baines and Stephen McBrides. 172–80 (Winnipeg, MB: Fernwood Publishing, 2014); Anthony E. Boardman, Matti Siemiatycki, and Aidan Vining, "The Theory and Evidence Concerning Public–Private Partnerships in Canada and Elsewhere," SPP *Research Paper* 9, 12 (2016).

76. National Audit Office (NAO), "PFI and PF2," report by the Comptroller and Auditor General, January 18, 2018.

77. NAO, "PFI and PF2," 30.

78. Bretton Woods Project, "Public–Private Partnerships: The Global Debt Iceberg?" June 29, 2016. www.brettonwoodsproject.org/2016/06/21111/.

79. Ian Fraser, "John Swinney Slams PFI Legacy," *The Times,* April 19, 2009. www.the-times.co.uk/article/john-swinney-slams-pfi-legacy-fqmtkj8lgt5.

80. Whiteside, "P3s and the Value for Money Illusion," 167.

81. Bordeleau, "Building State Infrastructure Privately"; Whiteside, "P3s and the Value for Money Illusion."

82. Stuart Murray, *Value for Money? Cautionary Lessons about P3s from British Columbia,* Vancouver: Canadian Centre for Policy Alternatives (2005): 32.

83. Chris Hurl and Alia Nurmohamed, "Building Walls within Walls: Making value defensible in Public Private Partnerships," *Economy and Society* 52, 4 (2023): 650-674; see also: Matti Siemiatycki and Naeem Farooqi, "Value for Money and Risk in Public–Private Partnerships: Evaluating the Evidence," *Journal of the American Planning Association* 78, 3 (2012): 286–99; Auditor General Ontario, "2014 Annual Report," Office of the Auditor General of Ontario (2014). www.auditor.on.ca/en/content/annualreports/arbyyear/ar2014.html.

84. Auditor General, "2014 Annual Report," 7.

85. Siemiatycki and Farooqi, "Value for Money and Risk in PPPs"; Boardman et al., "The Theory and Evidence Concerning PPPs."

86. Murray, *Value for Money?* 52.

87. John Loxley, *Ideology Over Economics: P3s in an Age of Austerity* (Halifax: Fernwood Publishing, 2020), 50.

88. Auditor General, "2014 Annual Report," 198.

89. Eve Chiapello, "Financialisation of Valuation," *Human Studies* 38.1: 13–35 (2015), 26.

90. Dexter Whitfield, "Alternative to Private Financing of the Welfare State," European Services Strategy Unit, University of Adelaide (2015). www.european-services-strategy.org.uk/wp-content/uploads/2015/09/alternative-to-private-finance-of-the-welfare-state.pdf.

91. Christine Cooper, Cameron Graham, and Darlene Himick, "Social Impact Bonds: The Securitization of the Homeless," *Accounting, Organizations and Society* 55 (2016): 63–82, 63.

92. Canadian Labour Congress, "For the Public Good: The Growing Threat of Privatization and Workers' Proposals to Protect our Future," Canadian Labour Congress Report (2021) 17.

93. Cooper et al., "Social Impact Bonds," 78.

94. Deloitte, "Paying for Outcomes: Solving Complex Societal Issues Through Social

Impact Bonds," 2012. www2.deloitte.com/content/dam/Deloitte/au/Documents/public-sector/deloitte-au-ps-paying-outcomes-social-impact-bonds-180914.pdf.

95. Cooper et al ""Social Impact Bonds," 78.

96. Cooper et al., "Social Impact Bonds," 79.

97. Heather Whiteside, *Purchase for Profit: Public–Private Partnerships and Canada's Public Health Care System* (Toronto: University of Toronto Press, 2015).

98. Deloitte, "GovConnect Public Health Transformation Platform," Deloitte website, n.d. www2.deloitte.com/us/en/pages/public-sector/articles/contact-tracker-tracer-covid-19-govconnect-public-health-transformation-platform.html.

99. Darius Tahir and Rachel Roubein, "Trump Officials Rush to Introduce Untested Vaccine Tracking System," *Politico*, September 13, 2020. www.politico.com/news/2020/09/12/trump-vaccine-tracking-system-412968.

100. Professional Institute of the Public Service of Canada (PIPSC), "The Real Costs of Outsourcing," January 23 2020. pipsc.ca/news-issues/outsourcing/part-one-real-cost-outsourcing.

101. PIPSC, "The Real Costs of Outsourcing."

102. Agar, *The Government Machine*.

103. David Rapaport, "An Unequal Partnership: The Privatisation of Information Technology in Ontario." *Work Organisation, Labour and Globalisation* 9, 1 (2015): 92–105.

104. Horrocks, "Experts and E-Government."

105. James Bagnall, "A Timeline of the Pheonix Pay Debacle: 29 Years and Counting," *Ottawa Citizen*, February 23, 2018. ottawacitizen.com/news/local-news/a-timeline-of-the-phoenix-pay-debacle-29-years-and-counting.

106. CBC News, "Miramichi Public Service Pay Centre Staff Struggling with Workload," CBC News, June 24, 2015. www.cbc.ca/news/canada/new-brunswick/miramichi-public-service-pay-centre-staff-struggling-with-workload-1.3126806.

107. Monique Muise, "Pheonix Pay System: Officials Say all Files Will Be Processed by Oct. 31," *Global News*, July 28, 2016. globalnews.ca/news/2853127/phoenix-pay-system-officials-set-to-provide-update/.

108. Jordan Press, "Liberals Add $142 Million in Spending to Solve Phoenix Pay Problems," *Globe and Mail*, May 24, 2017. www.theglobeandmail.com/news/politics/liberals-add-142-million-in-spending-to-solve-phoenix-pay-problems/article35098786/?ref=http://www.theglobeandmail.com&.

109. Julie Ireton, "IBM Contracts Cost for Failure-Plagued Phoenix Payroll System Jumped to Total $185M," CBC News, September 21, 2017. www.cbc.ca/news/canada/ottawa/phoenix-ibm-contract-union-pay-government-1.4295827.

110. CBC obtained access to these in 2017 through access to information requests.

111. CBC News, "Phoenix Cost Soars by Another $137M, Paid to IBM," CBC News, May 15, 2019. www.cbc.ca/news/canada/ottawa/phoenix-costs-137-million-ibm-1.5135545.

112. Ireton, "IBM Contracts Cost."

113. Ireton, "IBM Contracts Cost."

114. Busemeyer and Thelen, "Institutional Sources of Business Power," 448–49.

115. Busemeyer and Thelen, "Institutional Sources of Business Power," 449.

116. Agar, *The Government Machine*, 377.

117. Standing Senate Committee, *The Phoenix Pay Problem: Working Towards a Solution*, Report of the Standing Senate Committee on National Finance, July 2018. sencanada.ca/content/sen/committee/421/NFFN/Reports/NFFN_Phoenix_Report_32_WEB_e.pdf.

118. Buy and Sell, Government of Canada, n.d. Accessed on March 01, 2022. buyandsell. gc.ca/procurement-data/contract-history/EN920-190988-005-XE-1.
119. Weiss, *Management Consultancy and the British State*, 151.
120. Weiss, *Management Consultancy and the British State*, 181–189.
121. Weiss, *Management Consultancy and the British State*, 188.
122. Agar, *The Government Machine*, 376.
123. Agar, *The Government Machine*, 378.
124. Agar, *The Government Machine*, 376
125. Agar, *The Government Machine*.
126. Horrocks, "Experts and E-Government," 111.
127. Corporate Watch, "Serco: Company Profile 2018," Corporate Watch Website, June 28, 2018. corporatewatch.org/serco-company-profile-2018/.
128. Serco Website, "About" Section, n.d. www.serco.com/about.
129. Jeff Gray, "Ontario Expands Role of Private Firms in Welfare Jobs Programs," *Globe and Mail*, September 22, 2022. www.theglobeandmail.com/canada/article-ontario-expands-role-of-private-firms-in-welfare-jobs-programs/.
130. Corporate Watch, "Serco: Company Profile 2018," Corporate Watch Website, June 28, 2018. corporatewatch.org/serco-company-profile-2018/.
131. Weiss, *Management Consultancy and the British State*, 250.
132. Weiss, *Management Consultancy and the British State*.

## Chapter 4

1. Ola Söderstrom, Till Paasche, Francisco Klauser, "Smart Cities as Corporate Story-telling," *City* 18, 3 (2014): 307–20; this concept is taken from Michel Callon, "Some Elements of a Sociology of Translation: Domestication of the Scallops and the Fishermen of St Brieuc Bay," *The Sociological Review* 32, 1_suppl (1984): 196–233.
2. Horrocks, "'Experts and E-Government."
3. Armbrüster, *The Economics and Sociology of Management Consulting*, 16.
4. Thomas Medvetz, "Murky Power: 'Think Tanks' as Boundary Organizations," *Rethinking Power in Organizations, Institutions, and Markets* (Emerald Group Publishing Limited, 2012), 113; see also: Andrew Sturdy, Karen Handley, Timothy Clark, and Robin Fincham, *Management Consultancy. Boundaries and Knowledge in Action* (Oxford: Oxford University Press, 2010); Paul Williams, "The Competent Boundary Spanner," *Public Administration* 80, 1 (2002): 103–24; Brooke Harrington and Leonard Seabrooke, "Transnational Professionals," *Annual Review of Sociology* 46 (2020): 399–417; Leonard Seabrooke and Eleni Tsingou, "Revolving Doors in International Financial Governance," *Global Networks* 21, 2 (2021): 294–319.
5. Medvetz, "Murky Power," 7.
6. Stephanie Yates and Etienne Cardin-Trudeau, "Lobbying 'From Within': A New Perspective on the Revolving Door and Regulatory Capture," *Canadian Public Administration* 64, 2 (2021): 301–19; Mark Hellowell, "The UK's Private Finance Initiative: History, Evaluation, Prospects," in *International Handbook on Public–Private Partnerships*, eds. G.A. Hodge, C. Greve, and A.E. Boardman (London: Edward Elgar Publishing, 2010); Jean Shaoul, Anne Stafford, and Pamela Stapleton, "Partnerships and the Role of Financial Advisors: Private Control over Public Policy?" *Policy and Politics* 35, 3 (2007): 479–95; Bogdanich and Forsyth, *When McKinsey Comes to Town*; Mazzucato and Collington, *The Big Con*.

7. Matt Taibbi, "Greed and Debt: The True Story of Mitt Romney and Bain Capital," *Rolling Stone,* August 29, 2012.

8. Lucia Graves, "Pete Buttigieg and McKinsey: Why a Background in Business Raises Doubts," *The Guardian,* December 5, 2019. www.theguardian.com/us-news/2019/dec/05/pete-buttigieg-mckinsey-business-democratic-2020.

9. Deloitte Canada, "Deloitte Canada and McInnes Cooper Welcome Former Cabinet Minister the Hon. Peter MacKay, P.C., Q.C," December 15, 2020. www2.deloitte.com/ca/en/pages/press-releases/articles/welcome-peter-mackay.html.

10. CBC News, "David Johnston, Former Governor General, Joins Deloitte as Adviser," CBC News, October 17, 2017. www.cbc.ca/news/politics/david-johnston-deloitte-1.4358001.

11. Geoffrey York and Robert Fife, "Criminal Charges Against McKinsey Cast Spotlight on its Business During Former Canadian Ambassador Dominic Barton's Tenure," *Globe and Mail,* October 7, 2022. www.theglobeandmail.com/world/article-mckinsey-corruption-case-dominic-barton/; Bill Curry, "E-mails Show McKinsey Involvement in Call with Barton While He Was Canada's Ambassador to China," *Globe and Mail,* May 18, 2023. www.theglobeandmail.com/politics/article-e-mails-show-mckinsey-involvement-in-call-with-barton-while-he-was/.

12. Terence Corcoran, "Terence Corcoran: Meet Dominic Barton, the Liberals' New Pied Piper of 'Subversive' Anti-Capitalism," *Financial Post,* February 24, 2016. financialpost.com/opinion/terence-corcoran-meet-dominic-barton-the-liberals-new-pied-piper-of-anti-profit. Perhaps not surprising, many of Barton's key recommendations reinforced the neoliberal policy program discussed in the previous chapter. This included establishing the Canadian Infrastructure Bank, which contributed to the normalization of Public–Private Partnerships at the federal level, "leverag[ing] government procurement to accelerate innovative companies," developing growth strategies for the energy sector, as well as other sectors with "untapped potential."

13. Rachel Gilmore and Sean Boynton, "'I am Not a Friend' of Trudeau, Ex-McKinset Head Dominic Barton says Amid Contract Probe," *Global News,* February 1, 2023. globalnews.ca/news/9451158/mckinsey-contracts-liberal-dominic-barton-committee/.

14. Wiki Leaks, "Macron Campaign Emails," July 31, 2017. wikileaks.org/macron-emails/.

15. France 24 News, "'McKinsey Affair': Prosecutors Probe French State's Use of Private Consultancy Firms," *France 24 News,* June 04, 2022. www.france24.com/en/france/20220406-mckinsey-affair-prosecutors-probe-french-state-s-use-of-private-consultancy-firms.

16. Duff McDonald, *The Firm: The Story of McKinsey and Its Secret Influence on American Business* (New York: Simon and Schuster, 2013), 284. "The national mode has changed ... Under Mr. Bush, working for Goldman Sachs, the greatest of Wall Street's then-great investment banks, seemed in itself to be a qualification for high office. This, after all, was an era where what counted was understanding the financial markets and globalization, and having great connections all over the world ... The new era may place a higher value on finding practical ways to improve the workings of vast bureaucracies" (McDonald, *The Firm,* 284).

17. Duff McDonald, "Behind the Singular Mystique of McKinsey & Co.," CNBC *Guest Blog,* September 25, 2013.

18. McDonald, *The Firm,* 285.

19. McDonald, *The Firm,* 285.

20. Wherry Aaron, "There Are Questions to Ask about Government Contracting — But MPs Don't Seem Interested in Asking Them," CBC *Politics,* February 02, 2023. www.cbc.ca/news/politics/barton-trudeau-mckinsey-analysis-wherry-1.6734624.

21. Daniel Guttman and Barry Willner, *The Shadow Government* (New York: Pantheon Books, 1976); Graeme Hodge and Diana Bowman, "The 'Consultocracy': The Business of Reforming Government," *Privatization and Market Development,* ed. Graeme Hodge (Northampton, MA: Edward Elgar, 2006).

22. Ian Cook and Kevin Ward, "Conferences, Informational Infrastructures and Mobile Policies: The Process of Getting Sweden 'BID Ready,'" *European Urban and Regional Studies,* 19, 2 (2012): 137–52.

23. Harvey Cashore and Kimberly Ivany, "Top Canadian Law Firm Endorsed Controversial KPMG Isle of Man Tax Dodge," CBC News, June 8, 2016. www.cbc.ca/news/business/dentons-kpmg-offshore-tax-dodge-1.3618257.

24. House of Commons, Canada, "Final Committee Meeting," *Parliament of Canada,* May 03, 2016. www.ourcommons.ca/DocumentViewer/en/42-1/fina/meeting-17/evidence.

25. Chris Hurl and Anne Vogelpohl, "Transnational Professional Service Firms and the Corporatization of Infrastructure Procurement," in *Pervasive Powers: The Politics of Corporate Authority,* eds. S. Aguiton, M. Deplaude, N. Jas, E. Henry and V. Thomas (London: Routledge, 2021); Chris Hurl, Valerie l'Heureux, and Susanne A. Kraemer, "Elite Networks in Public Private Partnerships: Mapping the Enabling Field in Ontario," *Studies in Political Economy* 103, 1: (2022): 36–54; Bordeleau, "Building State Infrastructure Privately"; Hellowell, "The UK's Private Finance Initiative.

26. Hurl et al., "Elite Networks in Public Private Partnerships."

27. Jean Phillipe Sapinski and William K. Carroll, "Interlocking Directorates and Corporate Networks," *Handbook of the International Political Economy of the Corporation* (London: Edward Elgar Publishing, 2018), 57; see also Michael Useem, *The Inner Circle: Large Corporations and the Rise of Business Political Activity in the US and UK* (Oxford: Oxford University Press, 1986).

28. James Kwak, "Cultural Capture and the Financial Crisis," in *Preventing Regulatory Capture: Special Interest Influence and How to Limit It,* eds. D. Carpenter and D.A. Moss (Cambridge: Cambridge University Press, 2014), 78: Yates and Cardin-Trudeau, "Lobbying 'From Within.'"

29. Shaoul et al., "Partnerships and the Role of Financial Advisors"; Hurl and Vogelpohl, "Transnational Professional Service Firms."

30. Mazzucato and Collington, *The Big Con;* Bogdanich and Forsyth, *When McKinsey Comes to Town.*

31. Brooks, *Bean Counters,* 436.

32. Weiss, *Management Consultancy and the British State,* 250.

33. Weiss, *Management Consultancy and the British State,* 136.

34. Ho, *Liquidated.*

35. Weiss, *Management Consultancy and the British State,* 105.

36. Weiss, *Management Consultancy and the British State,* 250.

37. Weiss, *Management Consultancy and the British State,* 80.

38. Harvey Cashore, Kimberly Ivay, and Katie Pedersen, "Major Accounting Firms Routinely Recruited Federal Justice and CRA Tax Enforcement Officials," CBC Business, April 11, 2016. www.cbc.ca/news/business/accounting-firms-recruited-cra-justice-staff-1.3526762.

39. Brooks, *Bean Counters,* 426.

40. Brooks, *Bean Counters,* 426.

41. Shaoul et al., "Partnerships and the Role of Financial Advisors."

42. Shaoul et al., "Partnerships and the Role of Financial Advisors," 482.

43. Unison, "A Web of Private Interest: How the Big Five Accountancy Firms Influence and Profit from Privatization Policy," 2002: 8. www.toronto.ca/ext/digital_comm/inquiry/inquiry_site/cd/gg/add_pdf/77/Procurement/Electronic_Documents/Miscellaneous/privateinterest.pdf.

44. Jonathan Barrett, "PwC Australia's Former CEO Among Eight Partners Removed Following Tax Leak Scandal," *The Guardian,* July 3, 2023. www.theguardian.com/business/2023/jul/03/pwc-removes-eight-partners-following-internal-investigation-into-tax-leak-scandal.

45. McDonald, *The Firm,* 326.

46. Thomas Gerbert, "Dans l'ombre, la firme McKinsey était au cœur de la gestion de la pandémie au Québec," September 30, 2022. ici.radio-canada.ca/nouvelle/1920666/mckinsey-quebec-covid-legault-gestion-pandemie.

47. Committee on Oversight and Accountability (US), "Committee Releases Report Uncovering Significant Conflicts of Interest at McKinsey & Co Related to Work for FDA and OPIOD Manufacturers," Press release, April 13, 2022. oversightdemocrats.house.gov/news/press-releases/committee-releases-report-uncovering-significant-conflicts-of-interest-at.

48. Brooks, *Bean Counters,* 437.

49. Williams, "The Competent Boundary Spanner"; Sturdy et al., *Management Consultancy.*

50. Busemeyer and Thelen, "Institutional Sources of Business Power," 7

51. Busemeyer and Thelen, "Institutional Sources of Business Power," 2.

52. Busemeyer and Thelen, "Institutional Sources of Business Power," 5.

53. Ramirez, "How Big Four Audit Firms Control Standard-Setting," 41; see also Tim Büthe and Walter Mattli, *The New Global Rulers* (Princeton, NJ: Princeton University Press, 2011).

54. Chiapello and Medjad, "An Unprecedented Privatisation," 462.

55. Ranjit Lall, "Timing as a Source of Regulatory Influence: A Technical Elite Network Analysis of Global Finance," *Regulation & Governance* 9, 2 (2015): 125–43.

56. Lall, "Timing as a Source of Regulatory Influence," 135.

57. Ramirez, "How Big Four Audit Firms Control Standard-Setting."

58. Manolis Kalaitzake, "Accounting for Success: The Big Four as Allies of Finance in Post Crisis Regulatory Reform," *Business and Politics* 21, 3 (2019): 297–326, 400.

59. Corporate Europe Observatory, *Accounting for Influence,* 21; see also Rasmus C. Christensen and Leonard Seabrooke, "The Big 4 under Pressure: Scanning Work in Transnational Fields," *Contemporary Accounting Research* 39, 4 (2022): 2941–69; see next chapter.

60. Kalaitzake, "Accounting for Success."

61. Bordeleau, "Building State Infrastructure Privately."

62. Hellowell, "The UK's Private Finance Initiative."

63. Shaoul et al., "Partnerships and the Role of Financial Advisors."

64. Hellowell, "The UK's Private Finance Initiative."

65. Bordeleau, "Building State Infrastructure Privately."

66. Hurl et al., "Elite Networks in Public Private Partnerships."

67. Financial Reporting & Assurance Standards Canada, accessed on September 01, 2022. www.frascanada.ca/en/public-sector/projects/public-private-partnerships.

68. Whiteside, *Purchase for Profit*.
69. Neha Sami and Shriya Anand, "Expert Advice? Assessing the Role of the State in Promoting Privatized Planning," *Professional Service Firms and Politics in a Global Era: Public Policy, Private Expertise* (2021): 273–92; Uttara Purandare, "Who Drives India's Smart Cities? Understanding the Role of Consulting Firms in the Smart Cities Mission," *Professional Service Firms and Politics in a Global Era: Public Policy, Private Expertise* (2021): 79–96.
70. Sami and Anand, "Expert Advice?" 282.
71. Sami and Anand, "Expert Advice?" 282.
72. Bipashyee Ghosh and Saurabh Arora, "Smart as (un)Democratic? The Making of a Smart City Imaginary in Kolkata, India," *Environment and Planning C: Politics and Space* 40, 1 (2022): 318–39, 319-320.
73. Ghosh and Arora, "Smart as (un)Democratic?" 320.
74. Busemeyer and Thelen, "Institutional Sources of Business Power," 7.
75. Roy Suddaby and Royston Greenwood, "Colonizing Knowledge: Commodification as a Dynamic of Jurisdiction Expansion in Professional Service Firms," *Human Relations* 54, 7 (2001): 933–53, 938.
76. Morten T. Hansen, Nitin Nohria, and Thomas J. Tierney, "What's Your Strategy for Managing Knowledge?" *Harvard Business Review,* April 1999. hbr.org/1999/03/whats-your-strategy-for-managing-knowledge.
77. Suddaby and Greenwood, "Colonizing Knowledge," 938.
78. Kiechel, *Lords of Strategy,* 65.
79. Kiechel, *Lords of Strategy,* 56–80. For the image, see the BCG website, "What Is the Growth Share Matrix?" www.bcg.com/en-ca/about/overview/our-history/growth-share-matrix.
80. Chris Hurl, "(Dis)Assembling Policy Pipelines: Unpacking the Work of Management Consultants at Public Meetings," *Geographica Helvetica* 72, 2 (2017) 183–95.
81. While we are not permitted to reprint these images in the book, plenty of examples can be found online. For example, see KPMG's Core Service Review, *Final Report to the City Manager* (2011), p. 20, available here: www.toronto.ca/wp-content/uploads/2017/08/9684-backgroundfile-39505.pdf. This matrix has been taken up in many other municipalities across Ontario. For instance, see KPMG's Core Service Review, *Final Report* for the City of Greater Sudbury (2020), p. 33 available here: www.greatersudbury.ca/city-hall/reports-studies-policies-and-plans/pdfs/kpmg-final-report-of-core-service-review/ or KPMG's Service Delivery Review, *Final Report* for the Town of Coburg (2020), p. 42 available here: www.cobourg.ca/en/town-hall/resources/Service-Delivery-Review-Final-Report.pdf.
82. Michael Briers and Wei Fong Chua, "The Role of Actor-Networks and Boundary Objects in Management Accounting Change: A Field Study of an Implementation of Activity-Based Costing," *Accounting, Organizations and Society* 26, 3 (2001): 237–69.
83. Mazzuccato and Collington, *The Big Con*; Eckl and Hanrieder, "The Political Economy of Consulting Firms"; Edward G. Pringle, "Do Proprietary Tools Lead to Cookie Cutter Consulting?" *Journal of Management Consulting* 10, 1 (1998): 3.
84. Cited in Mazzucato and Collington, *The Big Con,* 226.
85. Romain Schué and Thomas Gerbet, "The Value of One Consulting Firm's Federal Contracts Has Skyrocketed under the Trudeau Government," CBC *Politics,* January 04, 2023. www.cbc.ca/news/politics/mckinsey-immigration-consulting-contracts-trudeau-1.6703626.

86. Mazzucato and Collington, *The Big Con,* 331.

87. Mazzucato and Collington, *The Big Con,* 331.

88. Michael Kapoor, "Big Four Invest Billions in Tech, Reshaping Their Identities," *Bloomberg Tax News,* January 02, 2020. news.bloombergtax.com/financial-accounting/big-four-invest-billions-in-tech-reshaping-their-identities.

89. Kapoor, "Big Four Invest Billions in Tech."

90. Artificial Lawyer, "Big Four Firm EY Buys Legal Innovator," *Artificial Lawyer,* August 07, 2018. www.artificiallawyer.com/2018/08/07/big-four-firm-ey-buys-legal-innovator-riverview-law/.

91. Deloitte, "GovConnect Public Health Transformation Platform," Deloitte Website, n.d. www2.deloitte.com/us/en/pages/public-sector/articles/contact-tracker-tracer-covid-19-govconnect-public-health-transformation-platform.html.

92. Rasmus Corlin Christensen, "Transnational Infrastructural Power of Professional Service Firms" (2022) https://doi.org/10.31235/osf.io/k9bd2. Christensen draws the idea of infrastructural power from Michael Mann, *The Sources of Social Power,* vol II (Cambridge: Cambridge University Press, 1993).

93. Seabrooke, "Epistemic Arbitrage."

94. Seabrooke, "Epistemic Arbitrage," 50.

95. Eckl and Hanrieder, "The Political Economy of Consulting Firms," 2319.

96. Eckl and Hanrieder, "The Political Economy of Consulting Firms," 2320.

97. Christensen, "Transnational Infrastructural Power of Professional Service Firms," 19; see also James Faulconbridge and Daniel Muzio, "Professions in a Globalizing World: Towards a Transnational Sociology of Professions," *International Sociology* 27, 1 (2012).

98. Ian MacDougall, "How McKinsey Is Making $100 Million (and Counting) Advising on the Government's Bumbling Coronavirus Response," *Propublica,* July 15, 2020. www.propublica.org/article/how-mckinsey-is-making-100-million-and-counting-advising-on-the-governments-bumbling-coronavirus-response#:~:text=Hiring%20McKinsey%20is%20a%20famously,the%20second%20one%20mid%2Dlevel.

99. NDP, "Liberals and Conservatives Look for Rich Consultants while Canadians Struggle to Pay Their Bills," NDP News, January 10, 2023. www.ndp.ca/news/liberals-and-conservatives-look-out-rich-consultants-while-canadians-struggle-pay-their-bills. As one public official noted about McKinsey: "According to managers and politicians, everything that comes from outside is always better, even if we had enough resources internally." Another notes: "[McKinsey] always says they have great expertise, but it doesn't make sense because we have expertise and we're completely pushed aside," https://www.cbc.ca/news/politics/mckinsey-immigration-consulting-contracts-trudeau-1.6703626.

100. Sabeel Rahman and Kathleen Thelen. "The Rise of the Platform Business Model and the Transformation of Twenty-First-Century Capitalism," *Politics & Society* 47, 2 (2019): 177–204, 178.

101. JoAnne Yates, *Control through Communication: The Rise of System in American Management* (Baltimore: Johns Hopkins University Press 1989).

102. Mazzucato and Collington, *The Big Con,* 294.

103. Daniel Faggella, "AI in the Accounting Big Four — Comparing Deloitte, PWC, KPMG, and EY" *Emerj Artifical Intelligence Research,* April 03, 2020. emerj.com/ai-sector-overviews/ai-in-the-accounting-big-four-comparing-deloitte-pwc-kpmg-and-ey/.

104. Faggella, "AI in the Accounting Big Four."

105. Jamie Peck and Nik Theodore, *Fast Policy — Experimental Statecraft at the Thresh-

*olds of Neoliberalism* (Minneapolis, London: University of Minnesota Press, 2015), 223.

106. Mazzucato, *The Value of Everything.*
107. Kornberger and Carter, "Manufacturing Competition."
108. MacDougall, "How McKinsey Is Making $100" Million."
109. Julia Belluz and Marine Buissonniere, "How McKinsey Infiltrated the World of Global Public Health," vox *Science,* December 13, 2019. www.vox.com/science-and-health/2019/12/13/21004456/bill-gates-mckinsey-global-public-health-bcg.
110. Belluz and Buissonniere, "How McKinsey Infiltrated the World of Global Public Health."
111. Belluz and Buissonniere, "How McKinsey Infiltrated the World of Global Public Health."
112. Madhukar Pai, "10 Fixes for Global Health Consulting Malpractice," *Global Health Now,* August 12, 2019. globalhealthnow.org/2019-08/10-fixes-global-health-consulting-malpractice.
113. Boussebaa, "Professional Service Firms," 1223.
114. Boussebaa, "Professional Service Firms," 1225.
115. Daria Volkova, "Boutique Consultancy and Personal Trust: Advising on Cities in Moscow," in Chris Hurl and Anne Vogelpohl (eds), *Professional Service Firms and Politics in a Global Era: Public Policy, Private Expertise* (2021): 97–114.
116. Volkova, "Boutique Consultancy and Personal Trust," 103.
117. Horrocks, "Experts and E-Government."
118. Horrocks, "Experts and E-Government," 122.
119. Busemeyer and Thelen, "Institutional Sources of Business Power," 457
120. Madison Marriage, Caroline Binham, and Martin Arnold, "Concerns Raised about 'Too Big to Fail' KPMG," *Financial Times,* July 20, 2018. www.ft.com/content/f660b6a2-8b75-11e8-bf9e-8771d5404543.

## Chapter 5

1. Busemeyer and Thelen, "Institutional Sources of Business Power," 449.
2. Hurl, "(Dis) Assembling policy pipelines."
3. Busemeyer and Thelen, "Institutional Sources of Business Power," 449.
4. Personal correspondence, 2016.
5. Personal correspondence, 2016.
6. Personal correspondence, 2016.
7. Royson James, "'Service Review' Lacks Core Credibility," *Toronto Star,* July 25, 2011. www.thestar.com/news/gta/2011/07/25/service_review_lacks_core_credibility.html.
8. Personal correspondence, 2016.
9. Chris Hurl and Janna Klostermann, "Remembering George W. Smith's 'Life Work': From Politico-Administrative Regimes to Living Otherwise," *Studies in Social Justice* 13, 2 (2019): 262–82.
10. Staff, "Shadowboxer: Dan Guttman, a Lifetime Investigating the Government's 'Shadow Workforce' of contractors," Guttman, Buschner, & Brooks PLLC, February 21, 2020. www.gbblegal.com/shadowboxer-investigating-the-governments-shadow-workforce-of-contractors/.
11. Guttman and Willner published a damning book in 1976, *Shadow Government.*
12. Guttman and Willner, *Shadow Government,* 31.

13. For instance, see: Craig and Brooks, *Plundering the Public Sector*; Paul R. Verkuil, *Outsourcing Sovereignty: Why Privatization of Government Functions Threatens Democracy and What We Can Do about It* (Cambridge: Cambridge University Press, 2007); McDonald, *The Shadow Public Service.*

14. See Chapter 2; Chris Hurl, "Accounting from Below: Activists Confront Outsourcing in a London Borough," *Critical Policy Studies* 16, 3 (2022): 352–70.

15. Susanna Wilkey, "easyCouncil Set for Barnet Residents," *Ham&High*, September 03, 2009. www.hamhigh.co.uk/news/easycouncil-set-for-barnet-residents-3402120.

16. Personal correspondence, 2016.

17. Barnet, *MetPro Rapid Response Internal Audit Report, Report to Audit Committee*, June 16, 2011, 8. barnet.moderngov.co.uk/Data/Audit%20Committee/201106161830/Agenda/Document%204.pdf.

18. Barnet, *MetPro Rapid Response Internal Audit Report.*

19. Charles Honderick, *A Tale of Two Barnets* (2012). www.ataleoftwobarnets.co.uk; Charles Honderick, *Barnet: The Billion Pound Gamble* (2012). http://www.billionpoundgamble.co.uk/.

20. Armbrüster, *The Economics and Sociology of Management Consulting.*

21. Mary Lu Carnevale, "Obama Taps McKinsey & Co.," *The Wall Street Journal*, January 07, 2009. www.wsj.com/articles/BL-WB-7104.

22. Elisa Braun and Paul de Villepin, "How Consultants Like McKinsey Took Over France," *Politico*, February 08, 2021. www.politico.eu/article/how-consultants-like-mckinsey-accenture-deloitte-took-over-france-bureaucracy-emmanuel-macron-coronavirus-vaccines/.

23. Daniel Boffey, "NHS Reforms: American Consultancy McKinsey in Conflict-of-Interest Row," *The Guardian*, November 05, 2011. www.theguardian.com/society/2011/nov/05/nhs-reforms-mckinsey-conflict-interest.

24. Schué, "The Value of One Consulting Firm's Federal Contracts."

25. Bogdanich and Forsyth, "When McKinsey Comes to Town," 626.

26. C. Wright Mills, *The Power Elite* (Oxford: Oxford University Press, 2000 [1956]); William Domhoff, *Who Rules America? Power and Politics* (Boston: McGraw Hill, 2002 [1967]).

27. Corporate Mapping Project, www.corporatemapping.ca/.

28. Strategic Corporate Research, strategiccorporateresearch.org/strategic-corporate-research/.

29. Jane Mcalevey, janemcalevey.com/.

30. Stephen P. Borgatti and Daniel S. Halgin, "Analyzing Affiliation Networks," in Peter J. Carrington and John Scott (eds), *The Sage Handbook of Social Network Analysis* (Thousand Oaks, CA: Sage, 2011): 417-433; William K. Carroll, *The Making of the Transnational Capitalist Class* (London: Zed, 2010); Seabrooke and Tsingou, "Revolving Doors in International Financial Governance."

31. See Borgatti and Halgin, "Analyzing Affiliation Networks"; Carroll, *The Making of the Transnational Capitalist Class*; Seabrooke and Tsingou, "Revolving Doors in International Financial Governance."

32. See also Chris Hurl, Valérie L'Heureux, and Susanne A. Kraemer, "Elite Networks in Public Private Partnerships: Mapping the Enabling Field in Ontario," *Studies in Political Economy* 103.1 (2022): 36-54.

33. See: Loxley, *Ideology over Economics*; Whiteside, "P3s and the Value for Money Illusion"; Murray, "Value for Money?"; Unison, 2003; Jean Shaoul, "The Corporate Takeover of Public Policy: The Case of Public–Private Partnerships in Britain," in

*Professional Service Firms and Politics in a Global Era: Public Policy, Private Expertise*, eds. C. Hurl and A. Vogelpohl (London: Palgrave Macmillan, 2021).

34. littlesis.org/.
35. Matt Hope, "Mapped: How a Big Oil Lobbying Network Makes Billions from Taxpayers as North Sea Wells Run Dry," *desmog*, Feburary 28, 2017. www.desmog.com/2017/02/28/how-big-oil-lobbying-network-makes-billions-taxpayers-north-sea-wells-run-dry/.
36. Tamasin Cave, "The Privatising Cabal at the Heart of our NHS," Spinwatch, April 01, 2015. spinwatch.org/index.php/issues/lobbying/item/5759-the-privatising-cabal-at-the-heart-of-our-nhs.
37. Cave, "The Privatising Cabal at the Heart of our NHS."
38. Hurl et al., "Elite Networks in Public Private Partnerships."
39. PwC, "Using Transparency to Build Trust: A Corporate Director's Guide," n.d. https://www.pwc.com/us/en/services/governance-insights-center/library/using-transparency-to-build-trust.html.
40. McKinsey, "Supply-Chain Recovery in Coronavirus Times — Plan for Now and the Future," March 18, 2020. www.mckinsey.com/capabilities/operations/our-insights/supply-chain-recovery-in-coronavirus-times-plan-for-now-and-the-future; McKinsey, "Building Value-Chain Resilience with AI," November 26, 2021. www.mckinsey.com/industries/metals-and-mining/our-insights/building-value-chain-resilience-with-ai; Hernan Saenz, "The Traceability Transformation: How Transparent Value Chains can Help Companies Achieve Their Sustainability Goals, *Bain Press Release*, September 16, 2021. www.bain.com/about/media-center/press-releases/2021/the-traceability-transformation/.
41. Transparency International UK, "Corporate Political Engagement Index 2018," n.d. www.transparency.org.uk/corporate-political-engagement-index.
42. Bogdanich and Forsyth, *When McKinsey Comes to Town*, 622–23.
43. Mazzucato and Collington, *The Big Con*, 335.
44. Richard Murphy and Salia N. Stausholm, *The Big Four — A Study of Opacity*, Brussels, Belgium: European United Left/Nordic Green Left (2017): 28.
45. Cris Shore and Susan Wright, "How the Big 4 Got Big: Audit Culture and the Metamorphosis of International Accountancy Firms," *Critique of Anthropology* 38, 3 (2018): 303–324. Shore and Wright note that these firms have pioneered "a new form of business entity that is neither a multinational corporation, a global partnership, nor a single firm. Their role, instead, is to act as coordinating entities for their network of global affiliates, who are to be unified around 'brand,' 'risk,' 'quality,' 'values' and 'ethics' by adhering to a common code of conduct" (310).
46. Christensen and Seabrooke, "The Big 4 under Pressure," 2954.
47. Christensen and Seabrooke, "The Big 4 under Pressure," 2954.
48. Christensen and Seabrooke, "The Big 4 under Pressure," 2963.
49. Open Data for Tax Justice, datafortaxjustice.net/.
50. Personal correspondence.
51. Alex Cobham Jonathan Gray, and Richard Murphy, "What Do They Pay? Towards a Public Database to Account for the Economic Activities and Tax Contributions of Multinational Corporations," *Data for Tax Justice*, February 2017. datafortaxjustice.net/what-do-they-pay/.
52. Dean Beeby, "Ottawa Hires Consultants to Advise on Airport Sell-Offs," CBC News, July 19, 2017. www.cbc.ca/news/politics/airports-pwc-credit-suisse-morneau-sale-equity-lease-c-d-howe-cdev-finance-canada-1.4210703.

53. Beeby, "Ottawa Hires Consultants to Advise on Airport Sell-Offs."
54. MacDougall, "How McKinsey Is Making $100 Million."
55. Information Commissioner of Canada, "2015 Chapter 1, Extending Coverage," n.d. www.oic-ci.gc.ca/en/resources/reports-publications/2015-chapter-1-extending-coverage.
56. Keith Reynolds, *Canada Infrastructure Bank and the Public's Right to Know* (Vancouver: Columbia Institute, 2017).
57. Loxley, *Ideology Over Economics*; Reynolds, *Canada Infrastructure Bank*.
58. Auditor General of Ontario, 2014, 20.
59. Loxley, *Ideology Over Economics*; Reynolds, *Canada Infrastructure Bank*.
60. Peter Fleming, "Never Let a Good Crisis Go to Waste: How Consulting Firms Are Using COVID-19 as a Pretext to Transform Universities and Business School Education," *Academy of Management Learning & Education* (2022): 9.
61. Anne Vogelpohl, "Consulting as a Threat to Local Democracy? Flexible Management Consultants, Pacified Citizens, and Political Tactics of Strategic Development in German Cities," *Urban Geography*, 39, 9 (2018): 1345–65, 1361.
62. City of Toronto, Executive Committee Meeting, July 28, 2011, DVD recording.
63. Bogdanich and Forsythe, *When McKinsey Comes to Town*, 533.
64. Including Open Secrets, Section27 (S27), Right2Know (R2K), MyVoteCounts (MVC), Corruption Watch (CW), #UniteBehind, Equal Education (EE), and Dullah Omar Institute (DOI).
65. News24 Wire WireService, "'They Are Stealing Our Future' — How State Capture Affects Its Faceless Victims," *The Citizen*, October 12, 2019. www.citizen.co.za/news/south-africa/state-capture/they-are-stealing-our-future-how-state-capture-affects-its-faceless-victims/.
66. Aziz Choudry, *Learning Activism: The Intellectual Life of Contemporary Social Movements* (Toronto: University of Toronto Press, 2015).
67. Alan Sears, *The Next New Left: A History of the Future* (Halifax: Fernwood Publishing, 2014).
68. Choudry, *Learning Activism,* 107.
69. Jacobsen to authors, 2016.
70. Burgess to authors 2016.

## Chapter 6

1. Christopher Hood, "A Public Management for All Seasons?" *Public Administration* 69, 1 (1991): 3–19; David Craig and Richard Brooks, *Plundering the Public Sector* (London: Constable, 2006); Matti Ylönen and Hanna Kuusela, "Consultocracy and Its Discontents: A Critical Typology and a Call for a Research Agenda," *Governance* 32, 2 (2019): 241–58).
2. Armbrüster, *The Economics and Sociology of Management Consulting,* 70.
3. Andrew Sturdy, "The Governance of Management Consultancy Use: Practices, Problems, and Possibilities," in *Professional Service Firms and Politics in a Global Era*, eds. C. Hurl and A. Vogelpohl (London: Palgrave Macmillan, 2021), 326; Matthias Kipping, "Hollow from the Start? Image Professionalism in Management Consulting," *Current Sociology* 59, 4 (2011): 530–50. McKenna, *The World's Newest Profession*.
4. Suddaby et al., "Transnational Regulation of Professional Services."

5. Christopher D. McKenna, "'Give Professionalization a Chance!' Why Management Consulting May Yet Become a Full Profession," in *Redirections in the Study of Expert Labour: Established Professions and New Expert Occupations,* eds. D. Muzio, S. Ackroyd, and J.F. Chanlat (London: Palgrave Macmillan UK, 2008), 215.

6. U.S. Securities and Exchange Commission, "Ernst & Young to Pay $100 Million Penalty for Employees Cheating on CPA Ethics Exam and Misleading Investigation," June 28, 2022. www.sec.gov/news/press-release/2022-114.

7. Armbruster notes: "Only in the past five years [i.e., since 2001] has there been a trend toward selecting consultants in systematic procedures and toward involving cost-calculating purchasing or procurement departments in the decision-making process" (61).

8. Sturdy, "The Governance of Management Consultancy Use," 326

9. Macdonald, *The Shadow Public Service,* 22.

10. Caspar Van den Berg, Michael Howlett, Andrea Migone, M. Howard, Frida Pemer and Helen M. Gunter, *Policy Consultancy in Comparative Perspective: Patterns, Nuances and Implications of the Contract State* (Cambridge UK: Cambridge University Press, 2020), 229.

11. Bill Browne, "Talk Isn't Cheap," *The Australia Institute,* October 04, 2021. australiainstitute.org.au/report/talk-isnt-cheap/.

12. Fleming, "Never Let a Good Crisis go to Waste," 6.

13. Sturdy, "The Governance of Management Consultancy Use," 330.

14. BBC News, "Accountancy Firm Price Waterhouse Banned from India," BBC News, January 12, 2018. www.bbc.com/news/world-asia-india-42662259.

15. D. Muzio, J. Faulconbridge, C. Gabbioneta, and R. Greenwood, "Bad Apples, Bad Barrels and Bad Cellars: A 'Boundaries' Perspective on Professional Misconduct," in *Organizational Wrongdoing,* eds. D. Palmer, R. Greenwood, and K. Smith-Crowe (Cambridge, UK: Cambridge University Press, 2016), 147.

16. Mike Raco, *State-Led Privatisation*; Colin Crouch, *The Knowledge Corrupters: Hidden Consequences of the Financial Takeover of Public Life* (Cambridge, UK: Polity, 2016).

17. Sturdy, "The Governance of Management Consultancy Use."

18. European Court of Auditors (ECA), 2022, 41. www.eca.europa.eu/en/Pages/DocItem.aspx?did=61461.

19. ECA, 27.

20. Marriage et al., "Concerns Raised about 'Too Big to Fail.'"

21. Sturdy, "The Governance of Management Consultancy Use," 325.

22. Amanda Iacone, "EY Consulting Split Aims to Free Firm from Ethics Crackdown," *Bloomberg Tax,* May 31, 2022. news.bloombergtax.com/financial-accounting/ey-consulting-split-aims-to-free-firm-from-ethics-crackdown.

23. Brooks, *Bean Counters,* 537.

24. Armbruster (*The Economics and Sociology of Management Consulting,* 2006) notes that many large corporations had begun establishing their own in-house consulting divisions in the 1990s.

25. Lawrence Dunhill and Rajeev Syal, "Whitehall 'Infantilised' by Reliance on Consultants, Minister Claims," *The Guardian,* September 29, 2020. www.theguardian.com/politics/2020/sep/29/whitehall-infantilised-by-reliance-on-consultants-minister-claims.

26. Michael O'Dwyer, "Public Sector Consulting Work Set to Grow Despite Planned

Spending Cuts," *Financial Times,* January 27, 2022. www.ft.com/content/2b67f0a3-4c0e-4234-85d0-fa4a2b65bd35.

27. Tom McIlroy, "Labor Plans to Use In-House Teams to Slash Bills from Big Four," *Financial Review,* October 13, 2022. www.afr.com/politics/federal/in-house-plan-to-cut-government-s-big-four-consulting-bill-20221012-p5bpay.

28. Michael O'Dwyer and George Parker. "UK Government Scraps In-House Consultancy as Departments Prefer Big Four," *Financial Times,* January 30, 2023. www.ft.com/content/a5fa45c5-448c-42ee-8d37-ffe90c42092f?desktop=true&segmentId=d8d3e364-5197-20eb-17cf-2437841d178a#myft:notification:instant-email:content.

29. Corporate Reform Collective, *Fighting Corporate Abuse: Beyond Predatory Capitalism* (London: Pluto Press, 2014): 180.

30. David McDonald, *Making Public in a Privatized World: The Struggle for Essential Services* (London: Zed Books, 2016); Isabelle Bruno, Emmanuel Didier, and Tommaso Vitale, "Statactivism: Forms of Action Between Disclosure and Affirmation," *Partecipazione e conflitto* 7, 2 (2014): 198–220; Mark Erickson, Paul Hanna, and Carl Walker, "The UK Higher Education Senior Management Survey: A Statactivist Response to Managerialist Governance," *Studies in Higher Education* 46, 11 (2021): 2134–51.

31. Michael McGann, Emma Blomkamp, and Jenny M. Lewis, "Everybody Else Is Doing It so Why Don't We? Analysing the Rise of the Policy Lab," *3rd International Conference on Public Policy* (ICPP3), 2017; Haris Alibašić and William Crawley, "Applying Good Governance through Policy Labs: Sustainable Solutions for Universities and Local Governments," *International Journal of Social Sustainability in Economic, Social & Cultural Context* 17, 1 (2021).

32. Amanda Clarke and Sean Boots, "A Guide to Reforming Information Technology Procurement in the Government of Canada," October 2022. govcanadacontracts.ca/it-procurement-guide/.

33. Fleming, "Never Let a Good Crisis Go to Waste," 8.

34. For a fuller discussion of these dynamics, see Mehdi Boussebaa, "Unsettling West-Centrism in the Study of Professional Service Firms," *Human Relations* (2022); Boussebaa, "Professional Service Firms, Globalisation and the New Imperialism."

35. Saint Martin, *Building the New Managerialist State.*

36. Kimberly Chong, *Best Practice: Management Consulting and the Ethics of Financialization in China* (Durham, NC: Duke University Press, 2018).

# Index